RCMP

vs
THE PEOPLE

RCMP

VS
THE PEOPLE

Inside Canada's Security Service

by Edward Mann, Professor of Sociology,
York University
and John Alan Lee, Associate Professor
of Sociology, University of Toronto
with a historical chapter by Norman Penner,
Professor of History, York University

General Publishing Co. Limited
Don Mills, Ontario

First published in 1979 by
General Publishing Co. Limited
30 Lesmill Road, Don Mills, Ontario

First printing

Canadian Cataloguing in Publication Data
   Lee, John Allan.
      RCMP
   ISBN-0-7336-1046-4
   1. Canada.   Royal Canadian Mounted Police
   I. Mann, William Edward, 1918-   II. Title.
   HV8157.L44   354'.71'0074   C79-094135-X

Cover Design/Peter Maher
Photograph/Paterson Photographic Works
ISBN 0-7736-1046-4
Printed and bound in Canada

Contents

Foreword

by Elmer MacKay, M.P.

Canadians, in my opinion, tend to be complacent when it comes to civil liberties, and unquestioning in their attitude towards police and law enforcement agencies. We tend to think of police excesses and security misdeeds as being confined to other countries, and are little concerned ourselves.

Recent revelations of wire-tapping, fake communiqués, breaking and entering, and other RCMP misdeeds, while not entirely destroying our complacency, have definitely undermined our illusions about an all-wise and benevolent police authority. On balance, this is a healthy and long-overdue development. No institution, whether it be Parliament, the judiciary, or our national police force, deserves unquestioning loyalty and trust. These must be earned, and standards must occasionally be brought under scrutiny.

The evidence given at four investigative commissions raises certain questions about the internal operations of the Security Service of the RCMP, and the resulting impact upon our civil liberties. There is increasing justification for reassessing certain police attitudes and techniques, and the nature of our security operations. Hard-hitting questions must be asked and definite decisions made.

Almost forgotten behind the more dramatic aspects of the controversy has been the treatment that police officers receive from their own employers. I am aware of members of the RCMP who have received unfair treatment at the hands of their own bureaucracy. I suspect that rigid discipline, inane regulations and lack of flexibility have all had an impact on the overt and covert behavior and attitudes of the force. We must ask ourselves how we can reasonably expect police officers to respect our civil rights, when so little concern or respect for their own exists.

Professors Mann and Lee have thoroughly researched the subject of secret police in Canada. They have consulted numerous books, articles and reports relevant to security and police matters. They have attended hearings and informed themselves firsthand by interviewing lawyers and other sociologists, as well as police and security officials. Their statements and claims, consequently, have the ring of solid research.

Mann and Lee have written an interesting and very topical book which students as well as ordinary citizens will find highly readable. They do not feel, I am certain, that they have the last word on what should be done. Nevertheless, while they will not achieve agreement on all of their ideas, they have set forth a series of proposals for improvement that deserves serious consideration in the continuing debate—a debate which is likely to go on for some time.

Preface

Alongside the tradition of scholarly publication in academic journals and texts, a growing number of sociologists have established a new investigative sociology focusing on controversial public issues. There is a great need for such action-research in Canada today. Numerous topics await thorough inquiry. For example, there has been little sociological research on malpractice in our professions, or on bureaucratic oppression of minority groups such as native peoples. There is almost nothing on malfeasance in trade unions; on manipulation of immigration laws to exclude refugees from right-wing dictatorships; on deviance in the post office. We are still waiting for insightful research on sharp practices in Canadian business; on religious promoters; on the role of secret societies such as the Masonic order.

A problem common to many such projects is that of getting inside information from large and powerful bureaucracies obsessed with secrecy. This was certainly the case with the RCMP Security Service! For much of our data we have relied on informants to whom we are extremely grateful, but who we cannot thank by name since they have spoken to us in strictest confidence. Our informants include RCMP members and former members, civil servants, members of Parliament, members of local and provincial police forces, and journalists. Nothing told us by any informant was taken at face value. Sociologists are a skeptical breed. We asked the same questions again and again, systematically comparing responses to sift out consistent kernels of fact from the varying chaff of opinion and hearsay.

We have also been severely restricted by Canada's oppressive libel laws, in which truth is not necessarily a defense. Indeed, the deletions we were urged to make by our legal advisers were a practical lesson in the limits on freedom of the press in Canada.

We are only too aware of the reluctance of most Canadians to be critical of the RCMP, so we have not asked the reader to rely completely on the credibility of ourselves or our informants. We have footnoted other sources already in the public domain whenever they were available, as well as conventional sources in the fields of sociology, political science and history. Some of our sources are not available to the average reader, but they can be confirmed by other researchers. For example, we have had access to top secret RCMP documents now in the hands of various journalists as a result of the Keable commission. While we don't expect our readers to believe everything they read in the newspapers, we have frequently cited journalistic sources, at least to demonstrate that we are not the only Canadians who consider certain facts to be true.

This book is an example of an ideal partnership and sharing of specialized skills of sociologists of quite different backgrounds. Edward Mann, the more experienced author by some fifteen years, had built up a wide circle of informants in police work and a reputation for protecting his sources. Thus the greater part of the recruitment of informants and legwork of interviewing fell to him. John Alan Lee could draw on journalistic experience, so the task of preparing a manuscript in less than six months fell to him. The authors shared their experience in the research, analysis and teaching of the sociology of deviant behavior.

We are pleased and grateful for the contribution of a historical chapter by Professor Norman Penner, who has also provided helpful editorial content in the rest of the manuscript.

We are much indebted to friends and colleagues who have provided ideas for the manuscript, including Tracy Rohm,

Alan Listiak, Alan Borovoy, Judy Botterill, John Hagan, Clifford Shearing, Raymond Favreau, Joe McAnthony, Michael McGee, and Douglas Fisher. We are especially grateful to Elmer MacKay for providing a foreword.

Far too many sociological books are riddled with jargon, or dull and circumlocutious, or badly organized, or all of these. We would like to thank our editor, Karin Judkins, who took an overly long and hastily organized manuscript and reworked it into a tightly presented argument.

When all those informants whom we cannot thank by name see this final product of their concern and our labor, we hope they will find their positions fairly represented, and will be pleased to have shared in research on a topic of great importance to all Canadians.

Edward Mann
Atkinson College
York University

John Alan Lee
Scarborough College
University of Toronto

ANY READER WHO IS AWARE OF WRONG DOING

by the RCMP or other Canadian police forces, is invited to contact the authors, who welcome such information for use in future studies. Confidentiality of sources will be completely respected.

1

Getting Inside the
Security Service

"Parliament has taken very little interest in the Security Service. It has set down virtually no guidelines. As a result a vacuum existed, and the organization, as big organizations do, set up its own rules—rules that would suit itself. And so it really got out of control."

The speaker is a former high-ranking officer of the RCMP Security Service, explaining the recent "wrongdoings" of the force. The fault, he claimed, lay not with the individual members of the service, but with a slack government and an inattentive Parliament. In short, the fault was with Canadian democracy, with every citizen who, most of the time, takes freedom for granted.

The more RCMP activities are investigated by journalists and royal commissions, the more wrongdoings are revealed. After a few days off the front page, the headlines return: "RCMP still carried on with a practice it had been told was illegal in 1954." "Mounties own up to phony letters." "RCMP removed tapes in custody of court, judge says." "Security Service used secret medical data to write disruptive letters." Official enquiries have uncovered hundreds of illegal break-ins and hundreds of illegal mail openings. The force has had more unfavorable publicity in the past several years than in its previous century of existence.

The Pandora's box of Security Service wrongdoings was opened in March 1976. Robert Samson, on trial for attempted bombing of a Montreal executive's home, defended himself by arguing, "I've done far worse things as a

Mountie." The press naturally began digging to discover what "worse things" he meant. When undeniable evidence was uncovered, the RCMP and the federal government admitted a few wrongdoings. But Canadians were assured that they were "only the rare excesses of a few overzealous corporals."

After the first admissions the government claimed that there was nothing more to reveal. "We have wiped the slate clean." But almost daily, inquisitive journalists and members of Parliament made new charges, often based on documents leaked to them by disgruntled Mounties. Again and again the government admitted the allegations, each time claiming that this time the slate really was wiped clean.

The Quebec government was not convinced, and appointed a commission under lawyer Jean Keable to investigate RCMP Security Service dirty tricks in the province. Soon the Keable commission was uncovering such damaging evidence that the federal government went to court to silence it—and eventually succeeded. The Keable inquiry has since resumed, but under terms severely restricted by the Supreme Court.

The tide of disclosures of Mountie misdeeds proved too great for federal authorities to ignore, so it was channeled into a royal commission. Once the commission was appointed, the government could answer complaints about the RCMP by insisting that the McDonald royal commission was investigating them.

Most Canadians find it difficult to criticize their beloved Mounties. The criminal investigation branch of the RCMP has earned the esteem of Canadians as a generally honest and efficient police force. The great majority of its members are dedicated to upholding the rule of law in Canada. They are friendly and helpful public servants, ready to assist the public in any emergency. These are the Mounties who serve as police forces in eight provinces and nearly two hundred municipalities.

But there is another branch of the RCMP that is almost invisible to the average Canadian: the Security Service. Even the number of its personnel and the size of its budget are secrets. Most of the "wrongdoings" of the RCMP have occurred within the Security Service.

In the autumn of 1978 it appeared that the McDonald royal commission became very disturbed by the secrets it was uncovering. The commission turned on the government which had created it, demanding documents the government did not want to reveal. It talked of summoning key ministers of the cabinet to testify.

As this book goes to press, the story is by no means ended. The McDonald commission has called several ministers. But there is no assurance that the public will share their revelations. Certainly Canadians cannot expect a report from the McDonald commission until 1980 or even later. But there is already enough evidence to demonstrate that the dirty tricks were not the rare excesses of overzealous corporals. What has emerged is a picture of predictable and probably inevitable illegalities which are the outcome of the structure and organization of Canada's Security Service.

Canada's Secret Police?

It is difficult for most Canadians to regard the RCMP Security Service as a secret police force. The term "secret police" evokes images of the Nazi Gestapo or the Soviet KGB. We associate secret police with totalitarian societies. Canadians find it difficult to grasp the fact that one's phone may be tapped, one's best friend may be a paid informer, and reputable organizations like OXFAM or large unions like CUPE may be spied on. We are reluctant to realize the mass of information and misinformation the RCMP Security Service has accumulated on millions of Canadian citizens.

There have always been some Canadians who have warned that the RCMP Security Service was acting like, and could become, a Canadian secret police. But these critics have usually been on the political left. "They've probably got something to hide!" most citizens would argue. "Why, they're probably the very subversives we want the Mounties to watch."

A few highly respected Canadians definitely *not* on the political left have criticized the Security Service. One critic was historian Arthur Lower, an esteemed professor at

Queen's University in Kingston, Ontario. In 1957 Lower warned in *Maclean's* magazine that the RCMP was becoming a secret police force, but few Canadians took notice.[1] In 1963 one of Canada's most popular journalists, Sidney Katz, sounded the warning again, with an article titled "RCMP— Inside Canada's Secret Police."[2] Again the warning was ignored.

Prime Minister Mackenzie King once called Canada a "fireproof house." Civil strife and war were things that happened in other countries, but not in Canada. In 1970 Canada lost its political innocence. In the afterglow of the Centennial and EXPO '67 came the October Crisis in Quebec. The modern world of terrorism and nationalist conflict had arrived on our doorstep.

In our neighbor to the south, the sordid side of the security police was being revealed. The overflow of the American media set Canada awash in a tide of leaks and revelations about the hidden world of the CIA. Even the golden image of the FBI became tarnished, when the death of Edgar Hoover led to incredible exposés of FBI wrongdoings. Finally there was the Watergate scandal and the fall of Richard Nixon. These American events are of concern to Canadians because it is public knowledge that the FBI and CIA have been involved in the training of the RCMP Security Service, and CIA agents have been active in Canada. There has been a close communication link between the RCMP, FBI and CIA for many years.

Many insights into the dirty work committed by the CIA and FBI in the name of democracy were provided by defecting agents who became authors. It is a striking contrast between the United States and Canada that so few Mounties have ever "blown the whistle" on the RCMP. In 1972, former Mountie Jack Ramsay published a searing critique in an article, "My Case Against the RCMP."[3] Since then a few other ex-Mounties, such as Don McCleery, have talked to the media. But not a single member of the RCMP Security Service has followed the lead of former agents of the CIA, FBI, or the British intelligence services, to take up pen or typewriter and unmask the hidden world of the secret police.

What is security for?

Almost every Canadian would agree that we must protect
our democratic way of life from internal subversion or external attack. In a nuclear age, the latter has become the task of
a military alliance under the protection of the American
"nuclear umbrella." The protection of our national security
within the borders of Canada has been the responsibility of
the RCMP Security Service, assisted in times of "crisis" by
the armed forces.

In a working paper prepared for the press and public, the
McDonald inquiry has asked the question: "What is security
for?"

> What is it in Canada that must above all be secure?
> Surely it is the process of democratic and constitutional
> government wherein social and political change is ac-
> complished through free discussion . . . . and the coer-
> cive powers of government are subject to the rule of
> law.[4]

The commission paper argues that "a security service must
be able to do its job, but do it in a way that does not undermine the very democratic process it is trying to protect." That
is the fundamental issue this study confronts: does a secret
security service subvert the very democratic society it is supposed to protect? The issue is not the occasional "bad apple"
in a security service. It is the organizational structure which
seems to emerge inevitably in any *secret* bureaucracy which is
given or achieves unchecked power. Our approach to the
problem will be considered within three key concepts: official
deviance, structured deviance, and the rule of law.

The Concept of Official Deviance

Most people associate the word "deviant" with criminals,
lunatics, or dirty old men. So did most sociologists until
recently. The vast majority of sociological studies of deviance
were of delinquents, criminals, the insane or the sexually
perverse. Almost no one paid attention to violations of the
law or of moral standards by the "establishment" in

society—corporate executives, military officers, politicians, or civil servants. Few sociologists examined the police as "deviant" and even fewer studied the ways in which powerful and secretive bureaucracies can undermine such foundations of democracy as freedom of opinion and a free press.

American sociologist Jack Douglas introduced the term "official deviance" in 1977 to expand the new field of sociological investigation which sprang up in the 1960s under a general approach called labeling theory.[5] This theory applied a notion as old as Shakespeare, that "nothing is good or bad but thinking makes it so." Labeling theory looked at the way any particular action came to be considered deviant, and abandoned the notion that any human behavior is bad in itself. Labeling theorists have inquired into the people and organizations—the policemen, judges, doctors, social workers or other officials—who have the power to "certify" a person as deviant (delinquent, criminal, perverted, maladjusted, crazy or whatever).

Eventually two important concepts have emerged. First, the officials with power to label others do not use this power entirely altruistically. They often use it in their own interest and in the interest of their organizations. If there are more "criminals," this becomes a justification for hiring more police and increasing the budget of the police force. If there are more "mentally ill," then the hospital can expand, promotions are in order, and salaries will increase. Second, officials themselves often deviate from the moral or legal standards they impose on others. Again, they do this in their own interest, though they try to excuse and justify their deviations in terms of some overriding principle, such as "administrative necessity," "the good of the patient," or the "public interest."

The all-embracing principle for justification of deviance by government officials in modern times is "national security." "I am not a crook," insisted President Nixon, rejecting the label we often fix on violators of the law. "I was acting in the interests of our national security." So too, Canadians were told, were the Mounties who broke in, stole, and even committed arson.

The Concept of Structured Deviance

Social scientists have traditionally tried to avoid moralizing. They attempt to explain and understand rather than blame and condemn. Sociological analysis of the simplest event soon reveals that the world cannot be reduced to good guys and bad guys. It is made up of complex human beings acting within a tangled web of conflicting social conditions.

Some deviant behavior is the choice of the individual. A man plans a murder, prepares his weapon and his alibi, and carries out the act in cold blood. But many deviant acts are the outcome of a complex set of circumstances and motivations. Was it the father's desertion of the mother, or the mother's lack of affection, or the unsympathetic teachers, or the delinquent school gang, or the lack of community sports facilities, or inadequate policing of the area, or the careless motorist who left his keys in his car, which "caused" a teenager to take a joy-ride and commit a hit-and-run homicide?

When sociologists find that a set of social conditions are so arranged that the people involved are virtually pushed into frequent deviant behavior, they speak of "structured deviance." Such deviant acts are apparently less the product of conscious choice by the people involved, than of the structure of their work and social lives. A parallel may be found in the example of a street corner that is the scene of repeated auto accidents. Eventually someone realizes that the problem is not just a series of careless drivers, but a badly designed intersection.

Our understanding of the dirty tricks in the RCMP Security Service is that of structured deviance. We have met few Mounties who are outstanding good guys or despicable bad guys. Most of them are just doing their job. Our objective here is to explain, in terms of the organization of the Security Service, how quite a few Mounties come to define their job as including illegal acts. James Q. Wilson, one of the most respected experts on police, has observed that the bad apple theory does not explain much official deviance in police forces. "It leaves unanswered the question of why there are so many more bad apples in some barrels than in others."[6]

When the bad apple (or overzealous corporal) theory is used as a basis for police reforms, the original problem remains untouched. The book *Fall of Scotland Yard*[7] reveals that this famous police force was aware of internal problems of official deviance from 1963, but laid the blame on a few individuals, who were then removed. The *structure* of official deviance remained, and by the mid-seventies was much more difficult to correct.

The Rule of Law

The early founders of democracy made a clear distinction between "the rule of law" and "the rule of men." The "government of law" is emblazoned over the American Congress. The RCMP motto is *Maintiens le droit*—"Uphold the right." The history of British parliamentary democracy is the story of centuries of struggle to compel the king to cede more and more of his power to legal institutions—Parliament and the courts. The rule of men was considered arbitrary, while the rule of law was considered to be equal for all citizens.

Justice is supposed to take no notice of the social status or economic power of the alleged criminal. Under the rule of law, justice is supposed to be blindfolded. In fact, she does quite a lot of peeking. As Anatole France once said, "The law in its majesty equally forbids the rich and the poor to sleep on park benches." Knowledge of the law and financial capacity to hire the best lawyers are obviously unevenly distributed. The poor, the powerless, women, immigrants and native peoples are often disadvantaged before the law. Nevertheless, the democratic ideal remains a law which is no respecter of persons.

The notion of the rule of law implies that the law is supported by everyone in society, and represents a general consensus of what most people consider right and wrong. Here again, the ideal and the real are often far apart. For example, how could a law which forbids abortion represent all Canadians today?

Despite disagreements, it is probably safe to say that most

Canadians, most of the time, support the basic criminal laws of Canada—that is, the laws which make murder, theft, rape, assault and other such actions legally *crimes*.[8] The rule of law as far as it affects these basic criminal laws is a rule of consensus, and most Canadians want the police to enforce these laws. In the process, of course, we expect the police not to commit crimes themselves. Indeed, we expect the police to behave better than other citizens.

A criminal law may be supported by a consensus of public opinion, yet not apply equally to everyone, For example, our laws on theft are aimed more at the petty rip-offs of burglars than the massive rip-offs of excessive corporate profits, fraudulent advertising and exorbitant interest rates. Laws are often used to protect the rights of those with great property and power, while ignoring the rights of the ordinary citizen. For instance, laws forbidding the blocking of traffic on a road or sidewalk may seem to be in everyone's interest. But while they are often used to harass and arrest striking workers or protest marchers, they are rarely used against corporations that want to close public thoroughfares in the interests of business.[9]

Laws against homicide would seem a clear-cut example of consensus laws enforced for everyone's benefit. Unintentional homicide (as in a car accident) may be labeled manslaughter under these laws, but there is no mention of such death-dealing acts as the manufacture of defective automobiles, botulism in canned foods, or severe industrial pollution. When corporations kill, there may be a fine, or only a warning. When individuals kill, they are imprisoned.

When we consider how laws are made in the first place, it is clear that some groups have more power than others to translate their wishes into law. When the laws are enforced, the police pay more attention to some kinds of offenders than others. (Vandalism by affluent youths and university students may be regarded only as "hijinks.")[10] Finally, when laws are administered in courts of justice, sentences vary according to the social background and biases of the judge. John Hogarth's exhaustive study of Ontario magistrates showed that the same offense may bring quite a range of penalties, depending on the judge.[11]

When it comes to laws affecting our national security, the rule of law is even more complex than in supposedly consensus-based criminal law. Appalling crimes have been committed by security police in the name of national security, and not merely in Nazi Germany or Soviet Russia. In the "democracies" of South Africa and Rhodesia, for example, the blacks know perfectly well that the rule of law is the rule of *white* law.

Closer to home, we must face the fact that at least some Canadians have not regarded all of the RCMP's actions as efforts to uphold the right. Native Indian groups have had frequent occasion to complain about unequal enforcement of the law. The most flagrant example of unequal rule of law in the name of national security was the dislocation of thousands of Canadian-born Japanese during World War II. In the hindsight of history, many Canadians have deplored that sad episode. But few Canadians outside Quebec have come to terms with the fact that many Québécois have little respect for a rule of law imposed by the army and the RCMP in October 1970 under the allegation of an "apprehended insurrection." Many Québécois see an English-speaking national security achieved at the expense of security for the Quebec nation. While this political problem is too complex to be considerd in detail here, we must at least keep in mind that no simple notion of the rule of law will suffice in understanding our subject matter.[12]

Taking on "Canada's Finest"

If Canada has a sacred cow, it is the RCMP. Let sociologists analyze and criticize any other institution they please, but not the Mounties. In 105 years of RCMP activity, Canada has produced only one really irreverent study of the Mounties.[13] Research into RCMP activities has been made extremely difficult by their refusal to allow scholars access to their documents unless they agreed in advance to submit their manuscripts for RCMP approval before publication.

A study of the RCMP Security Service is a quite different problem than the conventional study of stereotyped deviance. Our problem was to get inside information on a large and powerful organization that is obsessed with secrecy. RCMP members on the criminal investigation side were more willing to talk with us than were Security Service members, since they are not bound by oaths under the Official Secrets Act. However, when our credentials had been established with a few former Mounties on the criminal side, we were given leads to other Mounties who had served in the Security Service. Our most important credential was our willingness to preserve the confidentiality of our sources.

Another concern not typical of more conventional studies of deviance was the possibility that the RCMP would not be pleased by our research efforts, and would strike back. We took it for granted that our phones might be tapped or our special documents "lifted." Our approach throughout was one of complete openness about the fact that we were studying the Security Service.

Our major goal in presenting this study is to make a credible argument to the reader—who is assumed to have the typical Canadian's favorable attitude to the RCMP. We have tried to relate our information to facts already in the public domain, and we have chosen the most widely reputed sources possible. Although numerous allegations have been made against the RCMP in left-wing and radical publications, we have almost totally excluded these sources. This is not because we believe them false, but because we know that many Canadians will not accept them as valid.

Proving that official deviance is built into the structure of the RCMP Security Service will be no easy task. At the peak of revelations of RCMP dirty tricks in March 1978, public opinion polls showed that the majority of Canadians still preferred to trust the RCMP, even in Quebec where many of the dirty tricks took place.[14] Polls indicate that a majority of Canadians still trust the federal government too. If the McDonald commission hearings continue to pit the RCMP leadership against the government it will be exciting to see who wins. The odds are on the RCMP.

Given the choice between liberty and order, Canadians will usually choose order. We are basically a non-questioning and conservative people, or what political scientist Walter Bagehot called a "deferential society." Our origins in reaction against the American revolution shaped us in a conservative mold.[15] We have preferred restraint to protest and tradition to experiment.[16] We have been eager to believe in the preservation of public order by the Mountie who always gets his man.

But Canadians also believe in democracy enought to have joined two world wars for the defense of freedom. We have sent our armed forces on numerous peace missions for the United Nations, to help others maintain freedom. Hopefully we will not allow our own freedoms to be eroded one by one for the sake of a law and order demanded by government bureaucracies and police forces. What is not clear is whether we need a secret police to protect the long-term security of our democratic freedoms, or whether such secret forces militate against the very democracy we seek to preserve. We will attempt to throw some light on this issue by examining the activities of the RCMP Security Service.

2

Shady Business That Backfired

A social scientist hoping to test a theory may encounter a problem less likely to trouble his colleagues in physics or biology. Objects and animals can be manipulated without consultation, but most people object to being manipulated without their permission. A scientist who can't set up an experiment has to find a "test case" already available. An astronomer can hardly manipulate heavenly bodies, so star-watchers take advantage of whatever phenomena occur, such as an eclipse of the sun. When the RCMP set up Operation Bricole they provided secret-police watchers with the equivalent of an eclipse. As a test case, Operation Bricole is just what the sociologist ordered.

Directors of intelligence and security services often complain that their failures are trumpeted while their successes go unheralded. Bricole went unheralded for four years; then all hell broke loose. One of the Mounties involved, Robert Samson, blurted out his involvement in the operation in court, and soon the press dug up the details. That wasn't difficult, because people in the know about Mountie undercover activities had suspected all along that Bricole was a Mountie caper.

Bricole means "odd job" or "shady business." No doubt some Mountie thought the name a good one; it showed a sense of humor. But *bricole* can also mean "rebound" or "backfire." Operation Bricole involved the theft of fifteen filing cabinets full of documents, carried out of an office in the dead of night. It was not the sort of theft to go unnoticed, and the owners naturally complained. They didn't expect their complaints to produce results, though, because they suspected the RCMP. Who else would steal one thousand pounds of files of no commercial value, while leaving untouched the money and equipment in the office? But the owners couldn't prove anything and the police and their political masters denied everything. There the matter rested for four years.

The police could consider the operation a success in several ways. They made a large haul of useful information about a "subversive" group. The group suspected that police had stolen the documents, so they became wary, and began to restrict their activities. People who might have supported the group fell away, fearful of harassment. And the group was hampered in its fund-raising and other membership activities. Without files, even the elementary bureaucracy of dissidence is hindered! The Mounties who planned the operation had every reason to congratulate themselves.

Looking for Action

It all began at a secret meeting in 1971 when the RCMP Security Service in Montreal asked higher-ups for a free hand to counter the threat of subversion in Quebec. The October Crisis was still fresh in everyone's memory, and the Mounties were convinced that there were still a number of FLQ members and supporters at large. Since their previous methods had proved ineffective, it was suspected that the FLQ would now infiltrate legal avenues of political action, such as the Parti Québécois and the federal civil service.

The RCMP felt that these underground operatives had to be identified and neutralized. The Montreal Security Service offered their supervisors in Ottawa a *quid quo pro*.[1] The field men would have full autonomy of action, in exchange for taking the fall if it came. Though the senior men would know in general what was going on, they would be spared the details. Later they would claim innocence if necessary. They would have what CIA and FBI leaders call "deniability."[2]

The eagerness of the local Security Service for action was

explained to us in 1978 by an ex-Mountie: "It was mainly the NCOs [non-commissioned officers] who were doing those things. They got impatient. They felt frustrated. They wanted some action."

More light was thrown on shady business by the comments of an ex-Mountie from the criminal branch. "Dirty tricks are done all the time. It's just a matter of course with organized criminals. You try to make them believe one of their members, one of their own guys, is betraying them or doing something dirty so they'll turn on this guy and perhaps dispose of him or make it tough for him. When you make a report on these sorts of things, you don't put down every little detail in your report, you know!"

Since training of RCMP Security Service men usually begins on the criminal investigation side, it would be easy enough to substitute "subversive organizations" for "organized crime." Sometimes Security Service men are sent on special courses run by CIA or FBI experts for training in investigative methods. Dirty tricks have long been part of the standard operating procedures of the FBI and CIA. The attempt to get incriminating documents on Daniel Ellsberg, author of *The Pentagon Papers*, is a classic instance; the FBI broke into his psychiatrist's office. In 1975 the FBI admitted to 238 break-ins in a five-year period.[3] Most of these were directed against radical political groups.

A free hand in Quebec did not provide the RCMP with immediate action. First they had to find a suitable target. As the year 1972 passed, so did the freshness of the October Crisis. The political situation in Quebec stabilized. Concern about separatism waned, since the Parti Québécois had only a tiny minority of seven members in the Quebec legislature.

RCMP men on the criminal investigation side were able to find excitement by pursuing members of the drug subculture, but on the political side there wasn't much action. Students of police attitudes have established that policing tends to attract men who like action, who thrive in an "ecology of danger."[4] One of the best-known studies showed that only four percent of a police force of 224 men chose "safe" jobs with a low level of action.[5] Psychological portraits of policemen produce a "picture of . . . an individual who is more suspicious than the average person, one who is ready to take risks and is prone to act on his impulses.'' This portrait is not suggested as pathology. ''What appears excessive in the 'normal' population may well be in the service of the [policeman's] ego.''[6]

It might be argued that the policeman's need for action tends to support the official explanation of RCMP wrongdoing as mere overzealousness. The Mounties weren't committing crimes, we were told; they were just a little too enthusiastic in their devotion to duty. But a structural analysis of official deviance recognizes that such consequences of the police hunger for action must be anticipated. The structure must assure that a reliable flow of information about what lower ranks are doing reaches the top. Political masters must be held responsible for knowing about and controlling the policeman's appetite for action.

A Suitable Target

The Montreal Security Service finally settled on the Agence de Presse Libre du Québec (APLQ) as a suitable target for action. The APLQ was a left-wing organization founded by two journalists whom the RCMP believed were earlier involved in the FLQ. The main activity of the APLQ was issuing a bulletin to supply newspapers and other media with information promoting the separation of Quebec from Canada. RCMP agents summed up the ideology of the APLQ bulletin as "separatist, and sympathetic to terrorism." Operating out of the same offices as the APLQ was the Mouvement pour la Défense des Prisonniers Politiques (MDPPQ), an organization dedicated to providing legal aid and other assistance to radicals and FLQ members in Quebec prisons. Both the APLQ's and MDPPQ's official activities were quite legal. It was what they might be *planning* that fascinated the RCMP.

In addition to restlessness and a desire for action, security men in Quebec were increasingly frustrated at the indifference of many public leaders in Canada to the threat of separatism. Was no one but the RCMP interested in protecting Canada's security as a single, unified nation? The FLQ was gone, but the Security Service believed many of its supporters were still busy subverting Canada.

An ex-Mountie told the authors in 1978: "We never dreamed that the separatists would become a legal party, and then the government. Once they were a legal party the [federal] government told us to lay off surveillance. This was really a blow because we were trying to protect the country. Separatists can't be trusted and the government wasn't letting us do our job."

The Mounties were not alone in their impatience. The Montreal city police were still smarting from their failure to track down the FLQ kidnappers during the October Crisis of 1970, so they too were eager to put the separatists in their place. In January 1972 the Montreal police stepped up regular surveillance of dissident groups. They subscribed to the APLQ bulletin through a neutral party, and made several attempts to recruit an informer inside the agency membership. When these failed, they tapped the APLQ phone. This continued until they learned that the Mounties were also tapping the line! It was decided to run a joint operation, and to bring in the Quebec provincial police too (the SQ, Sûreté du Québec).

The SQ were able to contribute their share of intelligence. They had been intercepting telegrams between members of the FLQ who had been flown to Cuba as part of the settlement of the James Cross kidnapping, and their relatives and friends in Quebec.[7] The possibility of proving a Cuban connection fascinated the three police forces. The RCMP disclosed that their telephone eavesdropping had revealed conversations about a secret letter from Cuba to the APLQ. The letter had been delivered by courier to the APLQ offices, and must now be in their files.

Blaming the Victim

Police trained to catch criminals do not readily become burglars; there has to be a convincing justification for action so much out of line with their ordinary role. In this case a suspected Cuban connection was probably sufficient. Cuba was communist, and was believed to be involved in subversion of various Latin American governments. In June 1972, the Toronto *Star* ran some feature articles on one Orlando Castro Hidalgo, a former Cuban spy who had defected. Why did the *Star* wait until 1972 to trumpet Hidalgo's revelations? He defected in Luxembourg in 1969, and testified to an American senate committee in October 1969.[8] Moreover, he had never been in Canada. Yet, he was now reported at length, and particular emphasis was given to his charges of Cuban spying in Canada. A reputable journalist with informants inside the RCMP indicated to the authors that the Hidalgo story was a deliberate RCMP plant to help justify their dirty tricks should they become known.

If the APLQ had a Cuban connection, then the blame would be on the APLQ and not on the Mounties who stole its files—or so the argument would run. This was indeed the justification for Bricole offered by the RCMP after the operation was uncovered four years later.[9] There would be charges of Cuban financial aid to underground FLQ cells and a flow of Cuban arms to Quebec terrorists. None of these charges has ever been substantiated, but the need to find "foreign agitators" and "foreign money" in countering subversion is a familiar secret police pattern (see chapter 3).

It is also easier to blame the victims if they behave as though they might be guilty. An informer inside the MDPPQ tipped off the police that members believed they were being watched and wiretapped, so they were taking precautions. Soon the police learned that the APLQ had set aside a security room for meetings and for storing documents. What more was necessary to show that they were up to no good?

Cops Playing Robbers

The original discussions of joint action by the three police forces slowly took shape in an elaborate plan. The nine men originally involved increased to twenty-seven—twelve from the municipal police, eight from the provincial police and seven from the RCMP. As the story broke several years later, it seems that none of the three forces, and no individual, was "in charge," though some would suggest the moving spirit was Robert Samson. The RCMP participation was authorized at the Montreal level, and was led by the same inspector later involved in Operation Ham (see chapter 3). None of the three police forces was legally obligated to carry out orders from either of the other two forces.

There were elements of boys at play as well as men at work in the operation. The elusive "Cuban letter" was touted as an indication of a spy network. This smacks more of a boy's fascination with spy novels than of modern counterespionage. As Miles Copeland, a pro-CIA analyst of espionage, explains in detail, "networks" of spies went out of fashion when the KGB (the Soviet secret police) lost too many operatives in the fifties.[10]

Secret meetings of lower-level members of the three police forces, without senior officials knowing much of what went on, added spice to the adventure. The choice of hockey bags to cart off the stolen files, and an RCMP member's basement to store them—with his wife and dog mounting guard—can hardly be considered serious defense of Canada's national security. It's these spontaneous elements of espionage which make James Bond adventures popular, but when real people are involved the evidence of game-playing in the Security Service is hardly reassuring.[11]

Though many police were involved in the break-in (picking a lock, standing lookout, tapping a telephone line), only five cops actually entered the APLQ-MDPPQ premises. Later, when Operation Bricole became public knowledge, only three of these men would be charged. They were charged not with burglary or destruction of private property, but merely with failing to obtain a search warrant. None of the other participants were charged at all, though in a criminal action of the same nature, organized by a group of thieves, all would certainly be pulled in and charged as accomplices.

There was a flamboyant derring-do about the timing and implementation of Operation Bricole. With no clear authorization from superior officers, the men decided almost at the last moment to go ahead with the plan. The precipitating event seems to have been a tip that everyone in the target groups would be away at a meeting on the weekend of October 6–7. It happened that the superior police officers

were away the same weekend too, moose hunting in the
northern woods![12] Thus approval for the break-in would have
to come at a low level. Was this mere coincidence? Later, the
RCMP and the federal government would seize on this
feature of the operation to argue that Bricole was a unique
aberration in security work, the result of local overzealousness.

Make-work

The five men carted away a thousand pounds of
documents. Since the raid was "slightly unofficial," the
documents could not be kept at police headquarters. So they
were taken to the basement of the home of one of the Mounties. Searching through their loot, the men eventually found
the Cuban letter—though no one could testify later as to who
found it, or when.

On November 1, nine men from the three forces met to
consider how to proceed. They decided that the documents
should be sorted, those of interest microfilmed, and the rest
destroyed in the provincial police incinerator. The men spent
at least a week filming, as well as reading the contents of interesting documents into a dictaphone. Then the dictaphone
material had to be typed up. Why all this duplication was
necessary (apart from keeping everyone busy) was never
made clear.

An analyst was assigned to develop "psychological portraits" of the alleged terrorists whose communications were
found in the documents. This analyst, a woman in her early
twenties with less than a year of experience with the force,
spent hours "analyzing" the letter from Cuba. In it the exiles
reported that Prensa Latina, the Cuban news agency, had
asked for news on the Parti Québécois, trade unions, and inflation and unemployment in Canada. They also wanted
background information on Canada's prime minister and
solicitor general. The letter requested an anonymous address
for the APLQ (rather than its offices), and repeated three
times that the letter should be destroyed after it had been
read.

This was the heady stuff of international intrigue to the

young analyst. Later she admitted to the Keable inquiry that she was not aware at the time that Prensa Latina was a legitimate news agency with an office in Montreal. Perhaps she didn't think to check the phone book. At any rate, she forwarded the letter to her superiors, with advice that it be brought to high official attention. Her superiors suggested that the prime minister himself should be aware of it.

Interviews with ex-Mounties throw additional light on the excitement which the Bricole group felt when they found this letter which mentioned Prime Minister Trudeau and Solicitor General Goyer. There were apparently quite a few members of the Security Service who had little faith in these gentlemen as guardians of Canada's security. The prime minister was suspected of active leftist leanings. "Look at how many times he's visited communist countries," one ex-Mountie said. Another blamed Goyer for making life more difficult for the Security Service by allowing Soviet embassy staff to travel farther afield from Ottawa than previously.

The Agence de Presse Libre discovered the theft after their weekend away, and sent a telegram to the RCMP asking if they were responsible. No reply was forthcoming. They then held a press conference, complaining of police break-in and harassment. Complaints were made to Quebec Minister of Justice Jérôme Choquette. He consulted the provincial police (he later testified), and denied any police involvement. At the public inquiries years later, the provincial police would testify that they had not been consulted by Mr. Choquette before he issued his denial. This would be one of many contradictions to emerge, but for the time being, the Quebec police forces were covered.

Meanwhile RCMP brass in Ottawa were trying to find out what had happened. The local Mounties secretly confirmed to the director of the Security Service in Ottawa that the RCMP had been involved in the break-in. Four days after the break-in, the victims complained to Solicitor General Goyer, the federal minister responsible for the RCMP and its operations. The complaint was received in his absence by an assistant and forwarded to the RCMP commissioner for comment.

Meanwhile, the director of the Security Service (one step

down the ladder from the commissioner) expressed his disapproval of the operation to the local Security Service men. The RCMP advised the solicitor general not to reply to the APLQ complaint but simply to ignore it. This advice was followed. The APLQ break-in soon faded into obscurity, until the day four years later when Samson's unguarded remarks revived its memory.

Thieves Fall Out

When Bricole finally backfired in March 1976, the first concern of everyone involved was to agree on one story which would put the participants in the best possible light. Boys caught at mischief and spies exposed in conspiracy face the same old problem: thieves tend to fall out. It happened in the Watergate scandal, which ended with each participant angrily accusing the others.

The greatest concern of the Mounties was that an inquiry into Operation Bricole would open a Pandora's box of similar operations. The RCMP probably had more to lose than the Montreal or Quebec police forces—not because the Mounties used such methods more, but because they had been caught much less often. The two Quebec forces had less-than-illustrious reputations, but the Mounties have enjoyed an idealized status in Canadian life.

The danger to the RCMP's image became evident from the first announcement of Operation Bricole by a CBC newscast of March 30, which publicly wondered how many other break-ins had been committed in the name of state security. The local RCMP saw the handwriting on the wall, and telexed the whole newscast to Ottawa (using secret cypher, despite the fact that millions of Canadians had heard the program!)

The threat grew larger as the Quebec solicitor general demanded an explanation from the provincial police force in order to make a statement to the National Assembly. The Montreal RCMP security officer who had approved Bricole four years earlier now advised Ottawa that an official inquiry would be launched in Quebec. The question was: would it be limited to this specific incident, or would it go into the whole principle of such operations—a fishing expedition which might end up God knows where?

The concern widened, and a letter was drafted for the RCMP commissioner to send to all commanding officers. (Whether it was actually sent is not clear, but its arguments indicate the lines of thought of high-ranking Mounties at the time.)[13] Now that Samson had been convicted, the draft noted, an inquiry into the RCMP could be anticipated. "The Force cannot encourage or condone any practices which are contrary to the Rule of Law," the draft warns. If the letter was actually sent, one wonders what some of the local commanding officers must have felt, knowing that for years the force had quietly overlooked "technical illegalities" by the hundreds. Would the force now cover for them, or abandon them to the wolves?

Men who had taken part in break-ins must have flinched if they read such ominous lines as: "The position of the Force . . . is enforcing the law as it stands . . . It is my honest belief that an examination into these matters shall indicate conclusively that any acts outside that framework are individual acts on the part of individual members and do not form a common pattern of prevalent, investigative practices on the part of the Force."[14] These lines certainly became the public and official position of the RCMP on its wrongdoings.

On June 1, 1976, the director general of the Security Service expanded on the same line of thinking in a top secret letter to the officer in charge of Montreal Security Service detachment, Superintendant Donald Cobb: "It is important that there be no 'bargaining' by this Force with respect to any criminal matters under consideration by the Provincial Law Officers of the Crown. When one of our members is charged with a criminal offence, the member alone stands charged . . . The Force does not and cannot become a party to any matters connected therewith."[15] The sociological message of both the draft letter and the director general's letter is clear: the RCMP would never admit that its dirty tricks were structured deviance.

The commissioner did not hide his concern to protect the

RCMP's public image: "I am aware of the impact . . . on public confidence in the Force," he wrote the solicitor general with admirable understatement.[16] The officers in Montreal were more immediately aware, for the cabal held together by four years of secret complicity was in danger of coming apart. An RCMP top secret telex (later made available to the Keable commission) reported that the Montreal police involved in Bricole were "apprehensive" and might identify Robert Samson as the "evil genius in the affair and infer they were really working in support of the RCMP."

Even at this grave juncture, Donald Cobb was not without humor. "Their [the Montreal police's] newfound acknowledgement of our complete jurisdiction in such matters would be touching were it not so evidently born of the fear we are preparing to save ourselves at their expense," a telex message noted.[17] It continued that the provincial police were equally worried. The federal solicitor general's comment that the RCMP played only a supporting role was likely to cause a "panic of recriminations that would have grave consequences far beyond the worst that can come" if the RCMP simply took its knocks. The telex noted that the provincial police were protecting themselves by suggesting in their story that the authorizing officer had checked to make sure the RCMP were participating before allowing his men to join the adventure.

The public, and we as authors, owe something to the recriminations among the various guilty parties. It was from the Montreal and Quebec police forces that the Keable commission got copies of RCMP documents such as those we are quoting; documents which the RCMP and federal Solicitor General Francis Fox fought with great tenacity to protect from public curiosity in the name of national security. The blanket of national security is a comfortable one, and the Montreal Security Service grasped it eagerly. They cabled Ottawa urging that the "federal Solicitor General, due to his additional national security role, could explain/justify/legitimize the Bricole affair as a matter of national security in which the MUCPD and SQ [Montreal and provincial police] supported the RCMP."[18]

Looking for Legitimacy

The legitimation of events is a vital process in modern society, and arouses bureaucratic machinery to urgent activity. The experts in words search for the correct euphemism, the right turn of phrase, and try to avoid any opening into which critics might push the smallest wedge of questions. It is not surprising that the major content of messages from Montreal to headquarters in Ottawa should be concerned with the legitimation of Bricole once it was uncovered. The argument was now developed that the MDPPQ was the primary target. This group was closely tied in purpose to the FLQ, and made a more logical hook to hang national security on—despite the fact that it was not MDPPQ files which were stolen. The Montreal and Quebec police sought legitimacy for the operation from a claim that the RCMP operated on national security considerations, and they were merely helpers. Since the right language can avoid telling the truth while not quite telling a lie, Bricole was described as the sole instance "of its kind." This avoided mention of hundreds of surreptitious entries to plant electronic bugs and wiretaps.

Legitimation is an exhausting activity, and at the end of the process one detects a sigh in the secret RCMP correspondence. Why should it be necessary to explain these things to the public anyway? Why aren't they obvious to any reasonable Canadian? Besides, the whole affair could have been carried out under the legal cover of a search warrant, if only the police had bothered to get one, so what difference did it make? The RCMP seems to have concluded that since a search warrant could have been obtained anyway, the only sin was administrative—the failure to do the right paperwork. The importance of legal safeguards seems to have been lost on the RCMP, MUCPD and SQ men involved in Bricole. As the details unfolded in the media, they probably wondered why they weren't heroes in the silent battle against subversion.

3

Ham Actors

In the early hours of the morning on January 10, 1973, four members of Section G of the Montreal branch of the RCMP broke into a computer center and "borrowed" tapes containing the membership list of the Parti Québécois, a legal and democratic political party with seven members in the Quebec legislature. The tapes were carried to a prearranged rendezvous, copied at another computer center, and replaced in their original filing cabinets. No clues were left of the break-in. As an espionage operation it was a complete success. For several years no one but a few Mounties shared the secret of Operation Ham.

The victims apparently had no idea that they had been the target of RCMP "dirty tricks." In this operation the Mounties went it alone; they sought to avoid detection by the Montreal police as much as by the Parti Québécois. Some of the same Mounties were involved in both Bricole and Ham, but the left hand did not tell the right what it was doing. Operation Ham remained a secret even after ex-Mountie Robert Samson blew the cover on Bricole.

It was the energetic Keable commission investigators who in late 1977 uncovered Operation Ham. As soon as it was discovered, the mandate of the commission was broadened beyond the APLQ-MDPPQ break-in. All parties in the Quebec National Assembly supported the extension of the Keable inquiry, even the Liberals. A battle broke out between the federal government and the RCMP on one side, and the Keable commission (backed by a Parti Québécois now in power) on the other. Which would best represent the interests of the people of Canada? And of Quebec?

Operation Ham is a different test case of secret police operations in an open society than that epitomized by Operation Bricole. It was not an easily legitimized probe against an openly leftist and perhaps revolutionary group. The Parti Québécois is a legitimate and broadly based political party seeking constitutional reform, not insurrection. Its leaders come from prestigious ranks of the business establishment, the civil service, academic institutions, the media, and the arts.

Ham is a useful instance of the general tendency for secret police, once well established, to expand their definition of the "enemy." Their targets often spread beyond real subversives and threats to national security, to include an ever wider swath of dissent and nonconformity.

A regular police force operating under law must restrict itself to a narrow definition of its targets. But a secret police beyond the control of democratic institutions, operating out of sight and without accountability, is restricted only by its own self-restraint, plus the limits of its resources. If the self-restraint breaks down, and resources stand idle which could be employed in a widened target area, then often nothing stands in the way.

Positive forces exist within a bureaucratically organized secret police to push them toward an expansion of their target. Files sit waiting to be fed new data. Men trained and predisposed to action seek new activities. Suspicions, once nourished, reach out to thrive on what others find innocent or harmless.

Since the Mounties are schooled in the theory of Canadian democracy,[1] their first inclination would be to respect the legitimacy of a democratically elected party such as the Parti Québécois. There would have to be a convincing rationale to compensate for the stress of acting against deeply ingrained ideas. There would have to be approval of initiatives from higher levels of authority than were necessary for Operation

Bricole, and more precautions would have to be taken to keep it clandestine. If the secret did leak, repercussions would be more serious.

Operation Ham was very carefully planned and executed. It was proposed, pondered, postponed, and finally, cautiously approved at a very high level in the force. Indeed, the original trail of legitimations leads all the way back to the Privy Council office.

Though Ham was a completely clandestine operation, it was by no means unique. The RCMP already had an established class of operations variously known as 300 operations, or PUMA operations, or in the jargon of the trade, "bag jobs."[2] The RCMP's worst fear was that disclosure of Ham would expose the existence of the whole class of PUMA or bag jobs. It would be clear that the force had elaborate technical resources for illegal break-ins. The question would inevitably arise—where else had these resources been applied? Bricole was the sort of prank which could be dismissed as a unique aberration of *individuals*. But Ham was clearly the work of an *organization*.

Most of the targets of bag jobs will never be known, but the likely ones appear to have been the New Democratic Party, the Praxis group of urban reformers in Toronto, native Indian groups, and even the offices of members of Parliament. Once Ham was in the open, others who had experienced strange break-ins or losses of documents, and had been unable to attribute them to any culprit, were now provided with a likely explanation.

In October 1977, Conservative MP Erik Nielsen read off a list of groups which had been investigated or infiltrated by the Security Service under the direction of the Police and Security Planning and Analysis Group, a government committee between the cabinet and the RCMP. He charged that the RCMP had become a political police force. The use of the Security Service for this kind of work, he claimed, was ruining the RCMP's reputation for integrity. Among the groups he listed along with the FLQ were the National Farmers Union, native rights groups, the Quebec teachers' union, the two major Quebec labor federations, and other broadly representative and democratic organizations.[3]

Setting the Stage

In terms of a bureaucracy, something really "begins" when a file is opened and the first scrap of paper is housed in it. Operation Ham apparently began with a letter from Unit G of C Division of the RCMP, in August 1972. Unit G was in charge of anti-terrorism in Montreal. One of its members had noticed that the Parti Québécois was promoting membership by advertising its "fully equipped . . . efficient organization." The ad featured the party's computer-issued membership cards. The membership form contained a good deal of useful information: the member's education, employer, residence, and telephone number. The enterprising Mountie had also learned where all this data was stored on tape at a computer agency. His letter suggested that an expert in the RCMP's own computer section should determine whether it would be possible to tap into this computer.

Thus the operation began, though it was not named until later, and we probably will never know why the name Ham was chosen. Perhaps it was in humor, to secretly spite certain journalists and members of Parliament who had from time to time called the RCMP's Security Service "ham-handed."[4] But what led an RCMP member to consider tapping the Parti Québécois membership list in the first place?

The idea must have been born in the aftermath of the October Crisis of 1970. The FLQ was gone, but separatists remained. The old wolves must now be hiding in sheep's clothing. Robin Bourne, the federal civil servant in charge of the Police and Security Planning and Analysis Group, would put the RCMP's case this way in 1978: "Well then, goddammit, we had these separatists. The nerve of them. They're trying to break up our country. And, you know, the clear distinction between the Parti Québécois and the FLQ was really not made until very recently. All we knew, legitimate or not, political party or not, was that they were intending to break up our country. So they were the enemy."[5]

Because the PQ was a legal party, espionage against it would be undemocratic unless justification could be found in the name of a higher value than democratic policing. That higher value was national unity. Neither the leadership of the federal government nor that of the Security Service were able to conceive of Canada as anything but a single unified and centralized nation. As journalist George Bain noted, the federal leaders seemed incapable of distinguishing between "democratic" separatists—Canadians who think of themselves as Québécois first and Canadians second—and terrorist separatists, those prepared to use violent force to achieve a sovereign Quebec state.[6]

Separatism was seen as a danger to national security, therefore separatism was *subversion*. The RCMP Security Service existed to combat subversion. At the time, this was not even legally defined. That came in a revision of the Official Secrets Act in 1974, when subversion was defined as activities directed toward accomplishing government change within Canada or elsewhere by force or violence *or any criminal means*. Since the separation of Quebec from the other provinces it agreed to join in 1867 was not provided for in the "constitution" of Canada (the BNA Act), any attempt at separation could be deemed in violation of the law—in other words, a criminal act. Therefore the RCMP as the right arm of the Canadian state could justify taking counter-subversive action against the PQ, which stood for a sovereign Quebec.

The Myth of Foreign Money

In February 1978, a *Globe and Mail* journalist interviewed a security advisor to the Privy Council Office of Canada. The advisor revealed that the Privy Council Office had initiated an investigation into Parti Québécois finances in 1970. Apparently the federal government could not believe that the PQ was financed by its own members. Foreign money must be supporting the separatists, and the federalists wanted to know where it was coming from.[7]

"Foreign money" is one of the classic myths in the establishment's explanation of dissident movements in North America. In the thirties, it was common to hear the charge that the communist party and its "front" organizations were funded by "Moscow gold." Members of the party at the time didn't think the charge very amusing, because they were usually hamstrung for money. Foreign money was also frequently blamed as the basis for the nuclear disarmament campaigns of the fifties and the anti-Vietnam War movement of the sixties. In the United States, President Nixon specifically instructed the CIA to find the foreign sources of the anti-war movement's funds, and cut them off. When the CIA reported that there were no such sources—the money was coming from angry young Americans—Nixon sent them back to look again. He couldn't believe no foreign money was involved.[8]

At the Keable commission hearings, the former deputy director general of the RCMP security force confirmed the story of the RCMP's search for foreign gold behind the Parti Québécois (presumably not from Moscow in this case —perhaps from France?) In fact, a specific figure was mentioned—$350,000.[9] This charge has never been substantiated.

Another argument advanced to justify secret police action against the Parti Québécois was "plugging leaks." But to understand this argument we must examine the secret structures where it was possible for the imaginative corporal's letter to find a welcome.

The Theater of the Absurdly Secret

The theater of the bureaucratic secret goes Samuel Beckett and Harold Pinter one better. Their "theater of the absurd" doesn't really care if the audience understands or not—but at least an audience is allowed to be present, to glean what meaning it can. In the drama of bureaucratic secrecy, the audience is banished—sometimes for a short time, sometimes for many years, and sometimes forever.

The political leadership of a modern state faces a major problem when making decisions: there are always several different, and often profoundly different, audiences to react to the action taken. In past ages, rulers could ignore most of the population. But today public opinion is a powerful political force rooted in the mass media.

Politicians and bureaucrats who must make difficult decisions will get through the day more easily if those decisions are not immediately known. Secrecy prevents harsh reviews of one's actions. It also helps prevent the critics from ganging up. But if bureaucracies are to preserve secrecy they must prevent leaks—the unauthorized disclosure of information. To protect their jobs, those who leak secrets must keep their identity secret!

The RCMP suspected in 1972 that some members of the federal government had separatist opinions, and might even belong to the Parti Québécois. Such civil servants could be a likely source of leaks about decisions which the government preferred to keep from the public. There was talk of a "Parizeau network"—a chain of informers passing federal information to Jacques Parizeau, who became finance minister of Quebec when the Parti Québécois won power in 1976. (Later Mr. Parizeau would claim that this "network" was nothing more than a group of drinking buddies whose interests were mainly fiscal policy matters.)

A list of the PQ members would enable the RCMP to identify separatists within the federal civil service. Then they could be watched. In time, those suspected of leaking information to the PQ could be quietly dismissed on whatever pretext. *Thus the very preservation of secrecy of operations which made it possible for the RCMP eventually to acquire the PQ membership list, became one of the rationales for acquiring the list!*

Bureaucratic secrecy can certainly become theatrically absurd. Distinguished American historian Henry Commager observed that the "metamorphosis of two old and familiar concepts into political institutions with a life of their own—the concept of national security and the concept of secrecy," was at the heart of American Watergate politics.[10] Historian Jacques De Larue, dealing with a more terrifying political malaise, wrote that "secrecy was a vital principle of the Gestapo" which "allowed a veil to be drawn" over Nazi horrors.[11] "Keeping your mouth shut" is a century-old principle of the RCMP. Former Mounties we interviewed repeatedly emphasized the training of rookies in "keeping your mouth shut."

In another theater called Parliament, the prime minister told reporters that he was shocked when he first learned of RCMP surveillance of the Parti Québécois and said that it must stop.[12] But he could not recall which year he was told.

Ed Broadbent, leader of the New Democratic Party, observed: "If the Prime Minister was shocked . . . then surely he must remember the year. Surely he must remember whether he was told if the RCMP had a list of PQ members. If the shock is there, how could his memory suddenly disappear?"[13]

The prime minister later contradicted himself by explaining to reporters that he felt no surprise that the RCMP had obtained PQ lists, because "you can get a list very easily."[14] Spokesmen for all parties, including the Liberals, contradicted the prime minister; it was extremely difficult to get party membership lists. The PQ said even their own leader can't see the list without permission from the party executive council.[15]

An alternative and very plausible explanation would be that the government knew of—or even ordered—the surveillance long before 1972, and perhaps as far back as 1970. Journalist George Bain reported that a leaked cabinet document revealed that eight days before the PQ elected its first seven members to the Quebec assembly (and months prior to the October Crisis), the federal cabinet set up a committee to inquire into what to do in the event that the War Measures Act came into force "by reason of insurrection" in circumstances where "demands for social change might be accompanied by criminal behavior, with or without violence."[16]

Quebec author Pierre Vallières uses facts uncovered by CBC investigative reporters to argue (in his book, *Assassination of Pierre Laporte*) that by and large the 1970 crisis was orchestrated by the federal government to undermine the growing support for the Parti Québécois. In the short run this objective was achieved; the Quebec Liberals under Bourassa were re-elected. An ex-police chief with many years of high-level administrative experience has told the authors that it is extremely unlikely that any force—even the RCMP—would have undertaken an undercover operation so pregnant with political repercussions as Operation Ham without orders from political superiors.

In 1978 Trudeau did admit that as a matter of policy the RCMP carried out surveillance on political candidates of various parties.[17] Indeed, the RCMP manual specifies reporting on candidates considered to be of security interest, "regardless of political party represented." This contradicts earlier statements by Solicitor General Blais that the RCMP gathered only statistical material which is generally available on political candidates.

The Plot

Someone will someday write a thriller based on the RCMP plot to steal the Parti Québécois membership tapes. The details make a great story, but they aren't really relevant to a study of structured deviance, so we will summarize many documents, and many weeks of espionage work, into a few paragraphs.[18]

Once the Montreal Security Service resolved to get the tapes by any means, it became obvious that they would have to steal them. There was no way to connect to the computer terminal electronically, and all the computer center employees proved too loyal to be recruited as inside men. So a former Mountie now employed with a business machines corporation was approached to act as a front man. He agreed to visit the computer center, ostensibly on business, accompanied by a "business colleague" who was really a member of the RCMP. This would give the Security Service their first opportunity to case the joint, as burglars say.

Next the team began to organize the elaborate resources of the RCMP to stand by for breaking the law. Locksmiths who were capable (as the Laycraft inquiry in Alberta later confirmed) of picking as many as twelve locks an hour were ready to move. RCMP experts on computer functions gave advice on the problems of compatibility between systems. The RCMP transport section would have vehicles ready, with untraceable license plates. Communications experts would be ready with walkie-talkies.

The RCMP can always count on a section of the population to cooperate with its illegal operations without asking questions. The front man and his Security Service "colleague" who visited the computer center arranged a cover story with a business contact just in case their visit aroused suspicion. The business contact didn't ask for an explanation; he was glad to help the Mounties. So were some proprietors of buildings near the computer center; they allowed the Mounties to post lookouts to ascertain the movements of Montreal police in the area. (The police were not to be told about the operation).

Once the team knew the internal layout of the center and the location of the desired tapes (discovered by the front man in casual conversation with the computer manager), the next step was a "surreptitious entry." The RCMP code-word for such operations is PUMA. In fact, several PUMAs were necessary to lay the groundwork for Operation Ham. The first located the burglar alarms which would have to be silenced before the computer center could be entered. The second got as far as the computer office, where the RCMP locksmith discovered a new type of lock he didn't know how to pick. Information on this lock was obtained for the next PUMA, which included a dry run of the final operation—getting the tapes out of the center to a waiting car, transporting them to another computer center where they could be copied, and returning them.

There were still numerous problems to be overcome. The burglar alarms had to be safely neutralized, so Mounties visited the company that had wired the building. This time the cover story was pornography; the manager of alarms installations was persuaded that the Mounties were moving in on a porno ring. He cheerfully obliged by telling them how to disconnect the alarms temporarily. He even provided the code number of the locks used, and a few loose keys he had lying around that might fit.

There were problems too with copying the data. The dry run included taking a PQ tape from the center, but Ottawa RCMP headquarters found the copy incompatible with their equipment and difficult to decode. (The actual run would take much longer than the dry run, of course, since there were ultimately eleven tapes to copy.)

In December 1972, after four months of planning and rehearsal, everything was ready. There was even a disaster plan in case the Mounties were caught: they would steal some business tapes from the center along with the PQ tapes, so that the break-in would appear to be industrial espionage. This suggestion came from a top-ranking Ottawa officer.

Documents presented at the Keable inquiry include approval of the operation signed by L. R. Parent, deputy director general of the Security Service, who later avoided testifying at the Keable inquiry by presenting a doctor's certificate that he was suffering memory loss. Penned in the margin of the approval is the comment: "D.G. has seen, 11/12/72." D.G. is presumably Director General, since Parent is styled "D.D.G." in the letter.[19]

Unfortunately for the impatient Montreal team, the computer center suddenly had a busy spell and remained open all night for most of December. One Mountie grumbled in a communiqué that unless they could break in soon, they'd have to try a whole new approach to get the PQ tapes. Finally the center was closed for the Christmas holiday. But now Ottawa officials began to have second thoughts. They postponed the operation.

Finally, on January 8, 1973, the big moment arrived. There was still one last-minute snag. The owner of the premises overlooking the center was weary of Mounties coming and going, and was no longer willing to let them use his windows for lookouts. The burglars had to use a parked truck instead. At a few minutes after midnight, the conspiracy bore fruit. A total of fifteen men swung into action. By six in the morning, the tapes were back in their filing cabinets, all clues were removed, the agents were on their way home to bed, and the RCMP's complete copy of the PQ membership list was on its way to Ottawa.

With the usual bureaucratic obsession for detail, the Montreal office sent several telex messages to Ottawa over the following week, summarizing details of the successful performance, and giving all the players a suitable notice. In all, the supporting cast and stage crew totalled sixty-six members of the force![20] Ottawa telexed back appropriate congratulations to everyone.

The scene now shifted to Ottawa, where the tapes were eagerly analyzed. But the cupboard was bare. RCMP officers admitted to the McDonald inquiry that no clues to sources of leaks in the federal bureaucracy or other evidence of

separatist subversion was uncovered.[21] There was no evidence
of foreign money. In July 1975 the tapes were destroyed, but
the worry lived on. "Should any of this information fall into
the wrong hands it would prove embarrassing for the government as well as the RCMP," officers reflected.[22] The play had
been successful, but pointless. It was theater of the absurd
after all.

The Canadian audience, admitted much later to the
theater, must still ponder how many other unannounced per-
formances have been executed. In a secret telex between the
Montreal unit and Ottawa headquarters on October 20,
1972,[23] it was reported that one of the non-Mountie collaborators in Operation Ham had signed a modified form of
oath of secrecy under the Official Secrets Act. The use of the
oath is justified in the telex by the precedent of previous
operations, "e.g. Bravo and Grub." What were these operations? To date, nothing in the McDonald or Keable commissions' public hearings has thrown any light on them.

"We never gave it a thought"

Three years after Ham, some of the men involved would be
carefully interrogated by two commissions. One after
another, they would echo a refrain which should trouble
anyone concerned with maintaining an open and democratic
society. How did each man account for the gap between his
responsibility as an officer of the law and the unlawfulness of
burglary? Quite simply: "We never gave it a thought."

Asked if he considered the legality of the operation, an
RCMP inspector calmly responded, "That kind of question
never entered my mind." As for the use of pretexts such as
that of a pornography ring, he explained that a plausible ruse
was needed, and he made no distinction between an innocent
and a defamatory pretext.[24] The superior officers who gave
the clearance in principle never considered the legality of the
operation. At the worst it was only "technically illegal," and
there was precedent of long bureaucratic usage: "Such operations have been fairly standard procedure since the 1950's."[25]
Could anything be more revealing?

The same rationale has emerged in other countries of the

"free world" when the cover has been blown on intelligence-gathering methods. CIA head Richard Helm and FBI leader William Sullivan both told Congress that they never gave it a thought when asked about the legality of their operations. They behaved no worse than the congressmen themselves, who year after year approved the FBI and CIA's budgets—and often used information gathered by them—without asking how that information was collected.

What the secret police in a free society *do* give thought to is not legality, but "flap potential." How much bad press, how much embarrassment, will an undercover operation generate if leaked or exposed?[26] When secrecy is shattered, it must be replaced by cover-up. Evidence must be tinkered with or destroyed, and those in the know must cooperate to get their story straight. They must also remind themselves of the official legitimacy of their actions, in terms of the facilitating ideology—national security. The objectors, protesters, and interrogators must be made to look impractical, unreasonable, unrealistic. As an RCMP officer put it, "It is important to turn the question of Ham around. In what way was Ham illegal?"

Thus one of the McDonald interrogators was reminded that technical violations of the law are necessary if the police are to do their job. The officers appealed to "pragmatic considerations," "overriding reasons" and "the climate of the times." They would be assisted in this effort by those who believe that the ideology of national security is an overriding consideration. For example, the Toronto *Sun* editorialized about Operation Ham: "It seems the act of a desperate security force, trying vainly to catch up on lost ground due to years of government policies that restricted adequate surveillance."[27]

In other words, the secret police were only trying to do their job, which the government had made difficult. There is the implication that if everyone had been doing his job, the PQ would never have achieved power in the first place and Canada wouldn't face a national unity crisis.

When senior officers and parliamentarians said they "never gave it a thought," did an outraged public reply, "You should have"? A few citizens were indignant, but by no means a majority. There were those who, like Justice James Hugessen of the Quebec Supreme Court, argued that crimes, even those committed in the name of national security, are crimes nevertheless and should be punished as such.[28]

But most Canadians apparently didn't want to give it a serious thought. The daily papers were deluged with letters.[29]

I see nothing wrong with the RCMP getting needed information from PQ offices by any means possible. The PQ were making plans for subversion. Subversion means destruction of a country and plans to tear apart my country is subversion, in my opinion.

Comparing the RCMP break-in to the Watergate break-ins is ridiculous. The PQ was and is dedicated to the break-up of Canada.

It gives us a warm, cosy feeling to know the security of our country is in such capable and efficient hands as the RCMP.

4

Rumors of Wrongdoing

"If I checked out every rumor I'd be chasing rumors every day of the week," a member of the Ottawa headquarters staff of the RCMP Security Service told the McDonald commission.[1] He was explaining why he did nothing about rumors floating through the office for months about the unorthodox activities of the Mounties. The rumors began in 1973, but it was 1977 before senior officials admitted that Operation Bricole was far from a unique and isolated event.

The Barn-Burning

The headline read "BARN-BURNING MOUNTIES DESCRIBE A COMEDY OF ERRORS." The target was an alleged meeting between militants in the Front de Libération du Québec and a few Black Panthers from the United States. The time was May 1972—several months prior to the APLQ break-in.

The source of intelligence about the meeting was apparently a tip from the FBI in Burlington, Vermont, that an "underground railway" was bringing American subversives into Canada. The definition of the Black Panthers as subversives or terrorists is itself a controversial issue. There have been many who hold that this organization was one of legal dissent, but was ruthlessly harassed by the FBI and local American police forces.[2] We cannot go into the question here, except to refuse to take for granted that a "Black Panther connection" automatically implied either subversion or terrorism and therefore justified whatever means were necessary to prevent them meeting with the FLQ. It is hardly necessary to add, since the recent uncovering of much FBI wrongdoing in the United States, that one needn't take the FBI's word on the Black Panthers.

The RCMP Security Service accepted both the FBI's definition of the situation, and a typical secret police solution for the problem. It developed that it would be impossible to monitor the forthcoming FLQ-Panther meeting. There was nowhere to plant electronic surveillance and there was no informer inside the FLQ group. The solution was to destroy the barn, and force the suspects to meet somewhere else where they could be eavesdropped. This type of solution was familiar to FBI and CIA agents. As pro-CIA author Miles Copeland acknowledged, the CIA were trained to get information in whatever way necessary, including "burglary, theft or any other kind of petty crime."[3] The RCMP-CIA-FBI connection is not particularly secret, and has been noted in the daily press[4] as well as in pro-RCMP books.[5]

Any gathering at the barn located at Ste. Anne de la Rochelle, eighty kilometers east of Montreal, was already suspicious to the Mounties. The farm was owned by Rosa Rose, mother of convicted FLQ members Jacques and Paul Rose. No ordinary farm, it was known as La Grange du Petit Québec Libre. It was used as a summer campground, a poetry and music center, and a meeting place for "leftist intellectuals and union organizers." These were suspect activities in Mountie eyes![6]

Burning down a barn on the basis of a tip amounts to fairly vigorous rumor-chasing, but only one member of the RCMP assigned to the task raised any question about its legality. He was quickly assured by the sergeant in charge, "It is justified . . . I really don't think we are committing any type of illegal act."[7]

Another man on the assignment preferred to deal with his doubts by not knowing what he was doing: "RCMP Inspector Bernard Blier testified yesterday that he spent all night with three colleagues on a clandestine operation in Quebec's Eastern Townships and never knew that he had participated in a barn burning episode."[8] It was only a few days later that he heard that the barn, known as an FLQ hangout, had been burned. "In my head I put together two and two" and came up with "perhaps three and a half"—a strong suspicion that he had been part of the operation! Such deductive powers in Security Service men are impressive indeed. Even then he didn't ask any questions and didn't report anything to his superiors, the inspector told the McDonald commission. (He was a corporal at the time of the operation.) However, the other three men involved testified that "they probably discussed what they were up to in Inspector Blier's presence."[9]

In the barn-burning escapade, as elsewhere in the unraveling of dirty tricks by the Security Service, there is the temptation to blame individuals. The media would rather highlight individual wrongdoing than undertake the difficult sociological analysis of the system. The courts and commissions are hardly organized for extensive investigations. Politicians would generally prefer to throw a few highly visible culprits to the wolves, and leave the structure untouched.

Notable protagonists of civil liberties in Canada, such as novelist Margaret Laurence and constitutional lawyer Walter Fox, have argued that there should be prosecutions of senior officers who authorized the dirty tricks.[10] Peter McWilliams, a former Crown prosecutor and now an author on criminal law, has argued "there are ample provisions in criminal and civil law that can be used to prosecute RCMP members . . ." which would apparently include both authorizing officers and the men actually involved.[11] Williams notes that such prosecutions took place in the case of the CIA and FBI in the United States. But it made no real difference in the continuing commitment of those forces to subverting democratic law and practice. (When one top CIA man was found guilty of perjury in testimony before Congress, the fine was a nominal $1000, which his former colleagues raised within a matter of minutes as a gesture of solidarity and appreciation for his protection of their collective interests.)

Not to punish men involved in dirty tricks does not imply that they should be rewarded. Yet the members of the barn-burning team were congratulated on a successful operation. Even in terms of the expected skills of a secret police force, this was a dubious evaluation. As noted below, the interaction of the men during the escapade was hardly professional. But far from damaging their careers, participation seems to have been rewarded: "The ends justified the means at that time, and Mounties who carried out shady jobs, such as break-ins to plant bugs, continued to have very good careers . . . . the four participants in the barn-burning are all still with the RCMP and some have since been promoted."[12]

Everybody's Doing It

One of the men involved testified at the McDonald inquiry that he didn't think the act was arson. "It was perhaps not right under the law but . . . I acted like everybody else." It is the "everybody else" which should trouble both the sociologist and civil libertarian. The tasks assigned to a secret police force in an open society, by their very nature, create situations where the rules of the organization—in this case, the "rule of law"—must be flouted. The individuals involved are not particularly culpable; "everybody else" is doing it, and "if I don't do it, someone else will." An important part of this situation is the training of the Mountie to obey orders without question. Mounties have been trained to believe that the RCMP Act overrides all other Canadian legislation, an RCMP witness told the McDonald commission.[13] Thus an officer's orders under the RCMP Act would authorize the violation of any other Canadian law!

The particular officer who takes the initiative to give such an order is not especially culpable either. He will generally be someone whose *position in the structure* accounts for the fact that he is experiencing more of the *structural strain* affecting the organization at that time than others around him. In the testimony of the men involved in the barn-burning we find manifestations of such strain.

First, there is the strain of "cognitive dissonance"—the conflict between two sets of competing definitions of the situation.[14] Barn-burning is arson, unless you happen to have the owner's permission. It might even be murder, if someone is inside the barn. But RCMP officers felt that not preventing an alleged meeting of subversives "could have a disastrous impact with repercussions—such as murder—which would have been impossible to control."[15]

It appears that the Mounties resolved some of their stress in a manner fairly typical of North Americans: they had a few drinks. "Arriving in the area too early, they killed some time in a hotel in Granby, Quebec, drinking a few beers while discussing the project."[16]

Another symptom of stress is to botch the job. Setting a barn on fire is probably not difficult even for an amateur. Yet it took four Mounties two tries and a comedy of errors to achieve it.[17] The chronicle of mishaps includes a car breakdown caused by driving over a rock and ripping out the transmission. Then the heavy engine oil (an odd combustible for experts to use) failed to keep burning the first time, so the men had to return to the barn after making their first getaway. Finally (right out of the movies!) the getaway car failed to start, so they had to borrow a pickup truck. The men did make certain no one was in the barn, and concluded that a nearby farmhouse would not catch fire because it was raining. Fortunately, they were right.

The Mounties later told the McDonald inquiry that they talked about the most worrisome detail—how to avoid getting caught. "We agreed if anyone saw us around we would go in different directions and we would each make our own way back to Montreal the best way we could."[18]

The RCMP had prepared the men to cope with the stress of deviant activity by training them not to ask questions. *But none of their training dealt with the question of what they should do if given an illegal order.* "I don't know what would have happened if I had refused an order," one participant explained. Another said he "couldn't recall an instructor ever telling him what to do if he received an order to carry out an illegal act."[19]

In an amusing sidelight to the pervasiveness of bureaucracy, the men were told not to file any expense accounts for the operation. The only written report was a repair requisition for the ripped-out transmission. However, the young woman who acted as analyst for Section G did tell the McDonald inquiry that she referred to barn-burning in a paper on possible seminars about "disruptive tactics," written in June 1972.[20] Perhaps it was felt that the men needed more training for their next barn-burning! As for the alleged meeting between the FLQ and Black Panthers, there is no evidence that it ever took place.

The Dynamite Caper

Was there one case of dynamite, or four? Was it taken to plant on a suspected terrorist, in order to frame him? Or was it to help an informer establish himself in a terrorist group? Why didn't the Mounties just buy the dynamite? Why was it stored at a Mountie's summer cottage? Why did two Mounties apparently spend two weeks poking around construction sites for sticks lying loose before they happened to hear of a shed they could break into? These are some of the inevitable questions which will probably never be answered.

The facts reported to the McDonald inquiry were these: In *May* 1972 two of the same men involved in the barn-burning were ordered by staff sergeant Donald McCleery to get some dynamite "through other than normal channels" so that it couldn't be traced. (At the Keable inquiry, McCleery denied giving such an order but admitted storing dynamite at his summer cottage after it was stolen.) The men spent two weeks checking construction sites looking for stray sticks of dynamite. Then a fellow RCMP member happened to remark that explosives were stored at a Richelieu *Construction* site south of Montreal. Late at night the Mounties sneaked across an open field into the site while an RCMP driver waited in an unmarked car. The two men broke into a shed and, it was testified later, carried off *one* case of dynamite. It was stashed under Donald McCleery's desk (this much he admitted) for several days, then transferred to his cottage.[21]

At the McDonald inquiry, the manager of Richelieu *Explosives* testified about a theft from his firm's warehouse. He reported that *four* cases of dynamite had been stolen on the night of *April* 26, 1972, as shown in company records of the time. The four cases weighed two hundred pounds, and one hundred blasting caps were also stolen. All dynamite cases are coded by law. The codes were reported immediately to the provincial police.[22]

The Mounties' account of the final disposition of one stolen case of dynamite was that in the fall of 1972, two members of the force dumped the case in the ditch beside a rural road. They anonymously phoned the provincial police to report where it could be found. At this point their story meshes with that of the explosives company manager, who testified that a case of dynamite with the coding number removed was reported to him in the fall of 1972 by the police. They had found it in a ditch. The case fit the description of the stolen dynamite. Nothing was ever heard of the other three cases, he reported.

Whatever the true story, the testimonies concur that some Mounties took some dynamite in 1972. But was it theft? RCMP counsel at the McDonald commission repeatedly objected to any question which implied that the dynamite caper was theft. "The corporal isn't a lawyer and isn't qualified to say if his actions are illegal," counsel maintained.[23] Presumably, only Mounties who are lawyers (and there are very few with that distinction!) would be in a position to apprehend a thief caught in the act.

One RCMP member who was involved had an interesting explanation for why he believed that his act was not theft. It was provided for in his job description, written by his sergeant, that he should obtain necessary materials when required. These neutralizations after the fact (whether one's counsel's efforts or one's own) illustrate a point made by John Hagan that in attractive circumstances, where the deviant behavior seems to promise a worthwhile reward against low risk, little neutralization occurs in advance.[24] It develops only as justification if and when one is caught. Thus the important rule of Mountie secret service operations is undoubtedly: "Don't get caught."

In many bureaucratic organizations there is a "displacement of goals." Employees lose sight of, or become confused about, the purposes of their activities, and become totally preoccupied with keeping the bureaucratic operation going. The goal is no longer that for which the activity was set up, but the activity itself. Whatever the original intention for finding dynamite on a construction site, after two weeks of looking the reason for a theft would become less problematic; now the need was simply to get the job done.

The commission counsel asked one of the corporals involved: "During those two weeks, did it occur to you that your mission was to steal dynamite?" The reply was, "I felt it would probably come to that." The task was merely a technical process to be carried out, without regard for purpose. This displacement of goals was emphasized when the corporal was later asked by Mr. Justice McDonald, the commission chairman, "If McCleery said, 'We need a diamond ring so that the source in the terrorist cell can persuade his friends that he has stolen a diamond ring from Birk's,' would the corporal have broken into the store?"

"No," came the reply, "a more experienced man would be needed for a complicated job like that."[25]

The Phony Communiqué

"FAKE FLQ MESSAGE IS FINAL IMPROPRIETY OF RCMP, FOX SAYS." Thus read a headline of January 10, 1978. With this final revelation the slate had been wiped clean, the solicitor general claimed. Later he was to clarify that he meant the slate in Quebec—since other "improprieties" were emerging elsewhere, such as Alberta (the Laycraft commission into RCMP improprieties).

If there was a crime at all in the fake message, Mr. Fox considered it only "public mischief."[26] The message was issued to the media in Quebec in December 1971 (well before the barn-burning and dynamite capers, as well as before Operations Bricole and Ham). It purported to be a communiqué from the Minerva cell of the FLQ, and urged the use of violence. It specifically attacked those adherents of the FLQ who were proposing peaceful methods of political change. But the communiqué was not written by the FLQ; it was written in a Montreal RCMP office. Mr. Fox conceded: "One could understand, I suppose, a communiqué that would be a call to peace or to lay down arms but it's very difficult to understand a communiqué that is proclaimed in these terms."

The communiqué was deliberately couched in the style of other FLQ manifestos, and employed the famous illustration of the nineteenth-century Quebec patriot with gun and tuque. "Mao, the true revolutionary, teaches us that power is at the point of a gun," read the communiqué.

> The Minerva cell disapproves of the new ideas of Pierre Vallières. Vallières has convinced us of the efficacy of violent revolution to liberate us from capitalist tyrants. Now Vallières, the ineffectual revolutionary, can only write words. . . . Vallières endorses the Parti Québécois. We know this petit-bourgeois party, comfortable with the establishment, is gathering all the bunglers. . . . What good is it to infiltrate the PQ when we can reach our goals by our own weapons?[27]

The RCMP tactic of issuing a false communiqué falls in the category of secret police methods well established by the CIA, British intelligence, the KGB and other such forces. It is called "disinformation," and attempts to disrupt enemy activities by supplying false or misleading information.[28] In the RCMP case, the stated objective was to create consternation and distrust among FLQ members as each attempted to find out which other members had issued it without authority. Angry accusations would be met by equally outraged denials. Mr. Fox claimed the communiqué "was aimed at creating disunity among extremist groups."[29]

There was one small fly in this soothing ointment of neutralization of Mountie mischief. In the conventional use of disinformation tactics by secret intelligence services, your own side should not be taken in by the misinformation, which is aimed solely at confusing and confounding the enemy. But in this instance, the Montreal Security Service neglected to tell their superiors (or so it was claimed) that the communiqué was phony. Likewise the Montreal police "showed no indication that they knew it was a fake," Mr. Fox admitted.[30]

Was the PQ the target?

The sociological mind is like the detective mind—it suspects the obvious. Peter Berger says that the sociologist looks behind official explanations and employs "debunking" tactics.[31]

What has generally been taken for granted is that the RCMP communiqué was directed at the FLQ. But what was the Quebec political climate in December 1971 when the communiqué was issued by the RCMP?

The climate of late 1971 in Quebec was one of a gradual return to ordinary political life. The FLQ efforts to precipitate the "liberation" of Quebec through kidnapping and murder had proved futile and reprehensible. The FLQ was shown to be not a vast network, an apprehended insurrection of considerable scale, but a disorganized and largely unconnected series of cells, numbering altogether only a few dozen persons. The great majority of Québécois were shocked and disapproving of the FLQ actions. Very few indeed would be impressed by an appeal to the teachings of Mao about power issuing from the barrel of a gun.

In 1971, there were no further separatist bombings, kidnappings, or other excesses. The killers of Pierre Laporte were tried and convicted. At the year's end, the leading theoretician of violence in the cause of separatism, Pierre Vallières, recognized his miscalculation of the mood of Quebec. The influential French-language newspaper, *Le Devoir* (whose editor-publisher in 1978 would become the leader of the Quebec Liberal Party), published a lengthy statement by Vallières.[32] He repudiated violent means of political change, denounced the bungling of the FLQ, and called on separatists to pursue their goals through legal political channels. In particular, he urged support of the Parti Québécois.

Two weeks later, in this climate of restored calm, the top security service men in Quebec sat down to compose a phony FLQ communiqué which would be so authentic in its style and appearance that it would fool (it was claimed) all the headquarters officers, the federal government, and many ordinary newspaper readers in Quebec. It would lampoon Vallières and urge terrorism. It would castigate the Parti Québécois as petty bourgeois, bunglers, and "accomplices to the fascists in authority."

In a stabilizing political situation, it is the task of secret intelligence services opposed to the trend of political development to "destabilize"—a euphemism used by the CIA. The trend of political stability in Quebec was not satisfactory to the RCMP. The mainstream separatist movement had survived the October Crisis and its aftermath, and was consolidating its strength within the Parti Québécois. It may even have appeared to the RCMP to be more of a threat than ever.

Our interpretation of the fake communiqué is that it was an effort by the Security Service in Quebec to undermine the hold of the legitimate separatist movement on the imagination of a growing number of Québécois. Those efforts would expand in the following year, 1972, into the dirty tricks we have already examined, culminating with the acquisition of the PQ's membership list. As noted earlier, the RCMP did not distinguish sufficiently between violent and lawful separatists.

A possible counter-argument to our analysis of the fake communiqué must be considered. It could be held that our analysis is too clever by half. Maybe we have read too much into a mere prank. Maybe the RCMP are not crafty enough to produce a communiqué which could be explained later as a disinformation tactic to disrupt the FLQ, but which in reality was a destabilizing tactic directed against the growing popularity of the Parti Québécois.

But the man who authorized the communiqué (and presumably had some hand in its preparation) was regarded as one of the brightest intellectual lights in the RCMP. He had an acute awareness of political reality, as demonstrated in his handling of the repercussions of Operations Ham and Bricole when they finally saw the light of day. Perhaps most important, he had the sophistication not to be taken in by his own act. He was capable of role distance, as demonstrated by his sense of humor.[33]

But it is not necessary for us to argue the intelligence and sophistication of Superintendent Donald Cobb. He was a cool head. While other RCMP officers seemed distraught by commission inquiries, Cobb seemed "relaxed before the two inquiries, his answers as lean and elegant as his appearance."[34] A former legal adviser to the solicitor general's department has reported that Cobb was a popular Mountie, and very probably in line for promotion to commissioner. "My information about him becoming the next commissioner is pretty direct . . . Cobb was being pushed for it. The minister's assistants were pushing it . . . . he was one of the most intelligent Mounties I've ever met."[35]

Since Cobb was a man on his way to the top, the revelation of his attitudes toward the role of the Security Service are particularly valuable—especially since they are likely to have been more candidly expressed after it was clear that he would never get there. Cobb seems to have seen his role as one which *Maclean's* editor Peter Newman described (in another context)[36] as "moving into the growing gap between law and justice." "Rather than sticking to the administration of laws and the apprehension of those who break them," Newman observes, the police are moving into the political arena.

"I don't like a police state in which police forces are powers unto themselves," Cobb told the Toronto *Star*.[37] But he apparently considered such power necessary. Cobb's neutralization of police deviance is a neat combination of courage and accountability. The policeman must be prepared to stick his neck out, "to choose between the law and neglecting his duty." Cobb does not condone illegal methods as an everyday practice, but "we are taught a basic methodology when we join the service, and we never associate certain functions with illegality." He had always been ready to answer for this choice, he said. "We have to prove that we can be trusted."[38]

It is valuable to consider the explanation Cobb himself provided for the fake communiqué when finally called upon to do so at the McDonald inquiry. He claimed it was issued to protect the Parti Québécois from infiltration by the FLQ! Cobb said it was the Security Service's "duty to protect democratic institutions" such as the PQ, so he felt justified in using "disinformation" (his term) to "confuse radical separatists so they wouldn't join the PQ."[39] In view of subsequent events, particularly Operation Ham, many will find this explanation of the purpose of the communiqué somewhat less than credible.

The last word on the fake communiqué may be given to

Justice David McDonald, the usually dispassionate chairman of the commission of inquiry into RCMP wrongdoing. When Donald Cobb appeared before the commission to explain the communiqué, McDonald delivered a stinging rebuke.[40] The RCMP action could only have frightened people, he said, and was an illegitimate interference in the political process. Cobb defended his action "as a way of protecting the public against violence" but admitted "there was a danger in extending police too far into politics." Commented McDonald drily: "I'm glad you recognize that."[41]

McDonald observed that it could be argued that the communiqué violated several criminal code provisions; not merely public mischief, but libel, forgery, and alarming the public, crimes that could carry a penalty of up to fourteen years in prison. Cobb replied that he didn't think he would be convicted because he was acting to serve a greater public good—protecting society against terrorists. In any event, Cobb's testimony was under the protection of the Canada Evidence Act. It can never be used against him in a court of law.

Unexplained Mischief

There is no space in this limited study to discuss the many other dirty tricks of the RCMP. The transcripts of the Keable and McDonald commissions (to say nothing of the Laycraft and Krever inquiries) run to tens of thousands of pages. If we have tended to concentrate on Quebec events it is because the most detailed documentation is available there (thanks to the Keable commission), and because Quebec politics will certainly remain a central issue in the survival of the Canadian nation for the forseeable future. But the RCMP has been violating laws across Canada, from numerous admissions of "surreptitious entries" in British Columbia, to the roughing up of suspects in the Maritimes.[42]

One of the most extensive Mountie violations of Canadian law was Operation Cathedral, the opening of private first-class mail without a search warrant. Both cabinet ministers and top officers of the RCMP claimed to be unaware of illegal mail-opening, which went on for many years. When the activity was exposed by a team of CBC investigative reporters, Solicitor General Francis Fox suggested the CBC was wasting the taxpayer's money by attacking the RCMP![43] The prime minister refused to get "wildly excited" about a little mail-tampering. If the RCMP could catch a terrorist even the "one out of five times" that they pried into private mail, "that's a good average," he claimed.[44] But the McDonald commission was later told that in more than twenty years of mail-openings, the RCMP had detected only one terrorist, and the mail-opening was not a major element in his capture. We still don't know who gave the lower-rank Mounties the orders to open mail illegally.

Neither journalists nor royal commissions have yet uncovered the full extent of RCMP involvement in certain mysterious break-ins. One of the most interesting puzzles is the Praxis affair. The Praxis Corporation was created in Toronto in the late sixties by a group of prominent community leaders and university professors. Its funding came from the Toronto *Star*'s Atkinson foundation, federal contracts and various public and private sources. The corporation became involved in such issues as day care, tenants' rights, working mothers' problems, and the poor people's movement.

In 1970 Praxis was involved in the organization of a national poor people's conference. On December 18, a few days before the conference, persons unknown broke into the Praxis offices and stole carefully selected files, all having to do with the conference. Then they started a fire—perhaps as a diversion, perhaps in the hope of a cover-up. Clearly it was the registration list for the conference which they wanted, as they hoped this would provide valuable information on "dissidents" across Canada.

Nothing more was heard for six years, but as events turned out, the files were busily moving from one place to another. On February 4, 1977, editor Peter Worthington of the Toronto *Sun* wrote a column headed: "I gave RCMP Praxis files." He revealed that he had been given the files two weeks after the 1970 break-in. He had determined that they did indeed come from Praxis, and had handed them over to the RCMP—without telling Praxis. He had offered them first to the Toronto police but they weren't interested.

Another sign of the files appeared in a memo circulated by Solicitor General Jean Pierre Goyer in June 1971. He circulated to fellow cabinet ministers an "enemies list" identifying Praxis "in the context of an extra-parliamentary opposition that seeks to organize and radicalize the underclasses of society and mold them into a revolutionary force."[45] This memo did not become public until 1977.

As soon as Praxis members (the corporation is no longer active but still exists with a board of directors) heard in 1977 of the RCMP's possession of the missing files, they contacted the force. After considerable maneuvering, the RCMP eventually admitted that it had destroyed some of the files, but still had others. These were returned—but not directly. They were given to "the proper investigating authority," the Toronto police, who in turn gave them to Praxis. The RCMP refused to disclose its information about the original theft, because—you guessed it—national security would be threatened.

5

Laundered Language

When Alice enters the world behind her looking glass, Humpty Dumpty assures her that if he uses a word, "it means just what I choose it to mean—neither more nor less." The problem, says Alice, is "whether you can make words mean different things." But Humpty has an answer for that—the only problem is who is to be master of the words.

In modern advertising, the master is the copywriter, and the result is a "hazard course in weasel words."[1] A few carefully chosen words can imply one thing, mean another, and still not actually lie. A familiar example is the headache pill that provides "a higher level of pain relief." This sounds like stronger medicine, a better cure. In fact it means that you take one pill instead of one-and-a-half pills of the rival brand. They're both the same medicine and two pills of the rival would put you farther ahead.

Top officers of intelligence services must be wordsmiths no less cunning than those on Madison Avenue. They must know how to say one thing and mean another without actually perjuring themselves. William Colby, former director of the CIA, frankly admitted this skill in a *Playboy* magazine interview in July 1978. But he expected the public to be cynical enough, after years of experience with commercial wordsmiths, to take nothing he said at face value: "I think the American people are conditioned enough through modern advertising, through modern political rhetoric, through modern headlines, to be willing to look through a certain

67

overstatement and work the truth out of it." Mr. Colby's difficulty was in persuading his interviewer to believe him when
he really *was* telling the truth. In one instance he denied an
allegation against his role as CIA director. The interviewer
noted that this denial might merely be playing with words.
"Then I *superdeny* it!" Colby replied. But when Brand X
doesn't get the clothes any cleaner than Brand Y, does the
word "superclean" mean anything?

Lawyers have become expert wordsmiths too, and more
and more court cases are decided on technicalities. The
royal commission inquiries into Mountie wrongdoings have
become battlegrounds between Humpty Dumpties, each
struggling for mastery over words.

One Mountie explained to the McDonald inquiry that "the
terms 'disruption, coercion and compromise' did not mean
that the Security Service would do anything illegal. This
would be understood clearly by the experienced, professional
member of the service."[2] Likewise, a citizen who was detained for fifteen hours—part of it facing into a corner—was
not imprisoned, kidnapped or even detained. According to
the RCMP he was merely "intercepted."

Even something as technically simple as a wiretap on a
telephone line is not always and everywhere a wiretap. The
Mounties explained to the McDonald commission that only
wiretaps which met the "strict definition" were reported by
the RCMP in statistics for legal regulation of wiretaps. Such
a wiretap was the mechanical attachment of a listening device
to a telephone line. However, an induction coil placed *beside*
the line could pick up the conversation quite nicely, without
being called a wiretap.[3]

Ask Me the Right Question

While secret police like William Colby may expect that the
public will "work the truth out," it is difficult to believe that
the bureaucrats intend that everyone will notice the catchwords. For example, in denying the obvious evidence that it
was spying on students and faculty on Canadian university
campuses, the RCMP issued a statement that, "It is not the
official policy of the Force to put undercover men on cam

pus."⁴ All well and good, but you didn't say anything about your actual practice, did you? It's just not your *official policy*.

Morton Halperin, one-time assistant to U.S. Secretary of State Henry Kissinger, has called this word game: "You did not ask me the right question so I did not give you the right answer."⁵ One form of this game, called "stonewalling," requires the player to give an answer to a question which is not quite the one put by the questioner, and then hope the questioner or public doesn't notice the sleight of hand. For instance, in answer to a question about whether there had been any RCMP surveillance of members of Parliament, Pierre Trudeau replied that while he was prime minister "no MP has been subjected to authorized electronic surveillance."⁶ But the point was that the RCMP never officially *authorized* such surveillance anyway.

Sometimes ministers caught up by the contradictions in their statements beg off on the grounds of getting confused by their own rhetoric. After stating in the House that he had been given a legal opinion that the RCMP's break-ins to plant wiretaps and electronic bugs were legal, Solicitor General Jean Jacques Blais reversed himself a week later, admitting that he did not have "a specific legal opinion relating to 400 surreptitious entries." In self-explanation, Mr. Blais said, "I am not advancing that my thought processes are absolutely devoid of obscurity."⁷

Solicitor General Francis Fox was quicker on the draw with the right words. When he resigned after admitting that he had "signed another man's name" to a hospital document, the word "forged" was never used. In an exchange with Leader of the Opposition Joe Clark over the RCMP "surreptitious entry" to get the Parti Québécois membership list, he shot back, "You called it a break-in. I did not."⁸

Bureaucratic jargon performs more than a mystifying function to keep outsiders from understanding what is going on. It also assists the insider to deal politely with unpleasant realities. Even killing is given a nicer name—in the CIA it was "executive action." "Surreptitious entry" neutralizes breaking and entering, trespass, burglary, and other criminal and civil offenses.

Admission of illegal activities can be obfuscated later by stonewalling. This process can become elegant word-fencing when the secret policeman has something he is determined to hide, while wishing to give the appearance of meeting the demands of a democratic society. The duel is most exciting when he finds himself pitted against an interrogator who knows how to ask exactly the right question, and is not thrown off the trail by answers to questions that were not asked. Keable commission lawyers proved themselves dogged and able in "torturing" witnesses. The torture consists of making the witness look as if he is refusing to answer the question. He could refuse, and be in contempt of court, or he could refuse until given the protection of the Canada Evidence Act, which allows him to avoid incriminating himself *legally*, by more or less admitting his guilt and turning "crown evidence." If the witness wants to avoid the penalties of contempt or the admission of guilt he must give the appearance of answering the question, without giving away what he knows.

The capacity to stonewall, like a musketeer's ability in fencing, will normally increase with the rank of the officer. There was evidence of this in the testimony of the various Mounties at the Keable and McDonald inquiries. Ordinary corporals became tangled in their own explanations, while the former director general of security showed a consummate skill in parrying blows from one of the best wordsmiths in the trade, lawyer Michel Decary.

Lower ranks of the RCMP are constantly reminded that obedience to officers is their first duty. Internal discipline is used against the men, but rarely against an officer. The officers are accustomed to giving orders and verbally defining situations. The men have only a narrow choice of reaction to these situations, usually obedience without question. Stonewalling is difficult under circumstances like those reported by an RCMP member to the McDonald commission. Mr. Blier was being investigated on his role in the "dirty tricks" in Quebec, by an RCMP officer, Mr. Pottier.

Mr. Blier said he was first read the standard police warning by Mr. Pottier. He could remain silent, but anything he chose to say could be used in evidence against him. When Mr. Blier said he did not want to make a statement, Mr. Pottier informed him that he did not have the right to remain silent under the RCMP Act. If he remained silent he could be charged with a major service offence and subject to discipline proceedings, resulting in dismissal.[9]

There is no safe exit from such a Catch 22 dilemma, for the member is reminded by an RCMP regulation dating from 1909: "Every member of the Force is to receive the lawful commands of his superior with deference and respect, and to execute them . . . without question or comment."[10] The admissions of lowly corporals have been relatively candid at the McDonald inquiry when compared to those of higher ranks. An ordinary member of the RCMP answered Mr. Justice McDonald's question on a dirty trick: "Did you ever consider if this operation was unlawful?" by admitting, "I considered it, but due to the reasons that it was necessary and needed at all costs, I presumed it must have been important."[11]

RCMP officers were rarely caught in such poor mastery of the technicalities of wordsmithing. A revealing instance is the joust between John Starnes, former director general of the Security Service, and Mr. Decary, lawyer for the Keable commission. The issue at stake was the letter sent by the Agence de Presse Libre du Québec to Solicitor General Jean Pierre Goyer in October 1972, shortly after the theft of APLQ office records. The APLQ were convinced the theft was police work. Quebec justice minister Jérôme Choquette had denied it was the work of any Quebec police force, and the APLQ wanted a statement from the solicitor general admitting or denying RCMP involvement.

The APLQ letter arrived at Mr. Goyer's office while he was out of town. It was passed by his assistant, John Cameron, to the then commissioner of the RCMP, William Higgitt, for comment. Ordinarily the RCMP would suggest to the solicitor general an appropriate answer to such a letter. In this case the RCMP recommended that Mr. Goyer *simply ignore the letter, i.e. not answer it.* This is what he did.

Mr. Starnes was informed of the RCMP participation in

the APLQ break-in shortly after it happened. Now, at the Keable hearing, the question Mr. Decary wanted an answer to was how much Mr. Starnes told Mr. Goyer. The solicitor general, of course, denied being aware of the RCMP's dirty trick. Mr. Starnes' choice at the inquiry was either to back up Mr. Goyer, his former political master (and have to explain why he withheld such sensitive information from him) or to contradict his former master, by saying that he had told him, thus passing the blame for not admitting the RCMP's dirty tricks for four years to the minister in charge. There is, however, a third choice for an adroit wordsmith: dodge the question. The transcript reads as follows, with Mr. Decary as Q. (question) and Mr. Starnes as A. (answer).[12]

Q. Before the meeting with the Solicitor General, did you actually plan on informing the Minister of the extent of the involvement of the RCMP, or not?

A. Obviously.

Q. You planned on giving him full details?

A. In full details, obviously.

Q. You are certain of that fact?

A. What fact?

Q. That you planned on informing the minister?

A. Of course because I stated it quite clearly in those telegrams. [evidence already before the commission]

Q. At the meeting did you in effect inform the Minister?

A. I can only repeat what has been said in the House of Commons on my behalf by the Solicitor General on the 17th of June 1977, as I told you earlier I have nothing to add to that and nothing to take away. Regrettably no notes seem to have been kept by any of us of the conversation. Now there it is.

Q. If I remember what you stated this morning basically it is that you do not remember having actually informed the Minister?

A. That is correct.

Q. Could it be that you did not inform the Minister?

A. Well that isn't what was said on my behalf in the House of Commons.

Q. Before this Commission, under oath, did you not, is it possible that you did not inform the Minister?

A. I would put it differently. I will put it in the way that Mr. Fox [the solicitor general referred to] put in on my behalf, and namely that I would be surprised if we had not discussed the matter.

The determined and skillful Mr. Decary was unable to budge the stubborn and wily Mr. Starnes from his position. Or, to make our point about the image-creating impact of words, we can put it the other way: the stubborn and wily Mr. Decary was unable to budge the determined and skillful Mr. Starnes from his position. He tried again a little later:[13]

Q. Now we read on page 6793 [of Hansard: Mr. Fox's statement concerning the APLQ letter]: "Commissioner Higgitt and Mr. John Starnes also recall having discussed the October 9th letter with the Solicitor General on a date they cannot now precisely establish." Do you recall having discussed the October 9th letter with the Solicitor General?

A. Well, I have no precise recollection of that, although obviously we must have because this is one of the matters that we would have raised with him. . . .

Q. Well then we should read: "Mr. John Starnes does not recall having discussed the October 9th letter." Would that be correct?

A. I don't think that would be correct either.

Q. What would be correct, Mr. Starnes? Do you recall or not? I want to be fair with everyone. Do you recall or not having discussed this letter?

A. I certainly cannot give you the details if that's what you're asking for but I have no doubt that we discussed the matter. We must have.

So Mr. Decary is back to square one. Mr. Starnes does not recall discussing the letter, but he would be surprised if he had not done so. As an American joke has it, the answer is a "definite maybe."

Mr. Decary had no more luck in attempting to discover how much Mr. Starnes knew about other illegal operations in his Security Service, such as the opening of mail. Mr. Decary's frustration is apparent in these lines:[14]

Q. Mr. Starnes, in order that we may proceed, first I'll explain to you, former Director General of the Security Service, what a PUMA operation is as described to us by Mr. Nowlan [an RCMP superintendent]. That is when a group of the RCMP go to a person's domicile or residence, either they copy information or gather information, or again cases where these documents or objects are taken out temporarily, copied and brought back. . . . Now when you were Director General did you have knowledge of such operations?

A. Yes, I guess so. However I think you offered the definition given to you by who?

Q. Mr. Nowlan, Superintendent, I believe. . . .

A. I am assuming we are talking about operations not illegal?

Q. I am talking about operations conducted by E section.

A. Pardon?

Q. E section.

A. Yes, I would have known in general terms. . . .

Q. Would you have known, in general terms, of all PUMA operations?

A. No, certainly not, absolutely not.

Q. Very well. How many did you know of?

A. Heaven knows. . . .

Mr. Starnes explained that he was aware of the fact that the technique was used, but not of the specific operations.[15] After more parrying, Mr. Decary returned to the offensive.[16]

Q. Such actions, PUMA operations, you knew only a few? Would that be correct? Is that your position?

A. I beg your pardon?

Q. You knew of only a few of what is known today as PUMA operations or 300 operations or whatever code name they fall under . . . I think you understand quite well?

A. Why would I know about that kind of an operation any more than any other?

Mr. Decary is likewise unable to trap Mr. Starnes on the contradiction between a statement based on his telegrams to Donald Cobb (censuring the APLQ break-in because he was not consulted in advance), and a statement that he did not expect to be consulted on such operations (thus could not have known about them).[17]

Mr. Decary was hardly more successful with Mr. Starnes' former boss, William Higgitt, commissioner at the time of the APLQ break-in. Mr. Higgitt was no stranger to security, having previously held the post of director general of the Security Service. Mr. Higgitt couldn't recall whether he had discussed the APLQ complaint with Mr. Starnes. "I can't be precise. I don't remember an actual meeting although it would be normal for us to have meetings." Asked if he recalled "a meeting around the third of November 1972 between yourself, Mr. Goyer and Mr. Starnes," his answer was: "I don't recall that specific meeting . . . my answer really is that I would be very much surprised if such a discussion had not taken place at the time."[18] Mr. Higgitt had an easier time because there is nothing *in writing* to show that he was aware of the APLQ affair in 1972, while there are telegrams (referred to above) from Mr. Starnes to the Montreal RCMP discussing the break-in.

Skirting the Truth Without Lying

There appears to be no evidence in any of the Keable commission hearings that either Starnes or Higgitt lied to the inquiry. Stonewalling is not lying; it is merely defining the truth in a very narrow way and making it difficult for those seeking it to know what went on. William Colby explained the CIA position on the matter. "It's up to the prosecution to ask the right question to force you to give them flatly false answers."[19] Merely misleading the questioner doesn't count as perjury, though Colby admitted it was "less than totally responsive."

The most generous interpretation of the obscurities and apparent contradictions in RCMP officers' testimony to the commissions would be that they were asked to recall matters on which few records were kept, and to which no great importance was attached at the time. The least generous interpretation of weak Mountie memories would focus on their experience as policemen. Policemen are society's agents for the control of dishonest people such as criminals and spies. In the course of their duties, policemen often become convinced that honesty is not the best policy for catching dishonest people. "Fight fire with fire" seems a more attractive policy, so the police adopt their own strategies of dishonesty.

In his study of municipal police forces, Jerome Skolnick notes that police must sometimes contrive to catch a criminal who would otherwise get off by tricking him into a confession or at least a damaging admission.[20] An inspector in the criminal investigation side of the RCMP told the McDonald commission that some deception was necessary.[21] For example, it would not be permissible to lie in order to get a warrant from a judge to plant an electronic bug, but deception of hotel clerks would be acceptable. "We have been taught the use of deception," he said. The justification for deception and tricks is that they are necessary to catch the guilty; respectable, law-abiding citizens will usually cooperate with a police investigation without being tricked or surprised. But what should be the position of citizens—or of the courts and royal commissions—to those police who admit to the trained use of deception? Is their testimony worth anything?

Effective stonewalling depends on conducting oneself with dignity and authoritative bearing. Those who are taught to use deception in the detection and apprehension of criminals will understand the basics of the process of interrogation and how to manipulate it to advantage. Most police have learned a trick or two from criminals they have tried to interrogate. Some of the maneuvers include appearing not to understand the question, asking to have it repeated, or rephrasing it in a way which disarms or deflects. Like Lucy of "Peanuts" cartoon fame, when asked a difficult question the stonewaller offers to answer a different, easier one.

Dirty Tricks Washed Clean

Politicians, commission lawyers, and the media have cooperated at one time or another in laundering the RCMP's questionable activities through the use of euphemisms. "RCMP wrongdoing" has been the common referent, rather than law-breaking or criminal activities. Even the label "dirty tricks" suggests something less odious than actual violation of the law. It's closer to "shortcuts," "working near the margin," or just "going a little too far."

The label is extremely important, because it implies motivation, and judgment about that motivation. The RCMP activities have not been called crimes because this would imply *mens rea*, criminal intention. It would also imply that they have been found to be crimes by a court of law. The latter is not the case—and would not necessarily be the case even if the McDonald commission concluded that some of the wrongdoing ought to lead to criminal charges. Verdicts would still be required.

We probably will never know how much discussion has gone on in RCMP offices concerning the question of motivation and *mens rea* in their wrongdoings. It is interesting that it did not appear on an RCMP secret list of "Questions which may be raised later on" dated February 2, 1977, concerning the embarrassments arising from Operation Bricole.[22] These questions related to the problems faced by the RCMP brass in coping with the exposure of an operation they had denied, and in particular, the role of the federal politicians in the cover-up. They are worth repeating verbatim to give some flavor to the problems the brass anticipated.

GOYER – Did he know? Did he take any part in not *pursuing RCMP participation in the raid further?*
HIGGITT – Did he act reasonably by being satisfied that it was a unique operation and that measures had been taken by his Deputy to prevent recurrence?
STARNES – Did he act reasonably in so assuring the Commissioner?
COBB – Why was he promoted on two occasions since 1972

when the RCMP was aware of his overzealousness in consenting to RCMP participation in the raid?

BREAKING AND ENTERING – What assurance do we have that it was a unique operation and that the Security Service has not been a party to other trespasses or other breaking and entering cases?

DISRUPTION – What does this term relate to? Was this practice widespread then and now?

COVER-UP – Does Commissioner Higgitt's reliance on the assurance of his Deputy at that time constitute a cover-up?

QUESTIONS OF HONESTY – Were members of the RCMP completely forthright and candid at any time that questions were raised within the Force or by Parliament and the Solicitor General?

The last question relates to the game of "Ask me the right question," but what is interesting is that none of the questions are about the intention of the burglars. It seems assumed that the motives for the raid involved no *mens rea*, no criminal intent. This is clearly held by the Mounties already cited, who saw themselves as committing no crime. Their motive was purely the service of their country. But deep down, were the Mounties concerned about *mens rea*?

We have only two pieces of evidence that they were, and we were never intended to see either one. The first is a top secret telex from a Montreal Security Service officer to his Ottawa superior, dated May 4, 1976.[23] It refers to information requested by the director general of the Security Service shortly after Operation Bricole was finally revealed to the public in March 1976. Items 2, A and B of the telex are worth quoting verbatim:

> 2. The brief dated March 15, 1976 and attachments were examined in order to determine whether or not they could be passed to the Attorney General for the province of Quebec. Several points were noticed which make us hesitate to pass this document in its original form. These are:
>
> A) The terminology used in the document is criminal terminology which tends to admit at face value that a crime was committed.

B) The document is written in the English language and should be translated in French prior to passing to the Attorney General. The terminology used could be changed during the translation. . . .

It is one thing to lose something in translation of poetry or prose from one language to another, because the same word is not available in the second language, but it seems the Mounties were concerned with a shady meaning, not a shade of meaning.

The second bit of evidence of Mountie concern with criminal intent is a top secret transit slip, "delivered by hand" on August 16, 1976.[24] It is from the commissioner of the RCMP to the director general of the Security Service—in short, the two top officers concerned with protecting the RCMP image as the Bricole cover-up continued to unravel. It begins: "Having reviewed the 'Bricole' file prior to the interview with Mr. Paul Benoit of the Quebec Justice Department I noted that the investigation in this case is far from complete." Further on, it continues:

Another disturbing factor, although not admitted during our interview with Mr. Benoit, is that it appears the plan was prepared with a view to the theft of documents to disrupt the organization concerned, not just to seek information. If such is the case there was 'mens rea' involved and if it comes out in court members concerned could be found guilty of Break, Enter and Theft.

For the sociologist, who sometimes has to play the role of detective, these documents (now in the public domain thanks to the Keable commission), are valuable clues to the microsocial processes of labeling. Men of high position in powerful organizations such as the RCMP and federal government, are clearly concerned that the right labels be applied to behavior which threatens the bases of their power. Power elites have considerable control over the applications of labels.[25] When the RCMP deliberately burns down a barn it is a dirty trick or wrongdoing, regardless of the admission of intent. When attempted by anyone else the act is arson. But as John Hagan notes, "upperworld indiscretions are not consensually defined as disreputable, much less criminal," to the same extent as those of ordinary citizens.[26] By avoiding labels which imply criminal intent the upperworld avoids definition of any of its activities as contrary to the social interest. Their motivations, whatever they may actually be, become interpreted as altruistic.

The Question of Self-Interest

In addition to *mens rea*, another important point must be argued and won in the battle over which words are used for the RCMP's secret operations. It is the RCMP's vested interest in employing labels which imply that none of the dirty tricks was done in the interest of the RCMP. The labels must imply that the activities were done in the interest of Canada and national security.

The question of disinterested, altruistic or patriotic motives is central to the process of labeling behavior which violates the generally accepted norms of everyday life. Labels make the difference between a legal execution and a lynching, between patriotic killing and assassination, between civil disobedience and civil insurrection. Robert Merton, in his famous typology of deviant behavior, makes the point that nonconformism, rebellion and similar labels are applied to behavior motivated for "disinterested purposes."[27] The same acts when intended to serve one's personal benefit are usually regarded as criminal.

Merton's theory of deviance is based on the notion that people who are motivated by the same goals often differ in the opportunities available to them to reach these goals. Most ordinary crime falls into Merton's category of "innovation" because illegal opportunities are used to obtain socially approved goals. (Instead of working for money, one steals). But Merton largely ignores the structure of opportunities created by a labeling process under the control of those with power in society. For example, buying undeveloped land at low prices, subdividing it and selling the plots for high prices, is not theft in Canadian law. Nor is speculating against the Canadian currency for the purpose of profit. These activities are much safer methods than theft for making money without working, but they are not available to every citizen. Those with power make sure that speculating is not labeled illegal, in order to protect their opportunities.

Not only do legal and illegal opportunities to achieve goals vary greatly; so do the opportunities to *resist labeling for deviance* when certain means are used.[28] Few physicians who become drug addicts will be labeled as such, much less harassed, charged and prosecuted by the RCMP. Most physicians have means to obtain drugs without using a pusher or stealing, and without having to pay high street prices. Thus the physician drug addict can resist the deviant label.

The RCMP has demonstrated that it is in a good position to use means which would otherwise be labeled deviant and even criminal, while successfully resisting these labels. Its ability for deviance disavowal[29] is perhaps greater than that of any other organization in Canada. One of the reasons for this is secrecy. Up until now few Canadians have been wise to what the RCMP is doing, so few are able to resist its capacity for deviance disavowal.

But the RCMP is not able to maintain its good image all on its own. As Peter Berger notes, "one cannot hold on to any particular identity all by oneself."[30] The identity must be validated by other certifying agents—those with the social power to apply labels and make them stick. (For example, psychiatrists are empowered to apply the label "mentally ill.") In the case of the RCMP, the cooperation of politicians is helpful, but probably not essential. Too many people are cynical about politics today, and besides, politicians are notoriously self-interested. It may be that more Canadian politicians rely on the RCMP to certify that they, the politicians, are "clean," than the other way round. (We are told that before anyone is granted a cabinet post he or she must be cleared by the RCMP.)

Solicitor General Jean Jacques Blais announced in a press interview that he was planning no disciplinary action against senior RCMP officials who authorized break-ins without warrants, illegal mail openings and other dirty tricks.[31] He said he "didn't think the reputations of these men had been tarnished." The media, obviously unimpressed by Mr. Blais' ability to wipe the slate clean, reminded him that just six months earlier, when he was postmaster general, he had been deceived by the RCMP on the mail-opening issue.

In sharp contrast, few journalists challenged the power of the present RCMP commissioner, Robert Simmonds, to absolve the politicians of any wrongdoing they might be accused of. Before the Justice and Legal Affairs Committee of the House of Commons, Commissioner Simmonds stated that he had checked the files, and found no evidence of any political approval of RCMP dirty tricks. Almost everyone took him at his word.[32]

If politicians do not provide the RCMP with the legitimacy to support its disavowal of deviance, what other powerful institution in Canada carries out this role? (We doubt the RCMP is already powerful enough to legitimate itself.) In actuality the support it needs comes mainly from the courts.

The power of the courts in Canada to certify labels (its own or those applied by other institutions) is considerably greater than in many other countries, where the courts are open to greater challenge and criticism. Many comments about a court decision which would be considered "fair comment" and "in the public interest" in the United States, are likely to put the critic at risk of charges of contempt of court in Canada. Canadian judges have guarded their freedom from public criticism with considerable success.

When former Minister of Consumer Affairs André Ouellet criticized the courts for acquitting Canadian sugar companies in a combines investigation trial, he was fined $500 for making "derogatory remarks." Two years later, Mr. Ouellet's opinion was vindicated when each sugar company was fined $750,000, but his conviction was not rescinded. Ed Ziemba of the Ontario Legislature has learned the same lesson about the awesome power of judges. He spent a week in jail for contempt of court after refusing to reveal the source of information given him in confidence as a member of the legislature. Later Mr. Ziemba spent a few more hours in detention for a second refusal, but was freed when the court decided his source was not essential to the case anyway.[33] These events prompted John Diefenbaker to propose action by Canadian Parliament which would protect legislators from contempt of court penalties if they refused to reveal sources (except in cases of felony or treason). But to date Canadian judges still have the power to label behavior or statements they disapprove of as contempt of court and to dictate jail sentences as they please. This unchecked power naturally makes us cautious about what we say in the next section.

The Vincent Decision

In June 1977, three of the men (one from each public force) involved in Operation Bricole were charged in Quebec court. The charge was not break and enter (which could carry a penalty of fourteen years imprisonment). They were charged only with failure to obtain a search warrant, and they pleaded guilty to this charge, which nevertheless carries a maximum penalty of two years in prison. The decision of Judge Roger Vincent is an interesting example of the use of language to provide labeling of the sort which the RCMP needs to legitimate its denial of deviance.

The learned judge noted that the defendants had pleaded good faith in a noble cause: national security and protection of the public. He heard witnesses who explained the defendants' motives and justified their belief that the APLQ and the MDPPQ might work against the security of the state.

"But," the judge warned, "the laws of our country do not permit, even for motives so noble and disinterested," that the police should use illegal means.[34] Except under emergency legislation in a crisis, they must have a warrant signed by a judge. This is a wise rule which shelters society from abuses it would otherwise be difficult to control, he observed.

However, the judge also took note of the defendants' long service. He noted the political and social climate at the time of the offense (the same appeal would be repeated again and again by apologists of the RCMP, especially in the federal government, despite much evidence to argue that 1972 in Quebec was far from a crisis year). The judge considered that a conviction would cause each of the men harm out of proportion with the purposes of a just and equitable sentence. Most important, he justified his decision with the consideration that the *public interest did not require a deterrent* in this case. The men had already suffered enough through being charged, appearing in court and pleading guilty. He thereupon granted an absolute discharge.

The Vincent decision could be interpreted as a valuable and powerful legitimation of a secret police seeking acceptance of whatever means the end may justify. The argument against a deterrent contrasts sharply with the argument for a deterrent in the secret trial of Peter Treu, the scientist-entrepreneur charged and condemned in 1978 with violation of the Official Secrets Act. The court recognized that Mr. Treu had shown worthy service of his country, and no apparent intention to commit acts of subversion, but had simply failed to obey the law. As a deterrent he was sentenced to jail for two years. (The conviction has since been overturned.)

Occasionally the Soviet Union is accused of staging a "show trial" of a political dissident charged with treason or a similar offense. The conclusion of these trials is largely decided in advance; the purpose being to provide for the public a visible certification of the policies of those in power.

The prosecution of the three men from the three forces involved in the APLQ break-in in Quebec appears to have been carried out largely for its publicity value; it served to clear the reputation of the RCMP. Of course we are not saying that the RCMP trial was a show trial—to do so might be in contempt of court, though we are always free to make such statements about Soviet trials.

The members of the McDonald inquiry into RCMP wrong-doing have no doubt struggled to prevent their hearings from turning into the same sort of farce as a Soviet show trial. Nevertheless, the press has from time to time commented on the strange incidents which occurred. One of the more amusing relates to an RCMP lawyer's defense of the "public's right not to know." Another involved the claim that an RCMP officer would not know when theft is theft. But perhaps the most bizarre sequence was when an RCMP corporal kept the commission guessing for half an hour because he refused to utter *one word* which he believed might still be classified as an official secret.

As reported in the *Globe and Mail* the word had already appeared in a Montreal newspaper: "The word is kidnapping and it was used by *Le Devoir* in 1972 to describe an incident in which a young law student was scooped off the streets by Mounties."[35]

The incident related to the Security Service's recruitment of informers. The corporal now testifying to the commission was not involved, but had seen an official report on the affair prepared shortly after it occurred by the woman analyst also involved in the Cuban letter affair. He told the hearing that when he saw the report he disregarded some of its language, in particular the woman's statement that Mounties "were going to terrorize" a potential informer to persuade him to cooperate with the RCMP. The corporal suggested that he thought the word "terrorize" a poor choice. "It was like another word that was misused," he said.

That casual aside set the fox among the chickens. The commission naturally wanted to know what the other word was. The corporal refused to utter it publicly, fearing that it had not been declassified. A little guessing game ensued. "Is this a public word or a secret word?" one commissioner asked. Before the scene descended to the level of a parlor game, an RCMP lawyer suggested that the corporal was mistaken. The word was not in the official report; it had been in the newspaper. The word was still not divulged. The commission was recessed while the corporal read through the official document, looking for the secret word; but it was not there! The RCMP lawyer ended the scene by explaining that the word was "kidnapping," and that it had appeared in *Le Devoir*.

Indeed this was no parlor game—though it might have seemed like a charade. The word "kidnapping" had obviously stuck in the corporal's mind, so that he was under the impression that he had seen it in the RCMP report, not in the daily paper. As Freud demonstrated long ago, we rarely forget anything in our experience by accident. Kidnapping was a label which the corporal probably wanted to deny and disavow, as he was already in the process of disavowing the word "terrorize." But an unskilled player in the game of stonewalling, he was careless with what he said. He didn't need to mention "another word that was misused" at all. Stonewallers never give anything away.

The correct choice of words is a mark of those who know how to exercise bureaucratic power effectively. In modern urban society it extends into every aspect of our lives. Advertising, editorials, government documents, legal documents—all are affected by the struggle to find exactly the right words. Contracts of many kinds depend on precise words. Much legal skill is devoted to locating the loopholes in someone else's words.

Those who would uncover truth in the twentieth century must pick their way with consummate skill through an obstacle course of obfuscating language. Those who would cover truth up must become master wordsmiths.

6

"Nobody Tells Me Nuffin!"

During the famous Profumo scandal in England a decade ago, Prime Minister Harold MacMillan explained to the House of Commons that he was unaware of information which the British intelligence service, MI5 (now called DI5), had had in its possession for months. MacMillan claimed that he was never informed of the questionable relationship between Mr. Profumo, the minister of war, and persons suspected of being sympathetic with communist activities. Members of the House were understandably skeptical that the secret police had never provided the prime minister with the slightest bit of information about Mr. Profumo's associates. A back-bencher interrupted MacMillan's speech to shout a complaint more appropriate to the factory floor than to the august chamber of Parliament: "Nobody never tells me nuffin!"

The organization of workshop, mine shaft and lumber camp often involves the "right" of the ordinary workman not to know what is going on. "None of your business," the manager tells the inquisitive worker. But there are also benefits for the worker in such a policy. When caught in a situation where he might have prevented an error or loss by taking initiative without orders, a worker can exculpate himself by saying "Nobody told me," "It's not my business," or "I just work here."

In most factories, it is the foreman's responsibility to define the work situation and to provide rules for conducting activities in accordance with the definition. If it is a question of a rush order, or a change in normal procedures, the foreman must alter the strategy. He usually does so with a minimum of explanation of the reasons. His special access to knowledge is one of the bases for his claim to power.[1]

The higher up one goes in a bureaucracy, the more one expects the officials to know what is going on. As Max Weber observed long ago, bureaucracies are organized into hierarchies of offices in which occupants have access to files and correspondence, as well as personal networks of information.[2] The bureaucracy regards knowledge as power. The rights and means of access to information increase with rank in the hierarchy. Theoretically, the people at the top of a bureaucratic structure should have access to, and at least a general awareness of, information relating to any activity of concern to any section of the organization.

The organization of political and military bureaucracies in the modern state still embodies this principle of greater knowledge at the top. The prime minister or president is considered to have the right of access to any document. Classification of documents is organized by layers: "Restricted," "Secret," "Top Secret," and "For the eyes of the prime minister (or president) only." The number of people with access declines as the rank rises.

However, the concern for national security alters the traditional bureaucratic control of information and knowledge. The principle of "the need to know" is introduced to minimize the leaking of secret information. Only those who have a demonstrated need for access to information in order to carry out their own activities effectively are given clearance. This principle reflects the attitude of the traditional foreman that those below him don't need to know why the order is rush, or who it is for. But the outcome is, in one respect, quite different. Now it is not only the workman below who doesn't know what is going on; it is often a man near the top. Yet there is also a similarity to the factory situation, for the man at the top can plead innocence and nonresponsibility. The sociological problem is how top officials, such as cabinet ministers, get away with this, for they certainly do.

The Person to See

In the traditional bureaucracy, such as a small corporation or an educational institution, the admission by a senior official that he did not know what was going on—that he lacked or was denied access to information about the activities of subordinates in the bureaucracy—would amount to an admission of incompetence. It would also lower his status as a power holder. In Weber's model of bureaucracy, those who want power must have access to information. If an official is supposed to have power because of the office he holds, but does not, a pattern of institutional deviance occurs under a rubric called "the person to see."

Suppose a person unfamiliar with the information networks of a given bureaucracy makes enquiries on the basis of the *official* structure of the organization. But someone familiar with the *actual* distribution of information and power in the organization quietly advises: "Oh, Mr. A doesn't know what's going on. The person to see if you want some action on that is Mr. B"—who may be in some other, apparently unrelated department. In many instances, the person to see may be a lower functionary, with no official power. For instance, in some university administrations, the "person to see" is not the chairman of the department, but his secretary.

When awareness of an information lack relating to bureaucratic status is accompanied by apparent indifference, rather than resentment ("Why didn't you come to see me? Why doesn't anyone tell me what's going on around here?") then one may suspect the emergence of a principle directly converse to normal functioning in a bureaucracy. Power no longer involves a need to know. Instead, at least in some areas of operating, power involves *the need not to know*.

A university chairman who doesn't know which forms are required for some procedure may be protecting himself from knowing about all the little deviations from official policy which make life politically tolerable, and administratively practical, within his department. The person to see is his secretary, who knows "where the bodies are buried." A corporate manager who keeps himself ignorant of incriminating details not only has an easier conscience—he has a ready excuse for the government inspector and the tax man.

Policemen, too, work in bureaucracies, and operate on both principles. They share information on a need-to-know basis; you keep your mouth shut if information you don't need to know happens to come your way. But, more important, you deliberately avoid self-exposure to information which could create difficulties or force compromises. Officials at the top make it clear, not only by avoiding asking certain questions, but also by a studied lack of curiosity, that they need *not* to know. If information is pressed on them which they wish to avoid, there are numerous devices available for maintaining a protective cover of ignorance. Reports can be returned apparently unread: "Didn't get time to read this. You take care of it." Conversation can be steered elsewhere. "Haven't got time for that—see X about it." As an ex-Mountie explained to the authors, "You got to know when an officer wanted to rule by the book. You just left certain details out of your reports. He didn't want to hear about them."

The need not to know provides a cloak of apparent official innocence for those at the top, especially those most visible outside the bureaucracy. At the same time, information is channeled on a need-to-know basis to those who are the persons to see. Such officials may garner power which exceeds that proper to their position in the hierarchy. However, they are still dependent on the approval, or at least the tolerance, of certain people at the top.

The person to see is not a new development in human organization. In monarchical systems the person to see was known as the *eminence grise* (gray eminence, or power behind the throne). In the Catholic church, a cardinal or member of the curia might be the person to see, though the Pope would act officially when a visible symbol of power seemed required.

Whether in the papacy or a traditional monarchy or a modern bureaucracy, the eventual fate of the person to see is the same. He (or she) may quietly exercise enormous power for years. But if the king, the pope, or the president of ITT needs a scapegoat in order to exculpate himself, then the person to see is thrown to the wolves. Washington reporter Jack Anderson provides a lively and detailed example of this in the defaming of Dita Beard, the powerful Washington lobbyist for ITT.[3] When the corporation was investigated by Congress for buying off politicians, Mrs. Beard was disowned by top executives who had previously allowed her great leeway and discretion within the organization.

Playing Both Roles

The Weberian concept of bureaucracy is still valid for powerful organizations. The senior officials are expected to have power, and the information necessary to maintain and exercise such power. Efficiency, ruthlessness, determination, and an ability to act quickly are highly prized, for example, in competitive multinational corporations. At the same time these vast economic empires increasingly involve political activities. Lobbying for concessions and accommodative laws, supporting political candidates and parties in exchange for favors, or opposing anti-corporate ideologies are all germane to the modern multinational's everyday operations.

Such activities inevitably come into sometimes severe conflict with democratic rhetoric and the legal system. Lobbyists are caught buying off members of the legislature, civil servants are exposed for overlooking corporate violations of the law, while consumer movements take flagrant exploitation and misleading advertising to court. At such times the all-powerful, all-knowing, hardheaded corporate executive may serve his own and his company's interests by suddenly becoming a bumbling half-wit who isn't quite sure what's going on inside his corporation. The executive at bay becomes a corporate pussycat until the heat is off.

Jack Anderson has provided a classic example of such a metamorphosis. The individual was Harold Geneen, probably the world's highest-paid executive at the time (in 1973 he was paid $800,000 and extras). As president of International Telephone and Telegraph he ruled a multinational empire that extended into six continents and was implicated in political maneuvers that ranged from financing Republican politicians to undermining the Allende government in Chile.

A 1971 report of the U.S. House of Representatives Antitrust Committee described Harold Geneen as a master corporate executive, in command of the smallest details of
policy-making at ITT. *Forbes* magazine noted that Geneen
read monthly reports from all divisions of the far-flung corporation and its many holdings. He also maintained his own
staff of traveling investigators who checked out the reports
for him. As Anderson concludes, Geneen was widely regarded as an organizing genius.

In 1973, ITT became involved in political scandals ranging
from payoffs of politicians to antitrust suits, and Geneen had
to appear before Congressional committees. Anderson
reports: "The new Geneen was as oblivious of happenings in
his company as if he had just awakened from a Rip Van
Winkle nap. He had only a slight recollection of Dita Beard
and only a vague notion of what she did for ITT. . . . He had
had nothing to do, really, with the famous ITT pledge to help
finance the Republican convention."[4]

It suited Congress to play the gentleman's game with Geneen, and no one challenged his Olympian detachment from
the day-to-day affairs of ITT. No doubt the senators
understood, from their own experiences, Mr. Geneen's sud-
den need not to know. He was able to claim, unchallenged,
an ignorance of the hapless Dita Beard and of her unfortunate memo, which had been leaked to Anderson after
someone failed to carry out her signing-off words: "Please
destroy this, huh?" Geneen's performance at Congress and
his subsequent handling of Mrs. Beard made certain that
wherever she sought work in the future, she would not be the
person to see.

Sometimes the person to see can save himself from ruin by
a form of blackmail. Since he knows where the bodies are
buried, he can threaten to go to a competing power with compromising evidence (to a rival prince, or, in modern days, to
the press). Unfortunately for Mrs. Beard and others who find
themselves out in the cold, one must have documents to
challenge a bureaucracy. Mrs. Beard was unable to prevent
ITT officials from shredding the files in the few hours between the first breath of scandal and her reaction to it.[5] When
Igor Gouzenko fled the Soviet Embassy in Ottawa in 1945, he

had the good sense to be prepared. For days in advance, he had earmarked incriminating documents, and on the night he fled, he knew which files to grab.

National Security—the Anonymous Scapegoat

In the traditional bureaucracy of monarchy or papacy, the top man could proclaim his innocence on the basis of "not knowing" only in prescribed and limited ways. If it turned out that he was unaware of what was really going on, it was usually necessary that he prove he had been fed *misinformation,* not *no information.* His not knowing could be blamed on a lesser official's deceit, but rarely on his own ignorance. There was always one safety hatch of escape from responsibility through "divine right." Both kings and religious authorities were assured some protection from challenge by claiming that their power came from divine appointment. But it wouldn't do for those with divine connections to plead human ignorance!

Modern bureaucratic officials and politicians do not hold office by divine right—though sometimes prime ministers and presidents behave as if they did. Some corporate presidents also act as if they had a telex to heaven, but for most occasions, some other legitimation is required. A scapegoat may still be found when the leadership needs to avoid taking responsibility but, as Anderson demonstrates, the modern press (if not the public) is skeptical of scapegoats. Some other device or term has to be found by which political and bureaucratic authorities can claim their innocence and their right not to know.

National security fits the bill perfectly. It is both amorphous and anonymous. It cannot be cross-examined by congressional committees. There is no danger that it will turn and bite back, or lead the investigating hounds to the real culprits at the top of the organization. National security has replaced divine right. It appeals to a mysterious, transcendental principle which is ideologically beyond challenge. Anyone who presumes to question national security is worse than a heretic; he can be labeled a traitor.

The progress of the emperor toward exposure for ideological nakedness in recent American and Canadian history provides a fascinating comparison. In the American case, President Nixon first hoped to avoid exposure by appointing his own special prosecutor, Archibald Cox. But Cox, backed by Judge John Sirica, refused to stay on his leash by respecting the "sovereign power" (as Nixon himself called it). He kept asking for more documents, especially the White House tapes. When the excuse of executive privilege collapsed, Nixon retreated to national security. Fortunately for America, he did not succeed in labeling as traitors those who refused to be cowed by the magic of national security.

In the Canadian case, the government also appointed its own investigators—the McDonald commission on RCMP wrongdoing. The solicitor general repeatedly assured Parliament that the commission would have full power to follow the trail of dirty tricks wherever it might lead. The opposition were dubious, and wanted the commission's mandate spelled out clearly to include the power to summon cabinet ministers.[6] The Trudeau government rejected these demands, insisting that the existing mandate included the power to expose any guilty party.

After proceeding with the speed of a lame bloodhound to examine every small fry involved in the RCMP wrongdoings, the commission was finally ready in October 1978 to begin calling the big fish as witnesses. This provoked something of a crisis for the federal government. On October 5, the government lawyer before the commission, Joseph Nuss, argued that the government was the sole judge of what documents made available to the inquiry could be classified as secret: "Perhaps I can first deal with the question of privilege. . . . even though the matter contained in a document, or even though the matter which might be the object of testimony bears upon the issue which the court is to determine, for reasons of a higher public interest, that material is excluded."[7]

However, Mr. Nuss and his client, the Trudeau government, were not about to repeat the mistakes of history by merely claiming executive privilege. It was the lampooning of Mr. Nixon as a would-be sovereign which reduced the legitimacy of his appeal to national security when he reached that last barricade. Mr. Nuss linked executive privilege and national security together from the beginning. He was very careful *not* to appeal to the government's executive privilege under the Federal Court Act. That appeal had landed the government in great difficulties with the Keable commission. The manner in which Mr. Nuss interwove executive privilege and national security is extremely significant for sociologists of ideology and is worth reporting in its exact words:

> There are indeed a whole series of communications called privileged. And I would offer as the best definition I can come up with: a privileged communication or document is one which although it may be relevant to the resolution of the issues, is excluded from evidence because of a public importance which preserves the confidentiality of that communication.
> . . . We submit that to make these confidential Government papers public would be a departure from solidly established principles which are consonant with and indeed are entrenched in our constitutional tradition.[8]

So far, the claim is one of executive privilege, the traditional right of the Crown not to be accountable in every respect to Parliament and the people. Of course this is legitimated in terms of the "higher public interest," which only the traditional Crown, enjoying its connection with deity, could divine and assess. But Mr. Nuss knows this argument won't go over well even with Crown-awed Canadians, so the conjunction of executive privilege (divine right) with the new magic words of the twentieth century, national security, is an essential maneuver:

> But I'm on this point because there is a conjuncture, if you will, at which you will have confidential Government papers and these papers will also be papers dealing with national security; therefore the national security

aspect is one which is grafted on to the confidential Government papers for the purposes of this particular discussion.[9]

Mr. Nuss's language is so nakedly revealing that one scarcely believes that it was used in legal argument before a commission. The question, of course, was whether this explicit attempt at grafting an old legitimacy (executive privilege) onto another which is now more viable (national security) would take and hold. The implications of the argument did not escape Justice McDonald, the commission chairman:

> So, with regard to those classes of documents, every line of every document is to be sealed from the public? . . . Let us assume that [a document] does not contain any matter of vital importance to the country, but assume it contains a statement of fact, which records knowledge of a criminal offence. . . . You are saying that even that line which is a statement of fact is to be kept from the public view?[10]

The government lawyer's reply was a simple "Yes." One week later, the McDonald commissioners handed down a unanimous decision, rejecting the government argument and insisting that they alone had the power to determine what documents would or would not be made available to the public. The hounds had broken their leash.

Not Knowing Justifies Not Accounting

William Colby, former director of the CIA, explained to *Playboy* magazine (July 1978) that he couldn't make any comment on certain books critical of CIA activities. He hadn't read those books, and he didn't intend to. That way he wouldn't have to talk about them, or venture any opinion on their charges. When you don't know, you're not accountable for the truth.

When the most powerful policeman in the country, Commissioner Robert Simmonds of the RCMP, appeared before the Keable inquiry, he dramatized his respect for "the truth, the whole truth and nothing but the truth" by taking the commission's Bible into his hands. He thumbed through apparently looking for a suitable inspiration, then "slowly he bent over, holding it in his hands, and kissed the page," thus providing just a subtle hint that deity still shelters power.[11] But as the hearing progressed, Commissioner Simmonds demonstrated the bureaucratic principle of the need not to know which enabled him to avoid responsibility for the whole truth. At issue was the Nowlan report, the result of an internal investigation by an RCMP superintendent assigned to get the facts on the Security Service's dirty tricks. The inquiry wanted to know everything that Mounties investigating themselves had uncovered, but the Nowlan report had been denied to the inquiry. The solicitor general considered disclosure of its contents dangerous to national security. (Naturally!)

Another way of finding out the report's contents was to ask the man at the top, who must surely have read it. But as it turns out: "Mr. Simmonds said that he doesn't have a copy of the report, has not seen it, hasn't asked for it, and has deliberately not asked for it 'to prevent myself from becoming emeshed in actions' that occurred before he became commissioner."[12]

The CIA's William Colby admitted only to not reading books by *critics* of the CIA. Mr. Simmonds went much further. He admitted to deliberately not knowing about internal reports presumably requested in the first place so that top officials would know what men in the field were up to. Moreover, the dirty tricks of the local men were being explained away as the isolated acts of a few policemen not carrying out official policy.

Mr. Simmonds added that his unfamiliarity with the Nowlan report was not because he lacked the security clearance to see such documents. "If I had asked, they would not have been denied to me." To lay to rest any doubts about the competence of a commissioner to govern an organization some of whose controversial documents he made a point of not reading, Mr. Simmonds explained that he was busy "plotting a course for the future of the RCMP."

Journalist Lawrence Martin, in an article focusing on contradictions by RCMP leaders and federal ministers, noted that Mr. Simmonds' blissful ignorance of the contents of the Nowlan report was not entirely unspoiled. Mr. Simmonds made a statement to a parliamentary committee in November 1977 that he had checked the RCMP files regarding allegations of wrongdoing, and found no evidence of their authorization by cabinet ministers. After his January 1978 statement at the Keable inquiry, cited above, he was asked how he could absolve the government of complicity in RCMP wrongdoing if he hadn't read the Nowlan report. Simmonds clarified his ignorance of that document; he had read some part of it but not all, "because it was too thick."[13]

William Higgitt, RCMP commissioner at the time of the dirty tricks in Quebec, showed an equally modest disinterest in, and ignorance of, the operational details of the force he governed:

Question: How could . . . the same body which is the rule of law to all Canadians . . . continue in such a practice? [of breaking the law]

Answer (Mr. Higgitt): This has not been easy of course; everyone acknowledges that. I really am not, I suppose, competent to deal with the intricacies of law that are involved. That's presumably for our masters to decide.[14]

The commissioner may be commended for admitting that for police to claim to uphold the law while breaking it is not easy—though one of the concerns of this study is that it may be becoming dangerously easy. But his modesty in knowledge of intricacies of the law is more than puzzling, since it is well known (and has been claimed many times by the RCMP itself) that its members are given an excellent training in the law. Morever, examinations for promotion in the officer ranks contain many questions on the intricacies of the law, and each new day's activities as commissioner would bring new experiences in the interpretation and practical application of legislation. Perhaps, like ITT's Harold Geneen, Commissioner Higgitt had just been aroused from the Canadian equivalent of a Rip Van Winkle nap.

In another instance of the RCMP's need—or perhaps more accurately, *want* not to know—the former director general of the Security Service, John Starnes, seemed unaware of the actions taken by his immediate assistant at the time of the APLQ raid, Mr. L. R. Parent, who had acted on Mr. Starnes' behalf during the latter's absence. The Keable transcript reports:

Question: When Mr. Parent makes his recommendation as a matter of fact in your absence, is he not expressing the position of the RCMP?
Answer: Not necessarily . . .
Question: Did anyone from the RCMP contradict Mr. Parent's statement, or recommendation?
Answer: Well I have no idea whether anyone did or not . . .[15]

Incidentally, Mr. Parent did not need to argue a similar ignorance of what was going on, at the Keable inquiry. He presented the commission with a doctor's certificate stating that he was suffering from a loss of memory.[16] Surely this is an unusual example of the use of physician as certifying agent!

The RCMP passed the buck to its political "masters," as the officers are wont to call them. The argument is apparently that the police ought not to be deciding policy, but merely administering legislation approved by Parliament. But when we turn to the masters we find a similar reluctance to know what is going on.

Before demonstrating this, it is worth raising the question of whether a lower-level official in a bureaucracy may be exculpated from acts of official deviance because he has followed higher-level instructions. This is a question central to the sociological, legal and political analysis of official deviance. The issue arose in the ITT case already cited, since ITT executives have been charged with perjury (not merely ignorance) in testifying about ITT involvement in Chile. This time the government (i.e. the justice department) has laid the charges. But as the Washington *Star* queried, "Can the government convict anyone who was carrying out instructions of the government?"[17] (It was the CIA, it is alleged, that issued orders to the ITT to pretend to know nothing about Chile.)

The Government Doesn't Want to Know

William Higgitt's testimony at the Keable inquiry illustrates to a fine degree the principle that the need not to know increases as one climbs the bureaucratic hierarchy. It is at the lower levels that one finds the dirty work being done. Ordinary members of the Security Service are personally familiar with the lack of social niceties when recruiting informers, disrupting meetings, framing suspects and stealing documents. The same is true of any organization where official policy requires unofficial activities. Vast enterprises, such as Soviet industries, could not continue in operation without the fixers, or *apparatchiks*, who get things done.[18]

But as one emerges into public visibility, it is essential to go through rituals of investiture which divest one of corporate sins practiced on the way up. What the worm knew is forgotten when the butterfly emerges. The case of William Higgitt is illustrative. As director general of the Security Service he was aware of something called Operations 300.[19] Somehow this knowledge was lost or transformed, so that when he testified as ex-commissioner, he claimed not to have been "made aware of those operations as such."

An RCMP informant described the process by which a man rising in the ranks learns how to stop knowing: he stops reading reports and asking questions which he knows will provide him with information he doesn't want to know. "We used to put in reports about twice a week. If our officers wanted to know what was going on, all they had to do was read the reports. But they didn't, they just filed them." It is a commentary on compulsive file-keeping in bureaucracies that even information which no one wants to know is still filed—at least until someone higher up decides to shred it.

Another device senior officers use to avoid compromising contact with the dirty work is to give orders without actually seeming to do so. When the dirty work is done and someone must be blamed, the senior official can claim that he never

gave such orders. The classic historical example is that of
Henry II's comment, "Will no one rid me of this troublesome
priest?" which led to the murder of Thomas à Becket. The
absence of a specific order, especially in writing, provides
greater deniability of responsibility for acts carried out by in-
feriors. The occasional candid admission of such techniques
provides a rare illustration:

> Following up on the statement of John Starnes, former
> head of the RCMP security force, that a [Privy Council
> Office] tip led to the RCMP theft of Parti Québécois
> membership lists, Mr. Lemieux [who was for nine years
> a security adviser to the Privy Council Office] said this
> of the manner in which such tips are passed out: "We
> would . . . say, 'John, perhaps you should look into it.
> But whatever you choose to do is, you know, your own
> business.' The message could hardly have been more
> clear."[20]

The message referred to the need of senior civil servants
not to know what is really going on. Very well, then, it must
be the government ministers themselves who know. But how
would that be possible, without the information being passed
up verbally or in files by senior civil servants? Solicitor
General Warren Allmand said shortly after the revelation of
operation Bricole by Robert Samson: "at this time we are not
aware of any other incident similar to the one complained of
by Mr. Samson."[21] He said he was investigating to see if there
were such incidents. (He obviously didn't mean that he personally was doing so; few ministers have the time or skills to
do their own detective work.)

Postmaster-General J. J. Blais claimed he didn't know the
Mounties opened mail until he heard it on the CBC.[22] Later
Mr. Allmand told the Keable inquiry, on the same question
of illegal opening of mail: "I directly asked that question and
I asked it more than once. They categorically denied that they
opened mail."[23] The Keable inquiry had a copy of a letter
from Mr. Allmand to Conservative member of Parliament
Allan Lawrence. It stated: "I have been assured by the
RCMP that it is not their practice to intercept the private mail

of anyone and I trust that the above explanation will set your constituent's mind at ease.''

The famous "letter to a constituent" provoked one of the few occasions on which a senior RCMP officer was caught changing his testimony in public. In February 1978, ex-Commissioner William Higgitt told the Keable inquiry that Allmand's answer to Allan Lawrence's constituent was not drafted by the RCMP. But in November, at the McDonald inquiry, Higgitt testified that the RCMP did draft the letter, knowing full well that the letter was "not drafted on precise statements of fact.''[24] The fact—which Allmand claims he was unaware of—was that the RCMP was opening hundreds of letters; indeed the force had an entire section devoted to this activity.

Mr. Higgitt's self-justification "under vigorous cross-examination by Mr. Allmand's lawyer" was that the letter was *technically correct* because mail opening was not a "practice" of the RCMP. He claimed it happened "only eight or nine times a year,'' despite other testimony to the contrary at the inquiry. In any event the example is a splendid one of "ask me the right question.'' Mr. Allmand had apparently not asked his senior RCMP officers if they *ever* opened the mail, but had accepted their assurance that it was not a "practice.''

A responsibility to tell the truth is apparently not an obligation to tell the whole truth. "Very often the RCMP would draft letters for its minister that contained statements reflecting less than the complete facts of a situation, but the minister would know much more about the true situation,'' Mr. Higgitt said.[25] Perhaps the Mounties meant that letter-opening wasn't "practice" for them any longer, because they were quite good at it now. After all, they'd had years of experience!

The opposition has not had much luck in discovering who knows what the Security Service is doing. It is difficult to believe that one of the most powerful institutions in Canada, the RCMP, is being allowed to run its own show, but this is the impression left in parliamentary debates.[26] Even one of the "small handful of justice department officials working closely with the RCMP" was reported to be unaware during parliamentary debate on wiretap legislation that the force was conducting surreptitious entries to place its equipment.[27]

When senior officials can be shown to have participated in activities where it is likely that they would lose their innocence of what is going on, the claim that "nobody told me nuffin" becomes questionable. Joe Clark made this point to the Solicitor General: "According to the minister, it has been standard practice for the Solicitor General of Canada to meet on a weekly basis with the director general of security services . . . Is it the contention of the government that the question of illegal activities by the security service was not raised during those meetings? Those meetings would have numbered well over 100 during this period."[28]

Official deviance may be cloaked at lower levels of bureaucracy only if there is a strict quarantine protecting the senior officials from contagion. Prime Minister Trudeau gave such a quarantine the status of official government policy, claiming that government ministers should not know what was going on in order to remove the possibility of political interference in police work. "It is not a matter of pleading ignorance as an excuse. It is a matter of stating as a principle, that the particular Minister of the day should not have a right to know what the police are doing constantly in their investigative practices."[29]

The Public's Right Not to Know

Many Canadians clearly believe that when it comes to the RCMP and its activities, what you don't know won't hurt you. Few Canadians have yet taken advantage of the meager provisions of the Human Rights Act of 1978 to request government files. RCMP lawyers have shown great sympathy with the public on this issue; they have no desire to foist unwanted information on the public. A revealing admission was made to the McDonald inquiry by RCMP lawyer Pierre Lamontagne: "I'm trying to protect the public's right not to know."[30]

Those who believe that what they don't know about RCMP files won't hurt them might ponder the case of Bernard Maguire, who was dismissed in July 1975 from his job as a radio technician with Canadian National Telecommunications.[31] After a year and a half of unfaulted performance, special training for new work, and two raises in pay, Maguire was suddenly fired without a clear reason being given. His union took up his grievance, and nine months later, CNT explained the firing. Maguire had failed to pass a security clearance, they said.

The union could find nothing in Maguire's background to remotely suggest disloyalty to Canada. He wasn't even interested in politics. The union turned to friendly members of Parliament in an attempt to uncover the reasons why Maguire was branded a security risk. Solicitor General Warren Allmand denied that the RCMP had anything to do with the case, and when Francis Fox took over this post he repeated the claim. Finally the prime minister admitted that Maguire had a right to know what he had been accused of.

A senior official of the security branch of the Department of Supply and Services in Ottawa saw Maguire and admitted that the RCMP was involved. Maguire was dismissed because CNT had a contract to build a communications network for the RCMP. Maguire wasn't actually working on that project, but he might some day, and the RCMP had objected to Maguire's security clearance. But there was still no explanation of *why* he was a security risk. The union's friends in Parliament kept pressing for information, with no success.

When the Canadian Human Rights Commission was established in 1978, one of the provisions was the right of citizens to see what was written about them in government files. This legislation is full of holes—files can be withheld for national security reasons, without any further explanation. Finally, in May 1978, three years after his dismissal, Maguire was allowed to see his file. But first he had to sign a promise not to reveal the contents to anyone else. If he did, he would face severe penalties under the Official Secrets Act!

Maguire refused to give up. Finally the government agreed to declassify some of his file—but not a crucial RCMP security clearance report. The declassified papers did contain a letter to CNT advising them that confidential sources had shown Maguire was a security risk. Moreover, the govern-

ment letter added and underlined that in "removing this subject person the *reason given must not be associated with the
lack of a security clearance.*"

Could anything prove more conclusively that what a citizen
doesn't know about the RCMP's files can still do untold
harm? Maguire was a "subject person" to be fired, with
specific instructions not to tell him the real reason. What's
more, after three years of inquiries he still didn't know who
had caused him to be denied clearance, or for what reason.
Elaine Dewar, a dedicated investigative journalist, went to
Solicitor General J. J. Blais to get a final answer to Maguire's
questions. As expected, Mr. Blais repeated the denials of his
predecessors. When he denied that a particular document in
Maguire's file even existed, Ms. Dewar told him she had seen
it herself. Blais' reply was, "You saw it? Oh my god!"[32]

The Know-Nothing Democracy

During the 1850s a political party sprang up in the eastern
United States to oppose the massive immigration of Roman
Catholics into the country, and to prevent Catholic representation in political office. It was a secretive party, and
whenever members were asked about it they replied, "I don't
know." The party became labeled the Know-Nothing Party.
The Know-Nothings disappeared after a decade, but more
than a century later their watchword seems to have become a
survival theme for certain citizens of western democracies.

The most persuasive demonstration of the survival value of
not knowing was provided by the German middle classes
after World War II. Many otherwise well-educated and well-
informed Germans who survived the Nazi regime were able to
claim that they knew nothing of Hitler's mass murder of the
Jews.

In George Orwell's *1984*, one of the hero's greatest problems is to forget that he saw a photograph which was not supposed to exist, but which somehow fell out of the interoffice
tube onto his desk. Should he destroy it without the approval
of higher authority, or should he pass it along to senior officials, and thereby incriminate himself for having seen what

no longer existed in their history? Therein lies the classic dilemma: "You saw it? Oh my god!"

How much do Canadians really want to know about the history of the RCMP? To help answer that question, we invited a colleague to contribute the next chapter.

7

How the RCMP Got Where It Is

by Norman Penner

Since the foundation of the North West Mounted Police in 1873, the Mounties have had two missions, one public and the other hidden. The public mission has been widely celebrated in the press, movies, novels, and in the bulk of Canadian history books. The Mounties have been portrayed as the keepers of law and order in the Canadian west, permitting the peaceful opening and development of that gigantic region and, as the horsemen in red tunics, they have been the nemesis of all criminals. They "always get their man."

But behind this image, almost invisible, the other mission of the NWMP and its successor the RCMP has been the surveillance and sometimes forceful control of all minorities that do not fit into the Canadian establishment's model of public order.

Until recently, only those who have felt the direct effect of this role of the Mounties have sought to arouse the public to an awareness of the secret mission of the RCMP. But because most of those complaining were radicals or "foreigners," their warnings went largely unheeded.

A recent book generally favorable to the NWMP asserts that historically it was particularly concerned with four minorities: immigrants from continental European countries, American settlers, Indians and Metis, and organized labor.[1] The author goes on to say:

> The police treated all these minorities differently from

the rest of the population, indeed there was a different approach for every group. This did not mean that the ideal of equality before the law was abandoned, nor did it mean that the powerless suffered from official discrimination. Differential treatment was based in part on the recognition that some minorities had disabilities and was intended rather to protect them than oppress them.[2]

The author gives many illustrations of the "differential treatment" meted out to these minorities even though he tries to put the best face on what can only be considered as racism and deep hostility to labor: "Many members of the police regarded Indians as inferior beings to be tolerated only as long as they stayed out of the way."[3] The force looked upon certain European immigrants as having "very meagre ideas of right and wrong from our standpoint."[4] The attitude towards labor is excused by the author on the grounds of lack of knowledge about this new social force, but then he goes on to indicate that, if anything, the Mounted Police attitude to labor got worse in the twentieth century.

These attitudes were not accidental or fortuitous. They matched the public mission of the Mounted Police in opening up the west. Confederation established the framework for the region's economic and political domination by central Canada. The purchase from the Hudson's Bay Company of the vast territory known as Rupert's Land, five times the size of the four provinces which at that time made up the Dominion of Canada, was the decisive step in achieving the aims of Confederation. Unlike the founding provinces, which were given important areas of jurisdiction, the Canadian west was to be held in tutelage, to serve the purposes of the Dominion, and to become an agrarian hinterland for the industries of the east. "It is an empire we have in view," proclaimed Father of Confederation George Brown, representing Toronto businessmen.[5]

The early inhabitants of the west—Indians, Métis, and a small group of English and French settlers—were completely ignored by the federal authorities. Their resistance was met and crushed by military force, and the North West Mounted

Police was created to keep the dispossessed down, or in more euphemistic terms, to preserve law and order. This is not to suggest that the pursuit of common criminals was not part of the function of the police, but here too, as the records show, the majority of the arrests were of Indian and Métis people, who indeed had become the dispossessed.

This was no ordinary police force. It was directly controlled by Ottawa, not by local authorities as was the case in the other provinces. In the words of Sir John A. Macdonald, it was to be modeled after the Irish Mounted Constabulary,[6] whose main purpose was also hunting down dissidents. The first NWMP Commissioner, Lieutenant-Colonel George Arthur French, had been an officer of the Irish Constabulary.[7] The NWMP was labeled semi-military, although it is difficult to see in their mode of operations and in their rigid internal discipline why the qualifying term "semi" was used. Another difference from an ordinary police force was that many officers of the Mounted Police were given certain judicial powers which meant that they could arrest, prosecute, and judge.

The basic, unstated purpose of the Mounted Police, like the Irish Constabulary, was to keep the country British. The Mounted Police interpreted this aim with more than ordinary zeal. How much of their suspicion and dislike of Indians, Métis, immigrants, and later of French Canadians, sprang from this zeal? None of these groups could be relied upon at a crucial time to display the appropriate patriotic fervor for the British Empire.

The involvement with labor began as part of the Mounted Police's task of ensuring that the transcontinental railway went through without interruption. Among other things this meant quelling sporadic Indian attempts to prevent the railroad from being built over what they considered their land.[8] But the biggest part of this task was keeping the workers in line: arresting some for leaving their jobs, bringing in scabs when strikes were called, forcing others back to work even when the contractor neglected to pay them.[9] The Mounted Police showed a strong bias in favor of the corporation.

The identification of the Mounted Police with the cor-

porate interest in labor disputes extended eventually to all
labor struggles in which the Mounted Police were called to intervene. Trade unions in those days had almost no protection
in law, and every dispute, even the smallest, was looked upon
by the authorities and employers as a miniature revolution.
Thus between 1876 and 1914, the Canadian Militia was used
thirty-three times against striking workers,[10] resulting in arrests, imprisonments, and physical injuries. The Mounted
Police also began to infiltrate the emerging union movement
with informers and *agents provocateurs.* This practice first
came to light in the trials of the leaders of the Winnipeg
General Strike of 1919. The main evidence presented by the
Crown was that of an RNWMP constable, F. W. Zaneth,
whose role in the trials is described by a former RCMP
deputy-commissioner:

> When some of these aliens had threatened to turn legal
> labour organizations into tools of their revolutionary
> movement, young Constable F. W. Zaneth had man-
> aged to get himself hired incognito as secretary to the In-
> dustrial Workers of the World. From that vantage point
> he could see exactly what went on. Zaneth's testimony
> regarding the subversive principles advocated by the
> revolutionary conspirators helped to convict them, and
> they were sent to jail for terms varying from six months
> to two years.[11]

However, not one of the accused at the Winnipeg trials was
an alien in the legal sense. Every one of them was born in
either Britain or Canada. But to the Mounted Police, every
radical was an alien and vice versa. Racist labels and
references abound in their dossiers and publications. The an-
tipathy of the Mounted Police to immigrants merged with
their hostility to labor, making these two groups their prime
targets.

The Winnipeg General Strike of 1919 was a turning point.
In October of that year the Borden-Meighen government introduced legislation which would turn the Royal North West
Mounted Police into the Royal Canadian Mounted Police. A
force which had jurisdiction in only two western provinces
and the Northwest Territories suddenly became nationwide in

its operations. Throughout the debate that took place then, and on subsequent occasions, almost the only argument that was used to justify this move was the government and police version of the Winnipeg Strike: it was a plot to overthrow the government and establish a Soviet republic in its place!

This interpretation, which has long been discarded by every historian, is dredged up in a recent book on the RCMP by a former deputy-commissioner of the force. It claims that on June 21, 1919, demonstrators equipped with small arms began shooting at the police, forcing them to return the fire. The judgment of historians on that episode is clear and unanimous, and is summed up in the latest and most definitive work on the strike: "They [the RNWMP] were certainly under attack from bricks, stones, and bottles, but the only shots fired that day came from police revolvers."[12] At the end of the shooting, two men were dead from police bullets and twenty-four other civilians were injured, most of them as a result of bullet wounds. Six RNWMP officers were also injured but none of them by shooting.[13]

A few members of Parliament were not taken in by this hysterical fear of a bolshevist takeover in Canada. They argued that the establishment of a Dominion police force with the powers to act anywhere in the country was contrary to the BNA Act, which placed the administration of justice in the hands of the provinces. Objections were also raised about the cost. It was charged that the government was not disclosing the real reason why the force was needed. A Quebec MP tabled a letter he had received from Lomer Gouin, premier of Quebec, who said:

> I must add that I felt an astonishment equal to your own when I read the announcement you refer to as I have always considered that police matters, in the province, are within the exclusive attributes of the provincial government, as being part of the administration of justice, of local and municipal matters in the province.[14]

The member who tabled this letter followed it with comments of his own as to what the new force could be used for:

> It can be used for raids on private houses, colleges, and

libraries, that may contain books or papers objec-
tionable to the [government] . . . In point of fact, that
very thing has been done in several parts of the
Dominion in a way as high-handed and unjustifiable as
if the Kaiser himself was directing the raids.[15]

Another debate took place on a government motion of
supply which called for $4,700,000 to run the new force.
Again the opposition raised doubts about the need for the
RCMP. In view of events in the 1970s it is worth noting that
the opposition in 1920 was led by the Liberals under
Mackenzie King, who charged: "It looks as if the Government were trying to make a standing army out of this police
force, only calling it police instead of militia or an army."[16]
Another MP argued:

This wild rioting, and striking, and unrest, is more in the
minds of the Ministry than it is in the minds of the
people. All the people are clamouring for is an election
which will enable them to get rid of the Ministry; if they
could get rid of the Ministry they would be glad to get
rid of the Mounted Police; we need neither very badly.[17]

The general election of 1921 set the stage for a renewed attack on the status of the RCMP. The government which had
created the force went down to a crushing defeat, dropping
from 153 seats to 50, and from 57 percent of the popular vote
to 30 percent. Many of the seats and votes which the Conservatives lost went to the new farmers' party, the Progressives,
which could be counted on to oppose any strengthening of
federal power, which many farmers believed was in the hands
of the central Canadian financial establishment. Also new
was the two-man Labour Group led by J. S. Woodsworth,
himself a victim of Mounted Police repression in the Winnipeg Strike. The unknown factor was the stand of the
minority government, led by Mackenzie King, who had given
indications on several occasions, as leader of the opposition,
that he was against the expanded role of the force.

The first session of the new Parliament got underway in
March 1922 and within a month J. S. Woodsworth introduced a motion "that, in the opinion of this House, the ac-

tivities of the Royal Canadian Mounted Police should be confined to Territories not included in any Province of Canada.''[18] An important point in the ensuing debate was the admission by the Liberal government's minister of militia and defence that the formation of a federal force like the RCMP was not strictly in line with the BNA Act:

> Speaking technically, on absolutely legal or constitutional grounds, my honourable friend is right that the provinces ought to look after the maintaining of order within their several territories. . . . I agree that constitutionally my honourable friend is absolutely right, but in working out the affairs particularly of a new country, we are not always safe in adhering to the letter of the constitution. Sometimes we even have to violate almost the letter of the law, to be practical.[19]

The creation of a nationwide police force dedicated to the defense of law and order was thus admitted to be violating the letter of the law.

Mackenzie King's speech in that debate was the kind of performance characteristic of his style as prime minister in the years that followed. Forgetting all his previous criticisms of the Mounted Police, he indicated that his government would not support the motion. The reason he put forward was patently ludicrous. He said that the new RCMP had absorbed the old Dominion Police, whose chief function had been to guard federal property and guide people through the Parliament Buildings. If this motion to disband the RCMP was passed, he asked, who would perform this function? This was his only argument! T. A. Crerar, leader of the Progressives, supported Woodsworth's motion on the ground that the establishment of a police force with such wide powers was unconstitutional, and that the administration of justice should be left to the provinces as set out in the BNA Act. The vote to disband was lost, 108 to 47.[20]

In later years the RCMP could boast about how the Liberal party had criticized the force from the opposition benches, but supported it to the limit after coming to power.[21] No convincing reasons have ever been given for this switch.

There appears to have been no appreciable difference between Canada's two main political parties on RCMP policy and functions. The force has been able to stand apart from both parties, sometimes playing one against the other, often standing above the government itself. The RCMP has followed its own policies, confident that it would not be interfered with by changing administrations, and certainly not by the particular minister appointed to nominal responsibility for the force.

An important factor in the growth of RCMP power has been the existence of repressive legislation during long periods in our history. The War Measures Act has been proclaimed three times in this century—1914, 1939, and 1970 —and has been in force for a total of approximately twenty years. During this time the RNWMP and the RCMP have had extraordinary powers over the liberties of ordinary Canadians and their organizations: powers to arrest, detain and intern people without trial, to take away citizenship and deport naturalized Canadians and others; to raid premises, to seize property, to abscond with whole libraries; to censor literature and ban publications. This is not to suggest that the government has had no responsibility for what the Mounties were doing; indeed the government always has the ultimate responsibility and authority. But because of the extraordinary and arbitrary nature of the War Measures Act, the government could get away with handing over the administrative aspects of the Act to the RCMP, giving them practically a free rein. It was RCMP dossiers that determined who was picked up, detained, and deported, who was deprived of citizenship, what organizations and publications were banned, what property was seized, and whose homes and offices were raided.

Next to the War Measures Act, the most repressive legislation in Canada was Section 98 of the Criminal Code, which remained in force until 1936. The section was first passed in September 1918 as an order-in-council, under the War Measures Act. It was rushed through the House of Commons a year later under the impact of the Winnipeg Strike, as peacetime legislation. Ernest Lapointe, when he became Minister of Justice in 1936, claimed that the legislation of 1919 was identical "word for word" with the 1918 provisions except that the phrase "while Canada is engaged in war" was removed.[22] Lapointe noted that Canada was the only allied country to retain repressive wartime legislation during peacetime. In effect the RCMP was given at its foundation the powers and functions of a political police, which in fact it became as a result of enforcing this section of the Criminal Code for seventeen years.

Section 98 declared unlawful any association that advocated or taught the use of force, violence, and "other illegal means" to bring about any governmental, industrial, or economic change in Canada. Persons belonging to such associations were liable to twenty years in jail. Attendance at a public meeting of such an association, or wearing its badge, or distributing its publications, was sufficient evidence of membership unless the accused could prove otherwise. Anyone who rented a hall to an unlawful association or a subsidiary of one was liable to five years in jail. The kind of power which Section 98 gave to the RCMP is well illustrated in Sub-section 2:

> Any property, real or personal, belonging or suspected to belong to an unlawful association or held or suspected to be held by any person for or on behalf thereof may, without warrant, be seized or taken possession of by any person thereunto authorized by the Commissioner of the Royal Canadian Mounted Police, and may thereupon be forfeited to His Majesty.[23]

Section 98 became the principal legal basis by which Prime Minister R. B. Bennett attempted to carry out his proclaimed aim "to stamp out socialism, communism, and dictatorship with the iron heel of ruthlessness," during the Depression years. It began with the arrest, trial, and imprisonment of the eight main leaders of the Communist Party of Canada in 1931. It was also used to arrest and charge Canadians engaged in struggles of the unemployed and in the trade union movement. Strikes could be defined as forceful means to bring about industrial and economic changes.

An example of the wide-ranging interpretation of Section 98 came out in the House of Commons after police fired on a meeting of unemployed workers in Regina on July 1, 1935.

RCMP Commissioner J. H. MacBrien had telephoned from Ottawa a few days before to instruct his assistant commissioner, S. T. Wood, to arrest the unemployed leaders. Colonel Wood replied "that so far as he knew the leaders had done nothing in the province to warrant their arrest," whereupon the commissioner ordered their arrest under Section 98.[24]

The RCMP also gained great powers under the Immigration Act, as amended during the Winnipeg Strike. This Act authorized the minister of immigration to deport any immigrant, whether naturalized or not, including those born in Britain, whom he considered undesirable. No trial was provided and the minister could order the RCMP to seize a person and hold him or her in custody "pending investigation." While the authority to seize and deport was vested in the minister, it was the RCMP, using its files and reports from informers, that decided who was undesirable. Hundreds if not thousands were deported in this manner during the 1930s.

Several deportation cases were debated in the House of Commons. For example, three prominent Winnipeg radicals were taken into custody in the early hours one morning in 1932 and transported immediately to Halifax, where they were held for deportation. Their lawyers were not permitted to contact them, nor were their families.[25] One was sent to Poland where he was arrested by the Polish authorities; another eventually came to the attention of the Gestapo in Germany; and the third was able to prove that he was born in Canada and thus could not be deported.

During the Depression, a mood of anti-communist hysteria seemed once again to grip the government and much of the press. Statements of Solicitor General Maurice Dupré illustrate this:

> May I add that this communist agitation is spreading and gaining ground all over Canada. We think therefore that the only legislation which adequately meets the situation is this Section 98; we look upon it as a rampart against communism.[26]

There was a hint of racial prejudice in the attitudes of some political leaders. The acting minister of immigration said of the three Winnipeg radicals whose case was debated in the House of Commons:

> As time goes on it becomes more obvious that the last place on earth to which these men want to be sent is their country of origin, and that is the place where they should be sent if they are not appreciative of the advantages and rights conferred on them when they were allowed to enter Canada and live among the British and native-born people of our country.[27]

RCMP publications and the public statements of senior officers emphasized the same themes. The RCMP was encouraging, if not actually financing, anti-communist organizations and publications. In a letter to MP Grant McNeil, in 1939, Commissioner S. T. Wood admitted that the RCMP had secretly affiliated to it three years previously a military-type organization called the Legion of Frontiersmen, which he said was ready to assist the RCMP "in the event of trouble or lawlessness."[28]

In response to pressure from many quarters, including the Trades and Labour Congress, the Liberal government passed legislation repealing Section 98 through the House of Commons in 1926, 1928, 1929 and 1930. But each time the change was vetoed by the Senate. In 1936 the motion passed through both houses and Section 98 was finally removed from the Criminal Code.

Less than two years later Mackenzie King set up an inter-departmental Committee on Emergency Legislation, consisting of representatives of eleven government departments and the RCMP, to prepare legislation that might be required in the "event of war or emergency, real or apprehended."[29] They drew up a series of far-reaching proposals which became known as the Defence of Canada Regulations, and these were proclaimed on September 3, 1939.

In addition to the almost unlimited authority contained in the War Measures Act itself, the Defence of Canada Regulations provided the government with specific powers to intern without trial, prohibit specified political and religious associations, restrict freedom of speech and press, and confiscate property.[30] In fact that section of the Regulations relating to property was lifted almost word-for-word from the clause in Section 98 quoted above in footnote 23. Most of these wartime regulations lapsed on August 16, 1945, but two months later the King government passed a secret order-in-council restoring the clause on preventative detention, and used this to arrest and detain secretly a number of Canadians suspected of espionage.[31] The most recent use of the powers to detain without charge or trial was Pierre Trudeau's proclamation of the War Measures Act in October 1970.

The extent to which the legislation and events from 1919 to World War II firmly established the RCMP's power is revealed in an article entitled "Tools for Treachery" by RCMP Commissioner S. T. Wood, published in February 1941. It is essential to recall that this article was written in the darkest days of the war against Hitler:

> Many may be surprised to hear that it is not the Nazi nor the Fascist but the radical who constitutes our most troublesome problem. Whereas the enemy alien is usually recognizable and easily rendered innocuous by clear-cut laws applicable to his case, your "Red" has the protection of citizenship, his foreign master is not officially an enemy and, unless he blunders into the open and provides proof of his guilt, he is much more difficult to suppress. Since Communism was outlawed, most of his work is carried on under cover of other organizations and associations pretending to be, or in reality, loyal to the Constitution. It is important to remember this for the reason that this type of fifth column activity is least understood by our Canadian people, and yet is doing most harm at the present time.[32]

The commissioner went on to detail the places where "fifth column activity" would likely be manifested: labor unions, strikes, unemployed struggles which attracted "the criminal and weak-minded classes" by their "promises of gain," youth movements, and civil liberties groups among the "so-called bourgeoisie."

Commissioner Wood's 1941 statement sums up the RCMP's attitude toward political dissent which appears to be reflected in the following instances of violence. The mileposts are "Bloody Saturday," Winnipeg, 1919; the Estevan Coal Strike, 1931; the Regina Riot, 1935; and the Vancouver Post Office sit-in of 1938. The RCMP's suspicion of dissent is illustrated by a memorandum from the RNWMP commissioner to his Manitoba superintendent during the Winnipeg Strike. The commissioner was replying to a report that a meeting of solidarity with the Winnipeg strikers was to be held in Brandon, the main speaker being the Reverend A. E. Smith, President of the Methodist Conference of that province. The commissioner called Smith a most "dangerous" person and instructed the superintendent to dispatch thirty-five plainclothes constables to the meeting, carrying concealed small arms.[33] The Mounties formed a major part of the audience!

The RCMP has for a long time supplied lists of Canadian "subversives" to police forces of other countries, particularly the United States. This has resulted in debarment from the USA of hundreds if not thousands of Canadians on whom the RCMP keeps secret dossiers. An extreme example was a report to the U.S. government that Herbert Norman, a senior Canadian career diplomat, had once belonged to a Communist Party branch at the University of Toronto. Even though the information was later shown to be in error, the charge was aired in a U.S. Congressional committee with great fanfare and publicity, and led directly to Norman's suicide.[34] Another instance was the threatened ban on Pierre Trudeau crossing the border due to some leftist connections in his youth.

The RCMP has often found support among MPs from the Conservative and Liberal parties for its extremist actions. In the debate on the Defence of Canada Regulations in June 1940, R. B. Hanson, leader of the Conservative Party, offered this proposal:

> My opinion is that the Royal Canadian Mounted Police should be greatly strengthened and be given practically the whole say, perhaps with certain reservations to which I shall allude later, as to who should or should not

be interned. . . . I earnestly suggest to the Minister that
he over-rule the recommendations of the police only in
the cases of extreme injustice.[35]

One of his fellow members, Howard Green from Vancouver
South, went even further:

It is the duty of the government to detain—to detain, I
repeat, every man or woman who is for the enemy or
who aims to wreck our institutions. Once they are detained they are no menace.[36]

It may be argued that these quotes are from wartime
debates which would constitute extenuating circumstances.
But in practice many differing situations were called
emergencies: general strikes, the Depression, outbreaks of
terrorism as well as war. In all these situations, voices of dissent were raised in the House mainly from CCF and NDP
members, who called for calm amidst hysteria, pointing out
that even in the most serious emergency, that of war, there
was no need for such violations of democratic liberty.

The most persistent critic of the RCMP in the House was
J. S. Woodsworth, Labour MP from 1921 to 1933, and CCF
leader from 1933 until 1940. He brought out every conceivable criticism, often stirring up an avalanche of heckling
and bitter opposition from Conservative and Liberal members. But Woodsworth always had some support within the
House, first from the Progressives, then from the so-called
Ginger Group, then the CCF, which he helped found, and on
occasion from individual mavericks within the two old parties.

Woodsworth spoke with the support of a labor movement
which felt keenly that the RCMP's tactics were aimed prin-
cipally at the working class. He denounced the RCMP practice of sending agents provocateurs into labor organizations
and he detailed the activities of the two main agents: Corporal F. W. Zaneth and Sergeant John Leopold. Both had
joined socialist, communist, and trade union organizations
not only to inform, but to suggest and promote activities
which would bring about untimely or illegal confrontations.
But according to Woodsworth there were many others like-

wise being paid to spy on the labor movement. "The result," he said on many occasions, "is that the whole labour movement is permeated by this system of espionage, and also by a sense of suspicion."[37] Although himself an opponent of the Communist Party and often the target of bitter slander by communists, Woodsworth made it clear that he regarded the defense of the political rights of the communists as essential to the preservation of the rights of all.

The transformation of the RNWMP to the RCMP took place under inauspicious circumstances. It was a reaction to the Winnipeg General Strike during which the government of the day fell victim to its own propaganda, adopting an interpretation of that struggle totally rejected by the verdict of history. It was the creature of an authoritarian government which was completely repudiated at the polls a short while after initiating this legislation. It was only made possible by an unexplained turnaround by Mackenzie King who had opposed the RCMP as leader of the opposition, but supported it after becoming prime minister. The RCMP grew from these questionable beginnings to its present power—a power which few Canadians have the courage or desire to challenge.

8

Recruiting the
Professional Spook

Members of the RCMP Security Service are not usually recruited directly into intelligence work; they must begin like any other Mountie. After several years of satisfactory service in the criminal investigation branch of the RCMP, they may apply or be chosen for security work. It is said that the Security Service looks for Mounties who show unusual "intelligence, ingenuity and tact."[1] Like most law schools and medical schools today, the RCMP can afford to pick and choose, and turns away many applicants. Its reputation, combined with a serious unemployment level in Canada, attracts enough applicants to generate a waiting list.[2] The RCMP wants recruits who take its image with deadly seriousness. What it doesn't want is any sense of humor or "role distance"—the capacity to stand back occasionally and laugh at oneself. The Mountie must be a cut above ordinary humanity, as illustrated in the RCMP lecture series for new recruits, *Law and Order in Canadian Democracy:*

> To be a policeman requires skill, intelligence, forbearance and compassion to live one's own life within the law, yet it requires much more than these to apply the law . . . to the acts of others. . . . The policeman needs strength of character to resist . . . the many human impulses excusable in the private citizen.

The successful applicant must pass what is claimed to be a much more rigorous assessment than is required by municipal police forces.[3] Background, personality, emotional stability, political leanings and ethical standards are all investigated. But the supreme qualification is "an ability to accept discipline."[4] An ex-Mountie with over twenty years of service characterized the ideal recruit as "a farm boy; tough, bright, ready, brave and strong."

The minimum educational requirement for recruitment into the Mounties is grade 12. In 1974 it was grade 11, and in earlier years the minimum was even lower. Recently the RCMP has made efforts to recruit university graduates, but with little demonstrated success. The RCMP doesn't release statistics on the educational qualifications of its members, and when Commissioner Harvison was once asked how many Mounties had university degrees, he replied, "I don't have time for all that research."[5] (A leading officer in 1979 gave an unofficial estimate of 15 percent.) In contrast, the FBI since its inception more than fifty years ago, and the CIA since its formation in 1947, have required a university degree with honors standing from every applicant.

Since the RCMP began to recruit on Canadian university campuses in 1969, it has met with a mixed reception. Campus organizations have often identified the RCMP with harassment of students and professors, and with ruthless entrapment of marijuana users. University groups have protested at RCMP recruitment locations, and students have flooded campus newspapers with anti-RCMP letters.[6] A 1978 applicant who had a college degree told the authors of his considerable embarrassment when they began "checking him out" with friends, neighbors and teachers. "They asked about my spending habits, my politics, even my sex life," he reported.

The year 1974 saw some radical changes in RCMP recruitment. Both women and married men were accepted as applicants. Previously only single men were recruited, and they had to remain single for the first several years of service, and even get permission to marry. The prospective wife of a member was "vetted" by Mountie superiors.

In 1974, special efforts were also inaugurated to correct the severe under-representation of native Canadians in the force. This longstanding flaw in Mountie recruitment was all the more glaring because such a large proportion of RCMP law-enforcement work in western Canada affected Indians. The force also began to seek more French-speaking recruits. The need for all these changes was demonstrated in a rare burst of candor by the RCMP in the solicitor general's report for the year. It was admitted that in 1974-75, only 84 of 1140 recruits held college degrees. And while the RCMP listed 2614 positions requiring bilingual skills, it hired only 173 francophones that year.

The 1974 changes were a belated response to criticisms of Security Service recruitment by the McKenzie royal commission report of 1969. The report was very blunt about the inappropriate nature of RCMP training for its then Security and Intelligence branch: "It is quite wrong that recruiting for a security service should be tied to a recruiting and training program generally oriented towards the requirements of a police force."[7] The Security Service was not a police force, the report argued; its function was to conduct intelligence operations, and it needed recruits of above-average intelligence to do so effectively.

As revealed repeatedly in testimony at the Keable commission[8] and confirmed by our Mountie informants, the Security Service has never had any special training programs to equip it members when they are transferred from the criminal investigation side of the RCMP. "You learn on the job," members have testified. Occasionally classes of a few days duration have been given by so-called experts, sometimes imported from the FBI or the CIA. "Some of these were a useless bore," several informants told us.

Mounties recruited (that is, transferred) to the Security Service are expected to meet stiffer loyalty tests than regular Mounties. This means loyalty both to Canada and to the RCMP. "Having a university degree doesn't make much difference, but being the son of an RCMP member does," we were told. (It is felt that the sons of Mounties learn discipline early.) Like the FBI and CIA, the RCMP Security Service "likes to get young guys so they can be properly formed." This term recalls the Benedictine and Jesuit concepts of "formation" of novitiates. Another Security Service informant used the word "molded."

One of the traditional methods of molding new members of any highly disciplined organization—a rigid insistence on correct uniform—was long practiced by the Security and Intelligence branch. Our "secret service" wore uniforms until 1962. They then changed to civilian dress, but still of a regulation type which identified them too easily. Ex-FBI agent William Turner comments on the same rigidity in the FBI, where Hoover long maintained a strict dress decorum. "FBI men stuck out everywhere" with their short hair and suits.[9] An internal critique of RCMP practices published in May 1978 by a House of Commons committee charges: "Often officers will issue orders that all plainclothesmen must get military-type haircuts or wear suits and ties."[10] The one exception seems to be the drug squads, where undercover members are allowed to grow long hair and dress like pushers.

The Horsemen

A common criminal slang reference to the Mounties is "the horsemen." Though the RCMP today owns more computer terminals than horses, the image remains. Behind it lies a traditional mystique about horses. Commissioner McClellan used to refer approvingly to Winston Churchill's dictum that "the outside of a horse is good for the inside of a man."[11] Some judges have commented less admiringly on a Mountie uniform which may hobble the pursuit of a criminal who is not wearing uncomfortable riding boots. Journalist Robert MacDonald wrote on the incongruity of requiring Mounties to march in riding boots with spurs, but one inspector said "it was one way of getting the boys [sic] used to them."[12] The inspector spoke of horses as "the great equalizer; horses take the cockiness out of anyone and teach a man self-control."

Mountie recruits (male or female) must live apart from ordinary society for up to six months of training at the Regina barracks. "The aim is to fashion them so they all look alike," a former officer told us. Recruits have to surrender all independence of thought and integrity of action, and become totally and unquestioningly obedient to superiors. Ex-deputy commissioner William Kelly does not soft-pedal this military discipline: "Regardless of which subjects are chosen for study one is invariably stressed: discipline. A police recruit leaves the relatively undisciplined life of an ordinary citizen for the strict discipline of a quasi-military organization."[13]

As in other highly disciplined and hierarchically organized social systems (which sociologists call "total institutions"), the RCMP training of a new recruit is designed to "strip and mortify."[14] Any manifestation of resistance to discipline is dealt with in "degradation rituals." Former Mountie Jack Ramsay described such a ritual in his controversial 1972 exposé of the RCMP.[15] Naturally enough, the humiliation was associated with horses, and was called "horse-troughing." Any recalcitrant recruit could be doused in the horse trough, dragged about in horse manure and finally buried in it, head and all. Ramsay reports that one such ritual led to a riot among junior recruits at the Regina training barracks. The ritual (and the focus on the horses) is said to have gone out of use, but evidence at the McDonald and Keable commissions of Mountie willingness to obey orders—including patently illegal orders—without question, suggests that whatever means are in use today, the same discipline is achieved. The continuing failure of the RCMP to attract large numbers of college-educated applicants is not surprising. College graduates are accustomed to being treated like adults, not boys, and few would tolerate the RCMP's obsession with discipline and obedience.

The reader may react to many of the details of RCMP recruitment presented here with the objection that things have changed in recent years. We expect the RCMP itself to make this objection in an effort to discredit our study.

But it takes a long time to rise through the hierarchy of the RCMP. The commanding officers are thirty- and thirty-five-year men. It follows that if the RCMP is left in charge of Canada's Security Service, the officers in 1990–2000 A.D. will be the men who were first trained (and in the Mounties' own language, molded for life) during the sixties and early seventies. Unless they return to college, many top officers in the year 2000 will not have had a university training. Most will be at the top because they have survived in a ruthless competition for promotion; the best survival technique is to become a yes-man.

The years between 1980 and 2000 will probably be years of great social change for Canada. Will the Mounties recruited in 1965 or 1970 be the best men to protect the security of Canada through these stormy years? Or will the very qualities of adaptability to rigorous military training and discipline which may long have accounted for the Mounties "incorruptibility" be their greatest handicap in adjusting to social change?

The RCMP has long pretended to the reputation and status of Canada's finest police force, and indeed, one of the best in the world. "We were taught that we were *the* best," one Mountie informant recalled. Mounties learn to look down on municipal police forces; several municipal policemen we interviewed on the subject of the RCMP confirmed their observation, to say nothing of their resentment, of this Mountie attitude.

A classic "type" of RCMP recruit is the clean-cut farm boy from Saskatchewan. One such Mountie who entered the force at eighteen years of age told us: "By nineteen I was really brainwashed. I was going to be a thirty-five-year man." By this he meant that he intended a long career in the RCMP, since it is possible to retire on a pension after only twenty years of service—which this informant did, having long since become disenchanted with "Canada's finest."

Cynicism and disenchantment are a common and indeed a logical outcome of early training in the RCMP, and in other police forces where the recruit is trained to believe in the supercop image. Arthur Niederhoffer, now a sociologist but for many years a New York cop, believes that "cynicism is at the very core of police problems" in North America.[16] It begins soon after the recruit leaves training and becomes a rookie policeman. The pain of the "reality gap" between the propaganda of training and the everyday reality of police life leads to a cynical distrust of higher officers and everything they taught. "The first thing a rookie has to learn on the job is to forget most of what he learned in training."[17]

From Rookie to Godfather in the RCMP

For most recruits the force is not just a job, but a career. The distinction is vital in the sociology of organizations. A career is something to be lived for and planned for, not merely a means of earning money for leisure-time enjoyment. Most professional occupations are careers, but certain non-professional occupations—such as police work—may also be careers. The goal is the same: a certain status in the community, and the self-respect of doing a job which is worth-while and interesting. Careers are expected to lead some-where, and they have a profound effect on the self-image of the worker. The RCMP recruit is promised that if he or she is obedient, hardworking, and above all, careful always to pro-tect the image of the force, promotions and satisfying work will follow.

Sociologist Erving Goffman introduced the concept of a "moral career" which individuals may pass through in a lifetime.[18] In a moral career, the individual's conception of himself changes with his status, and with the contingencies of his life which are often beyond his control. The experience of a moral career is not limited to respectable occupations. To the respectable community, a teenage gang leader who suc-cessfully pulls his first big job for a criminal gang, then becomes an accepted member of the mob and finally a gang leader or godfather, has had a deplorable moral career. But in his subculture he has gone from success to success, and is now the envy of many. He may even be celebrated in novels and movies!

The Mountie also goes through a moral career. For a very few members it will include high social status—perhaps even the post of deputy commissioner or commissioner. But for many the career may be from rookie to a sort of "god-father." The godfather is a leader who has adopted the code that the needs of the organization may justify any action.

There is a loss of morale whenever a member of a disci-plined organization is unhappy about where and who he is, in relation to where and who he wants to be (and was led to expect to be by his superiors). James Q. Wilson of Harvard University, one of the most respected analysts of police organization, has noted that the problem of morale, for the individual cop, is the problem of finding "some consistent and satisfactory basis for his self-conception."[19]

When the problem of morale is related to the problem of corruption and dirty tricks, Wilson argues that "the rotten apple theory of misconduct does not explain why rotten apples should appear so frequently in one class of barrels . . . and so rarely in others."[20] Dirty tricks by Security Service members cannot be satisfactorily explained as the work of a few bad apples; they are directly related to the career expectations of Mounties, their moral careers in the Security Service, and thus, the structure of quasi-military discipline.

Jack Ramsay, one of the first Mounties to blow the whistle on corruption and poor morale in the force, wrote of his own experience in a personal way which also reflected the organizational pressures shaping his moral career:

> I want people to know what the Mounted police have become, instead of being constantly reminded of what they used to be. . . . I couldn't sign a petition, discuss politics, or attend a political rally . . . I know of members disciplined for 'conduct unbecoming' . . . for associating with juvenile delinquents they were trying to help. I even know of members who had to quit when the Force disapproved of their choice of a wife.[21]

Ramsay reported the cynicism which gradually oppressed him as he learned to survive and cope with life in the force through deception and sham. The Mountie who wants to rise to the top may find himself compelled to become a sort of godfather who gives orders for dirty work which underlings must carry out. He in turn must take the rap for the dirty work of his superiors, just as a local godfather must cover for the boss of bosses in the Mafia. The rule of secrecy assures that no one reveals the dirty work.

Sociologist Seymour Lipset has argued that if we want policemen with something of the qualities of dedication found in the social service professions, then we must train them like professionals. But, as an RCMP member told the House of Commons Justice and Legal Affairs Committee, "an electrician, plumber or carpenter receives far more exten-

sive training.''[22] He might also have added that the training
for a master plumber (to say nothing of the professional
training of a dentist or pharmacist, or even a mortician or
hairdresser) is likely to be more relevant to the job, than
horsemanship and parade marching are to the career of a
Mountie.

Much of the six months of barracks training for recruits
was faulted by our Mountie informants. ''The RCMP would
be a more effective force if self-discipline were emphasized
instead of unquestioning obedience to officers,'' an informant complained. ''To be a good detachment man you have
to be a self-starter, yet you've been trained to do only what
you're told.''

An official task force appointed by the Ontario government to study its provincial police reported: ''Command
structure implies that the important decisions are taken at
senior levels, and that officers in the field follow orders. This
is inconsistent with the modern requirements of [the
policeman's] role,'' in which discretion must be exercised on
the spot.[23] This is certainly true of the criminal side of the
RCMP, and even more applicable on the security side.

Numerous Canadian studies on policing, like those in other
countries, have referred to the increasing ''professionalization'' of police forces.[24] But it is generally agreed among
sociologists that extensive training in a specific area of expertise is essential to professional status. While certain occupations within the RCMP (such as psychologist or pathologist)
involve such professional qualifications, it is significant to
note that these are often civilian employees of the force. (Few
such professionals would put up with Mountie boot camp
and bootlicking!)

The Illusion of Professionalism

When the word ''professional'' is applied to police forces,
it is almost always inappropriate. Except for highly skilled
professional civilians employed by the police—for example in
forensic labs or computer sections—the police are not, and
do not act like, professionals. Unquestioning obedience to
superior orders, *merely because of rank*, is absolutely con-

trary to professionalism. Whether one is a lawyer, physician, architect, engineer, dentist, psychologist, sociologist or other professional, the ability to continue in practice depends on the respect and assessment of one's peers in the profession. Discipline in a profession is self-discipline, usually supported by a committee on ethics or malpractice within the college or organization of one's peers.

When Canadian studies such as the Morand report[25] or the Marin commission[26] use the term "professional" to refer to police work, they are clearly not referring to long training, or to professional standards of practice and self-discipline. Rather they are equating the term with a trend toward efficiency, bureaucratization, and technological improvements in police work. Often these reports have borrowed the term "professional" from the police themselves, who increasingly pretend to professional status.

There is a reason why the police claim professional status, and it is not merely to dignify their work. *"The term professionalism, as used by the police, generally implies a self-regulating guild seeking insulation from civilian control."*[27] The claim to professionalism shores up police resistance to civilian review boards. After all, physicians, lawyers and sociologists are not subject to such intrusions into their professional expertise, the argument goes, so why should the police be thus regulated? They are the "experts in their field" and should be treated as such.[28]

In the case of the Security Service this is a particularly dangerous claim, because they are already largely independent of any civilian or public accountability. There is no way a member of the public damaged materially (for example, by loss of employment) or in reputation by the RCMP can sue for malpractice, the way one may sue a physician. Moreover, one usually chooses to be the client of a professional, and one usually has the right to change practitioners if dissatisfied. Few Canadians choose to be clients of the Security Service, and only the Service, not the citizen, can end a contact or close a file. Despite these caveats, members of the Security Service definitely like to think of themselves as professionals. They see themselves as a cut above the ordinary Mountie. Informants used such terms as "the cream of the crop," "brighter," "more literate," "individualist," and "self-starters" to describe Security Service members.

The claim to professionalism in a certain field of activity is really a claim to control an occupation.[29] For example, the Ontario psychologists have stirred up great controversy and resistance by seeking government licensing as exclusive practitioners of psychological therapy.

The RCMP has long sought a monopoly on security work in Canada. It strongly resisted the proposals of the McKenzie commission in 1969 that security and intelligence services be taken away from the RCMP and organized into a separate service (presumably modeled on the CIA). The Security Service has strenuously opposed civilian inquiries or legislation which would increase public interference with its exclusive prerogatives.

Professional status for the RCMP Security Service would imply even more individual initiative by its members, and even less accountability for its activities, than is presently the case. We have already observed the all-too-predictable outcome of such professionalism in the Central Intelligence Agency. As described both by ex-agents and by presidential inquiries, CIA operatives who were allowed to operate like professionals produced a frightening variety of "services" for their "clients."[30]

Claims to professional status are likely to draw more applicants than offers of an ordinary "job." Today's high school and university graduates are often dissatisfied with the prospect of a mere job; they want careers. Professions promise careers. Indeed, an RCMP recruitment pamphlet is headlined: "A rewarding career with the RCMP." It offers "a life of variety" and "an opportunity to work with people," a "chance to be proud of yourself," travel, and "work side by side with other young people whose ideals and aspirations are much like your own."

One of the marks of a self-styled professional police force is the claim to efficiency and competence in its field. "A modern and progressive organization utilizing the most sophisticated methods," an RCMP recruitment pamphlet describes the force. It promises members the opportunity to become specialists. The same claims also lead to the generation of clearance rates on criminal charges (the rate of convictions to arrests). These rates prove police "efficiency" and substantiate the claim that the experts should be left alone.

A Security Service faces a difficult problem in justifying claims of efficiency. Espionage and counter-espionage rarely end in a definite conclusion with publicly announced arrests and convictions. Thus the Security Service has been forced from time to time to produce evidence of subversion to justify its existence. The fake FLQ communiqué is only an extreme example of this. There is pressure to make as much as possible of every garden variety of potential subversion, and to suggest new sources of threat. The RCMP strives to gain as much mileage as possible from the most ordinary espionage, such as that of garden, garage and kitchen staff of the Soviet embassy.[31]

A former RCMP officer assured us that "given the right kind of personnel, properly recruited and trained, we could do better work with one quarter of the numbers now in the Security Service and get better results." Much of the member's time is taken up in routine office work, processing security checks, clipping newspapers and journals. "Efficiency of a man might be measured in terms of getting new information for a file, or setting up a new file. A fatter file would count too . . . for example, growing from half an inch to an inch thick." (Those were his exact words!) The best evidence of an efficient Security Service member would be the recruitment of new human sources, a former officer explained, carefully avoiding the word "informer." Similar attitudes to efficiency have been reported for the CIA and the British intelligence services.[32]

The Security Service's frustration in demonstrating professional expertise is increased whenever the government in power allows other "reasons of state" to override their reports of alleged subversion. The Trudeau government's priorities for trade with Cuba, China and the Soviet Union have produced substantial anger in the Security Service. "They're more concerned with wheat sales than with protecting Canadian security," one of our informants charged.

It is particularly galling to Security Service members to be reminded that the Service has not (at least publicly) ac-

complished much in the apprehension of spies in Canada
since the Gouzenko case of 1946. (And even that case came to
the RCMP, not the other way round.) The RCMP has
detected only two illegal spies (as opposed to legal members
of embassy staffs) since World War II. One was an unimpor-
tant KGB agent, the other a Japanese Red Army terrorist.
Peter Worthington's observation in the Toronto *Telegram* remains true: "Canada is the only important Western country
that has never caught a real spy, has never turned up a big-
name traitor."[33] Maybe there aren't any such spies in
Canada—but the RCMP will never admit that.

Pitfalls of Being a Supercop

When there is consistency between various aspects of status
in a career, sociologists speak of "status consistency."[34] For
example, the educational level, salary, title, and powers of a
high-ranking officer should all be greater by the same degree
than those of an ordinary constable. When some aspects of
status are out of step, or inconsistent, the result is discomfort
which sociologists call "status anguish." For example, a cop
with a low rank and pay who is given unusual powers or
responsibilities, or a high-ranking officer who is paid no
more than a corporal, will experience status anguish.

Status anguish is kept to a relatively low level in the Canadian armed forces by varying the pay, powers and responsibilities according to rank. The tradition in the RCMP has
been quite different. A Mountie is expected to be able to do
almost anything—and to be willing to do it out of loyalty to
the force—without demanding extra pay or a promotion. A
Mountie with more than twenty years' service explains:

> It's assumed by the top brass that an officer can func-
> tion anywhere . . . so they will slip a guy with no special
> training at all into a new detachment and he doesn't
> know what the hell to do. While I was working in [a
> Canadian city] they sent down to me a guy from
> Whitehorse who'd been up there eight or nine years. We
> were working on organized crime at the time, and he
> didn't know the first thing about it. I lost the whole first

year after he got there just getting this guy educated for his job.[35]

Another veteran described how "the RCMP expects you to be able to do anything, and they move you around from one assignment to another whether you like it or not." Journalist Mary Trueman of *The Globe and Mail* raised the thorny problem of transfers with Commissioner Robert Simmonds, and reported: "The Commissioner has also shown firmness in the area of transfers. He has turned down a number of appeals on transfers . . . He responds that he must have had good reasons for these refusals. 'I never make a decision that touches on a man's career without reading his whole file, even though it takes hours.' "[36]

Father knows best, especially when he has the unchallenged power of the RCMP commissioner, from whose decision there is no appeal, not even the federal cabinet. In this respect the average Mountie suffers worse working conditions than, for example, a municipal policeman, who at least cannot be transferred out of his city.

"I would be very disappointed if I thought the motivation of most of our people was just advancement, rather than purer thoughts," Simmonds told the press in 1978. Yet the perception of injustices in promotion was one of the most frequent complaints of our Mountie informants. "There are no promotional exams until you become an officer," a former RCMP officer explained. "Even the Ontario Provincial Police have promotion exams at lower ranks. In the RCMP you can get into the officer ranks by apple polishing." He added that exams in the officer ranks seem intended not to measure ability but to prevent political influence, yet "the Commissioner holds the balance of qualifying points, so you may score high but not get the promotion if he doesn't like you."

The lack of focus on "purer thoughts" was indicated by the immediate outcry against an RCMP memo ranking the priority of members for promotion, in September 1978. At the top were bilingual applicants; second place was given to French unilinguals.[37] But the vast majority of Mounties are English-speaking, even in Quebec.

The memo was an attempt to improve the representation of French Canadians in the higher ranks of the RCMP. But the proposal did not go over well, and was withdrawn two weeks later. One of our informants noted, "There are eleven possible promotions for me into the officer ranks, but nine of these require French, which I don't have." It is interesting that RCMP recruitment materials promise "promotion based on abilities" but don't mention (in English-language materials) the ability to speak French. Considering the extremely small proportion of English Canadians graduating from high school or university with fluency in spoken French, recruitment efforts would be truly handicapped if the new proposal was made a requirement. Meanwhile, few French Canadians seem interested in joining an organization with an English-speaking ethos, and a record of elevating only one French Canadian to commissioner.

Keeping Up the Image

"The major consideration in promoting a man is whether he will advance the image of the RCMP," a veteran Mountie stated bluntly. A member's "presentation of self"[38] as assessed by his superior officers is crucial, and counts for more, it is claimed, than any political connection. "A man might get to the inspector level if he can get a friendly member of Parliament to use pull for him, but he'll stop dead there. "The highest ranks resent members who turn to politicians for help," we were assured. However, a perception by superiors that a member has left-wing political views would be a definite handicap, while activity in the Masonic order often provides good connections for promotion.

Policemen may be more highly motivated toward seeking promotions than members of other occupations. Men who are often recruited from the lower levels of society, but who become the enforcers of middle and upper-class laws and privileges, will tend to experience inconsistency between the obligations of the job and its status. They will strive for a higher status in order to reduce the mental pain of the inconsistency.

The ordinary policeman is near the mid-point on American sociological scales of occupational prestige ranging from physicians, judges and professors at the top, to charwomen and laborers at the bottom.[39] In a Canadian study of occupational prestige, policemen ranked at 35 points on an 80-point scale.[40] However, in both cases a police captain is much closer than an ordinary constable to other respected occupations such as accountant or teacher.

An ordinary policeman who finds too little room for advancement in his own local force may seek employment in any of thousands of other municipal, state or provincial police forces in North America. Police skills travel well. But the case of the RCMP is rather special. All promotions for the federal force, eight provincial forces, and nearly two hundred municipal forces are within a single massive bureaucratic system. Nor is there a great deal of room at the top. Officer ranks totaled less than five hundred members in 1977.[41] This is about three percent of the force, not including civilians. At the same time, being an officer in the RCMP is much grander than in most local forces. Like old-style armies, the RCMP has maintained rigid social distinctions between its officer clique and its ordinary members.[42]

There are two basic ways to cope with the anxiety arising from such conditions: struggle harder to meet the qualifications for promotion by over-conformity in upholding the RCMP image, or cynically opt out of the race, merely filling one's job until it's time to retire. Neither response is likely to provide an optimal police for Canada. Those driven to upward mobility are likely to harden into right-wing attitudes toward social questions, and a "survival of the fittest" social ethic.[43]

The Intelligence Community

The most noble appeal to recruits into the Security Service is undoubtedly that of membership in the international intelligence community. As part of this community, the aspiring Security Service member will join with others in the loyal and dedicated defense of freedom and democracy. Those who defend the ambitions of Security Service members or their equals in other parts of the intelligence community inevitably cite the most honorable motives.

Henry Tadeson, one of the top twenty officers in the RCMP in 1978, retiring after thirty-five years of service insisted, "Our motives were honorable. There has been no suggestion of personal gain or corruption in our activities. There has been no criminal intent in these acts."[44] William Colby, former director of the CIA, co-authored a book around the same theme: *Honorable Men*.[45]

Members of the Security Service, privy to secrets their fellow Mounties in criminal investigation may not share, undoubtedly see themselves as a profession with international links. They are part of the never-never world of the CIA, DI5 (formerly MI5) and the KGB.

Yet in that world, the RCMP man cannot help but suspect himself to be a country cousin. The average Mountie does not have the kind of social resources to fall back on which his typical counterpart in the CIA or DI5 has. The British and American services have long been recruited largely or exclusively from university-educated applicants, generally coming from advantaged social backgrounds. The predecessor of the CIA was the OSS (Office of Strategic Services); in Washington parlance it was nicknamed the Oh So Social.[46] Top CIA men are largely drawn from Ivy League colleges. The Company, as the CIA is known, is a sort of gentleman's club.[47] The history of the British secret service is much the same.

Fine manners and "noblesse oblige" have long been marks of social standing in western security services.[48] Their Soviet counterparts are also known for cultivating a veneer of sophistication. CIA men at embassy parties are likely to mix comfortably with their opposite numbers, ex-CIA members report.[49] RCMP members don't get many opportunities to mix at this level in the intelligence community. Officially the Security Service is strictly a domestic operation, with no agents in other countries. While this is something of a myth, because the RCMP does maintain an espionage presence at least in Canadian embassies abroad (and is often a critical factor in decisions to allow political refugees to gain asylum in Canada),[50] the RCMP is not in the big league of the spy world. Individual members of the Security Service must often feel déclassé when dealing with their more sophisticated counterparts in other services—especially if they stem from a rural or working-class background and never made it past grade 11 at school. In Canada it is External Affairs, not the Security Service, that attracts the educational and social elite. And while those scarlet tunics, boy scout hats and riding boots may dazzle the tourists, such accoutrements are more likely to be the object of jokes rather than admiration when professional spooks of other countries gather together.

9

Discipline in Scarlet and Gold

"Canada would be in great shape if even a tenth of the population lived like Mounties," an RCMP informant declared. "The military life is good for you."

G. S. Howard, a former Mountie, wrote that "the initial training may be severely militaristic but in the end the trainee, if he survives, is no longer a boy, but a man!"[1]

"I have been under discipline all my life," Commissioner Robert Simmonds once said, "I started out at eighteen in the Royal Canadian Navy."

The RCMP began as a quasi-military organization and rapidly tightened discipline. By 1875 (two years from its founding) a high desertion rate was an obvious symptom of unrest among the men.[2] The top brass responded by making desertion punishable by a year in prison, with no right to a lawyer and no appeal. At the same time, other avenues for protest against unsatisfactory conditions in the force were closed off. A refusal to obey orders was made punishable by immediate arrest and up to six months detention, again with no lawyer or appeal. Making an anonymous complaint to any government representative became a serious offense. Communicating any item of RCMP business to the press without the commissioner's approval was likewise forbidden. These prohibitions and penalties are still in force.[3]

The force extended its control into almost every aspect of the Mountie's personal life, including any "infamous or scandalous behavior, disgraceful, profane or grossly immoral conduct." Drinking on the job, and even fraternizing unduly between officers and men were punishable after an "orderly room" hearing without the right to a lawyer or appeal to the regular courts. In these internal military-style courts an RCMP member could even be punished for remaining silent when questioned. The Canadian Civil Liberties Association argued at the Marin commission on discipline in the RCMP (1976) that the Mounties are among the few in our society who can be jailed for not answering questions in a police investigation. They can be tried for discipline offenses *in camera* with no right to legal counsel.

"There is no more compelling evidence of the injustice experienced by Mounties accused of infractions of the RCMP rules than the weekly General Orders bulletin," reported one Mountie. The officers have absolute authority over the men. The General Orders never report a charge brought against an officer. The most frequent charge against a man is "making a false statement" to an officer. Several Mountie informants complained that a member charged with an infraction of rules is considered guilty until he proves himself innocent. Penalties can range from loss of pay to transfer, demotion, or confinement to barracks (i.e. imprisonment) for thirty days to a year.[4]

A standard number or quota of orderly room cases or disciplinary hearings is apparently considered by some officers as the mark of effective leadership. "With a subdivision this size we should be able to average four orderly room cases a month," an officer is reported to have said.[5] Cases are not difficult to generate since it is impossible to live by all the rules of the force. An RCMP member is considered to be on duty, at least in the sense of not reflecting badly on the image of the force, at all times. He is also not permitted to drink on duty, so technically he can never drink. One long-service Mountie reported incidents where officers wanted to "get" a man. "The officer would know the man was at a social gathering that evening. He'd wait until the man got home, then call him in on some pretext. Of course the man would arrive at the office with liquor on his breath and could then be charged with reporting for duty under the influence of alcohol."

The RCMP doesn't blush at such contradictions in its rules. Another example is the provision that a man charged with an infraction "is not required to answer; neither does he have the right to remain silent." An instance was reported during the RCMP's internal investigation of dirty tricks at the McDonald inquiry: "RCMP Inspector Blier said he was interrogated more than eight hours last summer and forced to make a statement about his involvement in 1972 attempts to recruit informers . . . He said he did not have any real choice in the matter. He could have refused to make a statement but he would have violated an order and could have been fired."[6]

Learning to Deceive

Contradictory rules and injustice in enforcing them compel those who want to survive in the force to learn to lie skillfully, an ex-Mountie said. The conditions under which Mounties work do not encourage respect for the right of citizens not to incriminate themselves. It is interesting to note the position of William Kelly, a former RCMP deputy commissioner, on self-incrimination. He argues that rules against the admission of evidence arising from interrogation and leading to self-incrimination are of comfort only to criminals. The innocent, he says, clearly do not need such rules. Moreover, if the innocent should occasionally be wrongly convicted, Kelly approvingly quotes an opinion that such a man "should consider it in the same light as if he had been wounded in battle fighting for his country."[7] In other words, it's just a bad break suffered in a worthy cause.

The orderly room procedure—and of course the overall enforcement of discipline within the Mounties, of which the orderly room prosecution is only the last resort—is predicated on the expectation that out of loyalty to the force Mounties will incriminate themselves whenever they violate rules. This code of honor has an ancient history. It may be found in Spartan Greece, in the monastic Christian orders, and in the modern communist practice of self-criticism.[8]

While such a lofty ethic of self-criticism may work from time to time, it is hardly likely to persuade most ordinary Mounties to incriminate themselves. Instead, they learn to lie:

"You lie, first to survive, then, as fear and guilt blunt conscience, to get ahead . . . [until] you no longer serve the ideal, you serve the image."[9] Ironically, the Mountie's everyday police activity makes it easy for him to learn to lie to survive. He sees the criminal doing it, and he learns in turn to deceive the criminal.

Members of the RCMP who themselves face inquisition by officers without the right to legal counsel or the right to remain silent, are much less likely to accord these rights willingly to citizens they arrest.[10] A confession is useful to any policeman holding a suspect. It confirms the legitimacy of the arrest, obviating the danger of a charge of false arrest. It also saves a great deal of time in searching for evidence which will stand up in court. It reduces court time, not only for the judge, but also for the policeman, who would otherwise have to appear as a witness. Accordingly, the ordinary policeman is under some pressure to minimize the citizen's right to remain silent and to obtain legal counsel.[11] For a Mountie who lacks such rights in his own orderly room, the pressure may be irresistible.

The RCMP rule against "conduct unbecoming to a member of the force" can be used by the force to prescribe the behavior of a member while not on duty, the Marin commission found. Several of our Mountie informants confirmed a widespread discontent with the force's interference in members' private and family life. However, the RCMP has been inordinately reluctant to allow social scientists to probe these aspects of its organization.

Coping with Role Strain

Policemen who are working under considerable personal strain because of unreasonable discipline are less likely to respect either the citizens they deal with, or the law itself. They will consume much of their energy in coping with what sociologist William Goode calls "role strain." Role strain results when the demands placed on a person occupying a role are significantly greater than the person can meet through conventional, socially conforming behavior.[12]

The work of the modern physician is often used as an example of role strain. The immense expertise required of a physician, the need to keep up with the latest drugs and techniques, and the inflated expectations of patients, set humanly unattainable goals for medical practitioners. The result is increasing malpractice. In the case of the RCMP, the image of supercop, the expectation that a Mountie can do anything, and the demand that he be a shining example of The Law while doing the dirty work of society, are all sources of role strain.

Goode enumerates a variety of escape hatches for the individual occupying a role with excessive demands. These include compartmentalization (separating the role from the rest of one's life), delegation of parts of the role to others, extension of responsibility (for example, a physician taking out malpractice insurance), and barriers against assessment of one's role fulfillment (for example, through secrecy).

Use of some of these strain-reducing mechanisms may lead to the form of deviant behavior sociologists call "innovation," but which most of us would simply label "shortcuts." A student with more assignments and examinations than he can cope with may come to depend on shortcuts such as cooperating on assignments, paraphrasing the work of others without giving credit, or purchasing "failure insurance" in the form of essays written by professional essay-writers. The student may also invent excuses to gain extra time to meet role demands.[13]

The implementation of strain-reducing mechanisms often leads to a cynical attitude toward the social structure which originally induced the strain. Police may stay in a force only long enough to qualify for the pension.[14] Just as the student may participate in the learning process only enough to get a degree, the Mountie may learn how to carry out his duties well enough to avoid penalties, while keeping his head down until his twenty years are done. The theme of "covering your ass" long enough to get out with a pension recurred in several of our interviews with Mounties, and may also be found in documents written by Mounties.[15]

Another means of coping with role strain has become the basis for a burgeoning profession in North America—that of psychotherapy. Role strain may be eased by merely talking about it, "getting it off your chest." For the Mountie, the therapist is not likely to be a psychiatrist, but a journalist. "Mountie watchers," as they are known, are journalists who have established reputations for listening to Mountie complaints and preserving the confidentiality of their complainants.

Jack Anderson, one of America's top investigative reporters, has described techniques of exploiting the role strain among government employees in order to develop journalistic sources.[16] Mountie watchers use the same techniques. They usually publish any tidbit of information they can get, no matter how insignificant. This signals their informants that they are being listened to, so that next time more important information may be revealed. Moreover, others suffering role strain in silence may be induced to come forward. Certain members of Parliament have also shown themselves to be sympathetic towards disgruntled Mounties. Don McCleery, one of the first Mounties to spill the beans on RCMP dirty tricks, "became one of Elmer MacKay's best sources" after he failed to get a satisfactory hearing on his dismissal from the force.[17] McCleery went first to the solicitor general. Warren Allmand was impressed enough by McCleery's argument to intervene with the RCMP commissioner, only to be curtly informed that there was no provision within the RCMP for further appeal by McCleery. In short, the solicitor general was told to mind his own business. McCleery persisted, and was advised by staff in the solicitor general's office that they could do nothing more for him. However, he might go to the opposition. "If someone in the opposition makes a fuss, we'll have to do something, but we can't initiate action against the RCMP on our own," a senior civil servant told McCleery.[18] Thus McCleery turned to MacKay, an outspoken member of the Conservative opposition.

A document read into the parliamentary record by MacKay provides some of the best illustrations of the effect of role strain within the force. It is by a former RCMP member.

> The power of the senior commissioned officer is so absolute, that should he be incompetent, then everyone below his command will operate far below a satisfactory

level. . . . Should a constable or NCO discover that a
high ranking officer is corrupt . . . he is risking his job,
his career and his pension should he expose misconduct.
. . . A constable discovering misconduct has no channels open to him whereby he can report his findings. . . .
As a result, the goal of each policeman is to protect his
own position.[19]

Maintain the Image

The leaking of secret documents may be considered in
some respects a socially positive by-product of an unjust
disciplinary system. A less happy outcome is the RCMP's
determination to maintain its public image at any cost. "The
worst sin is anything that reflects badly on the reputation of
the RCMP," an ex-Mountie reported. Such sins are more
often defined in moral terms, especially sexual terms, than in
terms of violations against democratic ideals or laws. "The
fastest way to get a transfer when you'd been refused one was
to get some local girl pregnant," an informant recounted.

The recent collapse of the RCMP image is not entirely due
to Canadian events; it is linked to the discrediting of the
FBI's image after the death of J. Edgar Hoover and exposure
of Watergate in the United States. Even the Toronto *Star*,
long an admiring supporter of the Mounties, would now have
difficulty saluting the RCMP commissioner as "police chief
of the world," or stating without an editorial blush, "By
other police forces, the RCMP are considered just about the
best."[20]

The maintenance of a good public image is not merely a
matter of ego gratification. Police work is much easier if
most people, most of the time, regard them as honest and
law-abiding. The public are more likely to carry out police
orders (even at so simple a level as obeying a traffic cop), and
also more likely to report infractions of the law and assist as
witnesses. Thus an effective police force will attempt to persuade the public that any police wrongdoing is a deviation by
individual officers, not an instance of official deviance or
"institutionalized malpractice."[21]

A good image is especially desirable for security police,

since detection of subversion is more difficult than detection of crime. A state which seeks to control dissent will need fewer police when the police are seen as being "on the side of the people." The RCMP would like to believe that it has this image. For example, an RCMP lecture series points out that the Canadian public often calls for fewer bureaucrats in government, but rarely for fewer police.[22]

The social reality may be somewhat different. Much to their dismay, Vancouver police found that the more students knew policemen, the less they liked them. In a controlled program involving five hundred students from grades 2 to 10, initial attitudes toward the police were tested. Then policemen made regular classroom visits to explain their work to an experimental group of students. At the end of two years the students not visited in class still had a favorable impression of the police. Those who had been given an opportunity in the classroom to get to know the police in person were more critical. They frequently found the police "cold and callous."[23]

Secrecy about much that the Mounties do may be essential to maintaining a good public image. Whenever events occur which might tarnish the historical luster of the helpful and protective Mountie, there is immense pressure to cover up. Informants provided us with examples which, of course, we cannot document without revealing confidential sources. (What's more, our lawyers have warned that to divulge the nature of these offenses might be grounds for libel.)

The top brass of the RCMP have shown, on occasion, the most ruthless determination to protect their image in a shroud of secrecy. For example, it was with great reluctance and under withering interrogation at the McDonald inquiry that former RCMP Commissioner William Higgitt admitted that Mounties who refused to carry out orders to commit illegal acts might be disciplined by a transfer.[24] Of course Mr. Higgitt insisted that the Mountie would not be "disciplined," but merely "transferred." ("It depends on where you are transferred," commented Commissioner Donald Rickerd.)

But a transfer—or the threat of it—is not nearly as powerful a weapon of discipline as the orderly room and internal trial of a Mountie. The use of this century-old method to punish a Mountie who leaked information to a public inquiry was reported in 1978. Corporal William Radey was charged "as a result of testimony he gave privately to Justice James Laycraft of Alberta on May 30, 1977."[25] The matter was raised in Parliament by MP Andrew Brewin, who said that if Corporal Radey was being denied legal counsel at a secret trial this was a breach of human rights.

The dedication of the RCMP brass to hushing up scandal was demonstrated in the events which followed the complaint in Parliament. Solicitor General Jean Jacques Blais promised to look into the matter, but on October 27 he wrote to Mr. Brewin that "while this NCO was one of the principal witnesses involved in the Laycraft inquiry I am informed that the service offenses referred to do not arise from the fact that he gave evidence nor from the substance of his evidence."[26]

Under further pressure in the House, Mr. Blais did add that "Corporal Radey was charged because he violated an order not to speak to the Laycraft commission lawyers." What a splendid example of laundered language! It was not the corporal's action in talking to the judge, but his disobedience of an order not to talk to a lawyer working for the judge, which led to his trial.[27]

Meanwhile, Justice Raymond Decary of the Federal Court ruled on October 30 that the RCMP could not proceed with the trial because Corporal Radey was not allowed legal counsel. The same day, MP Elmer MacKay asked the government not to appeal against the ruling.[28] But the RCMP was resolute; Corporal Radey's disobedience of an order was not to go unpunished. One week later they announced an appeal against the Federal Court decision.[29] As we went to press the matter was still not resolved, but the point is clear—the RCMP will go to almost any lengths to discipline a Mountie who violates the secrecy of RCMP operations.

The RCMP's determination to punish a member who disobeyed an order in the apparent public interest of talking to a judge, is in sharp contrast with the *promotion* of Mounties involved in dirty tricks. This apparent double standard of discipline has at least some support from the Canadian public, which has generally appeared more upset by the discrediting of the RCMP image than by police disrespect for the law.

Sociologist Richard Henschel calls self-justified police violation of the law "self-righteous criminality."[30] The National Commission on Causes and Prevention of Violence (United States, 1976), found an increasing tendency toward self-righteous police criminality among lower-ranking policemen. Frustrated by courts and lawyers which they considered to be too soft on criminals, lower-ranking cops who had to deal with criminals directly were simply taking the law into their own hands. Of course, "the law" in this case was the law as they saw it, not what the Supreme Court ("a bunch of crook-coddling liberals," in one policeman's expression) interpreted as law. The frustration of an honest and diligent policeman may certainly be understood when one sees sly lawyers and slow courts letting off a crook with little or no penalty. But obviously direct justice at the hands of the police is not an acceptable solution.

In the case of the RCMP, the internal investigating procedures themselves smack of blatant self-righteousness, and often serve merely to frustrate and anger those whose infractions are being investigated, as well as their colleagues. Mounties accused of dirty tricks in the Quebec division were investigated first by two RCMP officers, whose objectivity about the changes was highly questionable. The result was the Nowlan report which Commissioner Simmonds found too thick to read.

The Roots of Mountie Anti-Unionism

The structure of totalitarian discipline within the RCMP has more effects than those already outlined. It is one of the major roots of a longstanding tradition of anti-unionism. We have already noted the history of RCMP attacks on strikers and the tendency to include trade unionists along with other dissidents in a general "subversive" category. Stuart Jamieson, in his study of labor relations for the federal government, concluded that the RCMP "has been felt with enough force to tip the scales of battle in hundreds of strikes and labour demonstrations."[31]

This presents an interesting sociological puzzle. Why would men who experience unfair and undemocratic discipline on the job align themselves against fellow Canadians seeking more democratic control of their workplaces? Why would they swallow the official line (as found in the RCMP lecture series, *Law and Order in Canadian Democracy*) that troublesome unions are "communist infiltrated"?[32] In 1918 Mounties were ordered not to join or in any way associate with any trade union, and this order remained in force until 1974. But this alone does not explain RCMP anti-unionism.

The answer lies in the theory of "false consciousness." Anyone who has seen the film *Gone with the Wind* will have witnessed a striking example of false consciousness. A battalion of black soldiers is shown marching through Atlanta. It is not fighting with the northern armies, against slavery; it is part of the Confederate army. The historical fact is that numbers of black slaves willingly fought for the plantation system. They were what Southerners loved to call "good niggers."

Through effective molding and discipline the RCMP has persuaded most of its members to be "good niggers." Obviously there are some pro-union men in the RCMP, and there have been attempts at unionization of Mounties, but they have always been effectively frustrated by senior officers persuading and bullying the lower ranks to be loyal to the force. The officers have been aided in their efforts by the recruitment and training practices of the force. Recruits from farming backgrounds are likely to be suspicious of unions anyway. Many farmers see unions as city organizations responsible for higher prices of fertilizer, machinery, transport and other necessities of life. But what of the recruits from the working class of Canadian cities? Some of these must have grown up in pro-union families and neighborhoods.

As Walter Miller and others have noted, the working-class, urban youth subculture possesses certain special characteristics.[33] Among these are an admiration for toughness and smartness, and a desire for excitement. The most effective teenage gang leaders display more than average evidence of these qualities. Indeed, if they are to remain in leadership positions, they are required to do so by their peers. The delinquent gang leader must be fearless and quick-witted.

The RCMP appears to have traditionally recruited from the working class much more than from middle class, professional or upper class backgrounds. Of course it did not recruit teenage gang leaders, but it did get young men who grew up in just such a tough and competitive environment, and who showed a strong drive for achievement and upward social mobility. These boys—for reasons of family background, religion or other factors—found "respectable" outlets for their energy (such as sports) which allowed them to enter a police force without a criminal record. However, the same working-class urge to form a gang of loyal peers is there. It is expressed in pride of membership in a brotherhood of "the finest," the RCMP.

Our informants repeatedly referred to one form of collective activity popular among RCMP members for many years—the Masonic order. Evidence suggests that this all-male secret society is especially powerful in bringing together conservative, patriotic Protestants with clubby needs and deep ambitions to get ahead—and that it is helpful to upward mobility in the army, politics and the Anglican church.[34]

The origins of the trade union movement in North America are closely intertwined with the Masonic order—for example, the Knights of Labour of the mid-nineteenth century was patterned on the Masons. But workers who wanted real social change in the workplace soon found themselves at loggerheads with those who sought only the collegiality of a secret society outside the workplace. The trade union movement shook off the pattern of secretive ritual and organization. The survival of a strong Masonic influence in the RCMP right into the 1960s is indicative of the ability of the force to safely siphon off collective sentiments among the lower ranks into socially insignificant activity in secret societies. Several of our RCMP informants referred to the importance of a Masonic connection.

Often an analysis of the anti-unionism of the RCMP stops

at the ideological level. We have attempted to show first the basic organizational reasons for the anti-union ideology, because ideology alone cannot explain its own success. There are numerous instances among the military and police forces of other countries where attempts at similar indoctrination have failed. Large sections of the Russian army went over to the Bolsheviks. German soldiers, in 1918, refused to fire on workers on strike or marching in protest. The French Gendarmerie refused to carry out orders to use violence to suppress the Paris student and worker revolts of the late 1960s.

But there has never been an occasion where RCMP forces directed against collective worker activity have gone over to the side of the workers. Indeed, the RCMP were called in to the 1919 General Strike in Winnipeg because the city police were considered politically unreliable by the federal government. The RCMP leadership actively lobbied for the right to take action against the Newfoundland loggers' strike of 1958-59. The minister of justice, Davie Fulton, refused to send more RCMP men into Newfoundland to be used by the Smallwood provincial government in its suppression of the strike. Mr. Fulton's stated reason was that he feared the RCMP would be depicted in the media as a union-busting outfit. The RCMP was outraged at the federal government and shortly afterward, Commissioner Nicholson resigned.

Resentment of the lower ranks against the internal discipline system in the RCMP became strong enough in the 1970s that a significant number of Mounties attended meetings to discuss formation of a union. Naturally the officers reacted with horror. Apparently to stop this trend, the RCMP in 1974 created a new staff relations system, a sort of "company union." Members elect representatives from each division, corresponding roughly to a province. The representatives gather in regional meetings in the presence of their commanding officers, and twice a year they meet with the commissioner. The system obviously has no independence from management in either communications or finances.

The major aim of the staff relations program is to cool out grievances among the lower ranks. To this end, Mounties are appointed at each rank, in each division, in a sort of officer-controlled "union steward" role. But rather than describe the program ourselves, we'll let a Mountie informant compare the old system with the new, which has now been in operation for more than five years.

> In the old system you were supposed to go and complain to the personnel officer. If I went to see my personnel officer I knew he'd be talking to the OC (officer in command) the very next day and I'd be up shit creek. Once a year that guy would call you and say, "How are things going with you?" And you'd say, "Oh they're great," of course. . . .
>
> Then the new system came in. If you're a corporal you're supposed to complain to a corporal who's your representative. But what can that guy do? He's only a corporal . . .
>
> Of course most guys won't go for a union. The great majority of the men are very anti-union.

A More Democratic RCMP

Would the formation of a union of ordinary members of the RCMP improve the force's role in Canadian society (and improve the Security Service if it remained in the RCMP)? Sociologists of police organization disagree on the effect of unionism. Some argue that police unionism leads to undemocratic actions, such as opposition to civilian review of police wrongdoing.[35] Others argue that unionism among the police promotes democracy for two reasons: unions provide experience in democratic representative systems, and they allow grievances to be settled by member participation. Police unionism may also reduce police frustration, which is then less likely to be directed toward the victimizing of suspects.[36]

The RCMP is definitely not what the Task Force on the Ontario Provincial Police calls "a constable-centered force."[37] The conclusion in this report was that an effective but democratic police force should involve "lower-level non-military structures of response to conditions at the community level."

The participation of civilians in various aspects of police activity is widely recognized by sociologists of the police as an essential ingredient of democratic policing. Berkely argues: "To insure maximum democratization, the lower levels of the police organization should also be opened to civilian influence. The more the police force is integrated with the larger society, the more it is apt to share that society's rules and values."[38]

The 19,000 members of the RCMP in 1978 included about 4,800 civilians. The proportion of civilians (about one quarter) has remained about the same over the past decade.[39] However, they do not represent the "civilian influence" Berkley advocates in a democratic police force. Almost half the civilians are clerical and administrative employees. Another third are civilian members of the policing forces, low men (and women!) on the totem pole of influence in RCMP law enforcement. Another tenth are simply operational employees such as motor mechanics and horse grooms. In fact, there are only eight scientific employees and several score of technical and high-ranking administrative employees who might have any influence on the officers of the RCMP. No civilian employee has any actual power to command. Even the former director general of the Security Service, John Starnes, reminded the Keable inquiry that as a civilian he did not have the power to discipline the Mounties caught in such illegal operations as Bricole. The tight control of the RCMP officer clique over the force's command structure has assured that its civilian employees have little effect in integrating the RCMP—and especially the secretive SS—with the rules and values of a more open Canadian democracy.

The issue of a non-military and constable-centered structure interfaces with the question of police-civilian community relations. For many decades, the RCMP has recognized this nexus. Its standing orders concerning the treatment of civilian complaints against RCMP actions (for example, the manner of carrying out an arrest) are part of its disciplinary code of behavior. The Marin commission was appointed to consider both aspects of complaint procedure: that of the civilian against the RCMP, and that of the Mountie against his superiors. As the Marin commission learned, the source of many Mounties' complaints against their officers was the disciplinary action taken by those officers following orderly room inquiries originating in civilian complaints. There could be no better evidence for the argument that concern by the Canadian public for the behavior of the RCMP must be closely tied to concern for the way the individual RCMP member is treated by the force.

10

The Hidden World

"The secret offers the possibility of a hidden world alongside the manifest world," wrote German sociologist Georg Simmel nearly a century ago.[1] Even the child delights in the secret world, learning at a tender age to taunt his fellows: "I know something you don't know."

The world of officialdom is already a demimonde to the average Canadian. When cloaked in bureaucratic red tape and secret documents, it becomes a wonderland where everything is classified except the toilet paper. Officials responsible for disposing of difficult and controversial problems get through the day more easily when actions are taken in secret. They need only wave the magic rubber stamp. No count has been taken in Canada, but in the United States 55,000 federal government employees have the right to stamp "Confidential" on a document. Eighteen thousand wield greater magic; their stamps read "Secret." The master magicians are the 3000 senior government servants armed with "Top Secret" stamps.[2]

Once stamped and classified, a document assumes a mystique not easily vanquished. Only those privy to the secret spells (such as "Cleared to see classified documents") are able to lay hands and eyes on the powerful talismans of bureaucracy. Anyone who dares to profane the classified document without such authority is liable to discharge and disrepute. However, in the United States he is not liable to anything like the penalties threatened in Canada. There is no

156

Official Secrets Act in the United States, so an enterprising reporter may publish secret documents if he can lay hands on them. A Canadian (or British) citizen who dares to reveal the secrets of government bureaucracy risks fourteen years' imprisonment.

Few Canadians have ever read our Official Secrets Act. It is difficult to believe that it was legislated in a free country, as some selections demonstrate (our italics):

3(1) Every person is guilty of an offence under this Act who, for any purpose prejudicial to the safety *or interests of the State,*

a) approaches, inspects, passes over, or *is in the neighbourhood of,* or enters any prohibited place;

b) makes any sketch, plan, model or note that is calculated to be *or might be* or is intended to be directly *or indirectly* useful to a foreign power . . .

(2) On a prosecution under this section, it *is not necessary to show that the accused person was guilty of any particular act* tending to show a purpose prejudicial to the safety or interests of the State . . .

4(a) a person shall, *unless he proves the contrary,* be deemed to have been in communication with an agent of a foreign power if

(i) he has, either within or outside Canada, *visited the address* of an agent of a foreign power . . .

(ii) . . . the name or address of, or any other information regarding such an agent has been found in his possession . . .

14(2) The court may order the exclusion of the public from any proceedings . . .

The accused is not considered innocent until proven guilty, but the reverse; the trial may be conducted in secret; and the accused may be guilty by association and by alleged motivation, without having committed any particular act. If someone among your acquaintances should be accused of being an agent of a foreign power, then you, having his name, address or other information about him in your possession, may be called upon to prove that you were not party to a conspiracy. Where the accused "is a company or a corporation, every director and officer of the company or corporation is guilty of the like offence unless he proves that the act or omission constituting the offence took place without his knowledge or consent.'' (Section 14-3)

The combined effect of the Official Secrets Act and a system of classifications of documents is this: any bureaucrat with a Secret stamp can create a criminal offense for anyone who reveals the contents of the documents. Thus it is not only the hidden world of official secrets which expands with each new document stamped Secret.[3] It is also the world of potential criminal offenses which grows for anyone affected by the document who would like to know what it says, or to make it public.

Canadians are not allowed to know even the bureaucratic rules by which the government documents are classified. There is no public information about which officials, or how many, are allowed to hide behind Secret stamps. We are only permitted to know that there are four categories of classification: Top Secret, Secret, Confidential and Restricted.[4] ''A web of seventy-two statutes at the federal level prohibit the release of information. This does not include the administrative discretion allowed under an estimated 14,000 bureaucratic rules,'' reports Canadian sociologist Barry Leighton.[5]

The most recent trials under the Official Secrets Act were those of Peter Treu, a scientist and businessman, and Peter Worthington, editor of the Toronto *Sun*; but secret trials have a history in Canada. The commission appointed to investigate the allegations of Igor Gouzenko in February 1945 was empowered to ignore the laws of habeus corpus and the right to counsel. The thirteen accused were held incommunicado for two to six weeks. During the first ten days neither they nor their relatives were even told why they were being held. In its report, the commission stated clearly that the Official Secrets Act shifts the burden of proof from the state to the accused.

Peter Treu was so unaware of the power of the Official Secrets Act that he couldn't believe—until he was sentenced to two years in jail—that anything serious would happen to him. He is alleged to have had possession of classified documents without the requisite clearance. He had enjoyed clearance for years, and claims he was never told that it had been withdrawn. The ultimate irony is the fact that some of the classified documents he was charged with possessing without authorization were documents he himself had written! The court decided that Treu was a loyal Canadian and no security threat, but sentenced him to two years as a deterrent to other possible offenders. (The conviction has since been overturned by the Quebec Court of Appeal. The government has announced it will not appeal this decision, but neither will it compensate Treu for his court costs or his loss of time.)

The details of the Treu case are tangential to our concern in this study, and are already well outlined elsewhere.[6] The case of Peter Worthington is more relevant because the issue was not one of possible carelessness, or lack of information, but of a deliberate challenge to the Official Secrets Act. The challenge began not in Toronto, but in Ottawa, in the House of Commons.

Conservative MP Tom Cossitt already had a reputation as a maverick ready to lambaste the Trudeau regime at any opportunity. Early in 1978 Cossitt began leveling charges against the government for carelessness and indifference in security matters. It was obvious that Cossitt had good sources of information. His charges hit home, and Solicitor General Jean Jacques Blais argued that the charges were "working against the interests of national security—if Cossitt had important information, let him give it to the RCMP to act on." In making this suggestion, Blais was apparently playing the gentleman's game, for he must have suspected that Cossitt's sources were disgruntled Mounties trying to put pressure on the government. Soon Cossitt admitted as much, and was accused in the House with possession of stolen RCMP documents. There were suggestions of an arrest, but it was finally decided by the government that Cossitt enjoyed parliamentary immunity.[7]

Peter Worthington of the Toronto *Sun* meanwhile obtained the same or a similar document, and published some of the contents in his newspaper.

It is a virtual catalogue of Soviet crimes, or attempted crimes, against Canada and Canadians in business, academic, journalistic, military, political areas. Among the revelations which should give Mr. Trudeau pause are: . . .
- The Soviet Union acquired a deep-water submarine with a classified, pressure-resistant steel hull. . . . The Soviets signed a contract with a Vancouver company to have . . . parts shipped to Switzerland and rerouted to the USSR. This "Swiss connection" is repeatedly tried.
- In 1971 a Canadian scientist went to the USSR . . . and was seduced by his Intourist guide. . . . The scientist returned to Canada and was persuaded to smuggle a highly classified new laser from the National Research Council to the USSR . . .
- Since 1970 five Canadian corporations have become partners of the Soviets in selling and servicing Soviet goods. Canadians serve a figurehead role . . .
- In 1975 GRU [Soviet military intelligence] officer Dmitri Ivanov tried to bribe an Agricultural department scientist to give secrets of a new rust-resistant wheat.[8]

The *Sun* presented these and fourteen other items as if they were hot news of Soviet subversion. The Trudeau government played its part in the game by charging Worthington with violation of the Official Secrets Act. The RCMP carried out its role by conducting an investigation and serving the arrest summons. The *Sun* reveled in it all, devoting four full pages of the March 19 issue to it: "Worthington steadfast: We won't back down." "Sun trial first of its kind." A "Free Peter" petition appeared, and Worthington was likened to Soviet dissidents Anatoly Scharansky and Alexander Ginsberg.

Not-so-secret Secrets

But, already on March 15, journalist George Bain had written in the Toronto *Star*, "Now that the hysteria has subsided, let's examine some of the secrets contained in that Top Secret Paper."[9] It turned out that the deep-water submarine was supplied on an open contract known to several government agencies. In fact, it was insured by the federal Export Development Corporation. The laser had not been smuggled at the behest of a Soviet spy. It was taken with full government approval to a scientific academy in the USSR as part of an international exchange program. It was neither secret nor classified, and was widely written up in scientific journals.

The five Canadian companies mentioned were in public business selling Soviet-made goods (tractors, automobiles etc.) in Canada—just as Canada sells goods in the USSR. As for the secret rust-resistant wheat, there are no secrecy restrictions on agricultural discoveries and the wheat had already been publicized in scientific journals.

In short, Bain suggested, the "vital secrets" whose revelation was so dangerous to Canadian security were not secret after all. Moreover, much of the information Worthington and Cossitt were accused of revealing had already been widely broadcast on Canadian television in a program which included none other than Robin Bourne, head of the Security Planning, Analysis and Research Group in the Solicitor General's department, and Canada's top civilian authority on security operations. The program also included references to the alleged seduction tactic for a laser, the submarine, and the Soviet companies in Canada. But, as Bain pointed out, no one was charging the television network with violation of the Official Secrets Act.

The stolen secrets caper is continuing in the courts. Mr. Worthington's defense counsel naturally wanted to subpoena relevant RCMP documents. But the federal solicitor general has refused to allow even the judge to see 548 documents on the grounds of national security.[10]

The Treu, Cossitt and Worthington affairs underline the criticism often made of bureaucratic secrecy: its result is often the protection of inept officials. Sir Winston Churchill said it first, during Britain's trial of a member of Parliament, Duncan Sandys, for revealing state secrets in 1938 in order to prove the military unreadiness of England under the Chamberlain government. Churchill said: "The Official Secrets Act was devised to protect the national defences and ought not to be used to shield ministers who may have

162 *The RCMP vs The People*

neglected the national defences. It ought not to be used to shield ministers who have strong personal interests in concealing the truth about matters from the country."[11]

The Cossitt and Worthington affairs are recent Canadian examples of a chronic problem with secretive officials—the exaggeration of the need for secrecy. In the United Kingdom, the name of the director of the security service is an official secret, although it is well known and published in the press outside Britain.[12] The government has the power to prevent British newspapers from publishing information classified secret even after it appears in foreign papers of which copies are sold in London. The object is to keep the natives in the dark.

The RCMP has its own fetish for secrecy. In 1977 it was still refusing to declassify documents concerning the death of Peter Verigin, a Doukhobor leader killed in 1924. When a film-maker sought the RCMP file while researching a film on the Doukhobors, the RCMP began investigating the filmmaker! When the *Vancouver Sun* published articles criticizing the RCMP wrongdoings in 1978, Ottawa headquarters requested copies. They were duly transmitted—in code![13] The Canadian government is more secretive than most. While other countries are introducing freedom of information legislation, Canadian governments have continued to hide behind any available cover. This stance was legitimated in 1969 by the McKenzie commission on the RCMP, which "viewed suggestions for increased publicity with some alarm." This commission, which marked something of a watershed in RCMP-government relations, contrasted sharply with trends in the United States, where the first freedom of information act was passed in 1968, and the United Kingdom, where the Fulton Committee on the Civil Service (1968) condemned bureaucratic secrecy.

The democratic tradition of the right of a free people to information is weak in Canada. We have ignored Georg Simmel's warning: "Every democracy holds publicity to be an intrinsically desirable situation, on the fundamental premise that everybody should know the events and circumstances that concern him."[14]

The Canadian citizen who wants even the limited disclosure of information permitted by Canada's Freedom of Information Act must take an adversary position. He must prove that he has a right to the information, rather than the bureaucrat having to prove that it must be kept secret.[15]

Crown Privilege

The Canadian government's power of secrecy is not limited to the Official Secrets Act. The government may also claim Crown privilege. Allen Dulles, one-time director of the CIA, greatly envied the power of the British government to claim the privilege of the Crown, which the American revolution had ended in the United States.[16] Crown privilege gives the government the power to withhold documentary evidence in court—even when the government is one of the parties to the litigation. This applies not only to documents in the possession of the Crown, but to those held by others.[17] The high court has ruled that Crown privilege may be applied "where the practice of keeping a class of documents secret is necessary for the proper administration of the public service." This leaves out almost nothing which the government might wish to keep secret.[18]

Prosecutions under the Official Secrets Acts of Canada and England are rare, since the threat alone usually suffices. In Britain the threat is sometimes formalized in a "D notice." This consists of a written warning that the publication of certain information *might* be in violation of the Official Secrets Act. Newspaper and magazine editors almost never ignore such notices although they have no strict legal power.[19] In Canada, it has usually been sufficient for officials to informally suggest caution to journalists. Every Ottawa journalist worth his salt knows some juicy stories he'll tell you in private—if he trusts you—but will never put on paper.

Even in cases where the Official Secrets Act has been employed, there is rarely justification for this particular legislation. A charge of theft would have been equally effective in the Worthington and Cossitt affairs—assuming that such a charge were substantiable in the first place. However, charges of violating the Official Secrets Act should not be assumed to be what they seem. It is doubtful that Mr. Cossitt or Mr. Worthington revealed anything of even minor interest (let alone vital concern) to Canadian national security; *their crime was in challenging the doctrine of official secrecy itself.*

Max Weber observed long ago: "Every bureaucracy seeks to increase the superiority of the professionally informed by keeping their knowledge and intentions secret."[20] The maintenance of the right to secret information—and to declare information secret—is more important to officialdom than any particular secret. The desire for the power conveyed by secrecy runs through all levels of government organization. In his study of local police forces, William Westley found that "secrecy stands as a shield against the attacks of the outside world."[21]

It has been argued that, as a result of democratic pressures, there is less government secrecy today than once existed. In the eighteenth century governments maintained secrecy on state debts, taxation income, the size of the army, and even the size of the bureaucracy. As late as 1800, debates in the British Parliament were secret, and press publication of them a criminal offense. The sessions of the United States Senate were formerly closed to the public.[22] However, to argue that we are better off today because such matters are no longer secret would be to disastrously misunderstand the function of power in modern society.

The Hungry Files

The history of human governments is the story of a long march toward the total dossier. When archeologists uncovered clay tablets beneath the ruins of Europe's most ancient civilization, the Minoans of Crete, they found Europe's first writing, now styled "Linear B." Scholars worked excitedly to decipher the tablets, hoping for insights into the highest thoughts of the Minoans—their poetry, philosophy, religion. Finally in 1953, Linear B was deciphered. The tablets, buried 3500 years ago in the ruins of the palace of Knossos, proved to be bureaucratic records: permission for a farmer to sow his grain, contracts for roads and shipping, regulations of every kind of the daily life of Knossos.[23]

It is hardly necessary to tell a modern citizen the extent to which government operates on the basis of documents. Nothing exists, nothing has really happened, until it is recorded on paper, or more recently, on computer tape. But most civilians do not realize the life taken on by the files themselves. Once created, a file is not an inert thing, but a positive force which may be as destructive as a bullet. Anyone who has attempted to correct an error in a government file knows this. After much struggle with officialdom it may be possible to include a correction in the file, but often the error will remain there too; not replaced, but added to, by the correction. The error retains its own unique reality.

The secrecy of much government information helps to give it a reality independent of the people who manipulate it. Out of the inequality between those who know and those who don't know what is in the files, grows "the typical error according to which everything [in the files] is important and essential."[24] The files are the source of bureaucratic power, Max Weber observed. The power that goes to the occupant of any official position grows largely from his right of access to the files he accumulates.

No one understood this better than J. Edgar Hoover, former head of the FBI. Hoover learned in his youth the value of a good filing system; his first job was file-card indexing for the Library of Congress. Later, he maintained in his private office potentially damning files on everyone of importance. As soon as Hoover died various men of power were greatly concerned to get their hands on his private files. The FBI file system was so complete that even when documents dealing with dirty tricks were marked Do Not File, they were not destroyed. Instead, they were filed under special guard in a Do Not File file![25]

In the process of an illegal wiretap, an FBI agent might overhear a friend of the president talking to someone with a shady reputation—perhaps even a member of the Mafia. Later, in his verbal reports to the president, Mr. Hoover would take care to mention this juicy detail, with a comment,

"Of course, Mr. President, that conversation need never be known to anyone." The president would then congratulate Mr. Hoover on his continued patriotic service and loyalty to the American way of life. "Hoover was a master blackmailer," said William Sullivan, until 1971 assistant director of the FBI.[26]

Ex-FBI agent William Turner considered the FBI in many ways a "paper police": the maintenance of dossiers consumed more of an agent's time than actual detection of crime.[27] A break-in at the FBI offices in Media, Pennsylvania on March 8, 1971, by a group calling themselves Citizens to Investigate the FBI, verified the crucial role of FBI files in maintaining surveillance of political dissidents of all kinds. The Media group released studies of the stolen documents, showing that only 45 percent related to crimes of theft and violence, and a further 1 percent to organized crime. The FBI, despite its television image, largely ignored the investigation of organized crime. Forty percent dealt with political surveillance, and another 14 percent with draft resisters.[28] Thomas Emerson, professor of law at Yale, has further documented the preoccupation of the FBI with collecting political dossiers. He estimated that about 2000 agents, almost a quarter of the force, were devoted to this task.[29]

Feeding the files is also the main preoccupation of British security services:

> The greater part of the Special Branch's job is building up dossiers. . . . There are thousands of files on communists, fascists, the IRA, and protest organizations right down to tenants' associations. Any of the people named in these files would be startled if he could see the Special Branch files. They give a detailed picture of him—his favourite pub, where he takes his holidays and his wife's family history.[30]

Canadians likewise would be startled to see the RCMP files, our Mountie informants have indicated. "An intelligence service is as good as its files," one ex-Security Service man pointed out. Another reported, "My job was to get whatever I could and put it into the files." Such files take on a life of their own. Once a name is entered, any data concerning that person or organization becomes germane. New names are generated and new files opened for the most casual of reasons. "You never know when you might need a piece of information," an ex-security man argued. "If someone happened to be in the same newspaper photograph as an individual for whom we already had a file, then I opened a file for the new name too."

The files also provide work to do. As indicated earlier, one of the measures of "efficiency" of an intelligence service is each agent's ability to keep feeding the hungry files. This is particularly important when a service like the RCMP depends heavily on informers. Its knowledge of petty crimes, sins and peccadillos can provide an opening for recruitment of new informers.

For the past decade, sociologists of deviant behavior have been quarreling over the validity of "labeling theory." Opponents of labeling theory have argued that deviant behavior exists whether or not it has been labeled as such. Their favorite example is "secret deviance"—behavior which violates social norms, but is known to no one but the deviant. But surely one of the most convincing demonstrations of the validity of labeling theory comes from the secret services.

When the secret bureaucracy of police or government labels a citizen as deviant, he *is* deviant, so far as they are concerned, no matter what he did or didn't do. What's more, he doesn't even have to know that he has been labeled as deviant, in order to be treated as such. He may go on for years wondering why he's having so much trouble. The case of Bernard Maguire has already been examined in chapter 6. Another example is that of Joseph Fabian, a Toronto citizen who has been detained by the police more than fifty times. It seems that Interpol has a record of an internationally known criminal who uses the alias Joseph Fabian, and looks somewhat like Toronto's Fabian. Toronto police use Interpol data from the RCMP, so whenever they have spotted Toronto's luckless Fabian, they have hauled him in.

Mr. Fabian, at the end of his patience, "borrowed" a computer printout from the desk of a Toronto police office in a desperate effort to get proof that the RCMP files should be corrected. He was thereupon charged with theft of police property! Finally Mr. Fabian appeared in court and was given an absolute discharge—but there's no guarantee the computer won't be after him![31]

The Tentacles of Bureaucracy

Secret files and the labels in them are not local and individual things, but parts of a communication network stretching across national borders and even across oceans. In today's world, a file can reach thousands of miles to trap and bedevil its victim. Within Canada, information collected by various police services, together with security intelligence, is organized into a computer network in Ottawa by the RCMP. Called the Canadian Police Information Centre (CPIC), it has 876 access terminals across the country—plus one in FBI headquarters in Washington (we have no such access to their files). Anything in any CPIC file can be obtained through any one of these terminals.[32]

In 1977, the CPIC computerized files contained more than one million *criminal* record files, with an average of 90,000 inquiries *per week*. There are also more than 600,000 files on other individuals—wanted, missing, charged, suspected—with an average of 230,000 inquiries per week. During the 1976-77 fiscal year alone, the RCMP received 435,063 fingerprints.[33]

At the head of a vast network of police bureaucracy is Interpol, located in Paris. The RCMP is Interpol's "Canadian connection." No public agency has control over the information which the RCMP provides to Interpol. Indeed, no international agency (including the United Nations) has any control over Interpol, which is actually a private corporation contracting its services to 125 national forces. Canada's participation in Interpol has never been approved by Parliament.

Article 3 of the corporate charter of Interpol forbids it to undertake any activity in cases of a political, military, religious or racial character, but this is merely bureaucratic camouflage. It is never difficult for police to label an act of dissent as a criminal act of some kind. Even religious activity may be labeled a "criminal matter" and relayed without verification. In the modern state, the labeling process is largely in the control of political, economic and military elites. Thus the same act may be given a criminal label (murder, kidnapping), or a political label (national defense, political hostage-taking), depending on elite interests.

The need for consultation and exchange of information among national police forces is obviously functional to a world situation where terrorists, drug traffickers, multinational commercial crime, the Mafia, currency speculators, and other criminal elements respect no national boundary. Today police face the same need to follow suspects across national borders as they once had to follow them across state or provincial boundaries. But this makes all the more vital a stringent control on the kinds of information exchanged among police forces, and particularly its verification by means which prevent the abuse of secrecy.

All sorts of worthy people end up in police files: antiwar demonstrators, striking trade unionists, militant women's liberationists, and religious evangelists. For example, the RCMP has publicly acknowledged its accumulation of masses of files on the Jehovah's Witnesses in Canada. They were considered troublemakers "second only to the Communist Party of Canada."[34] These are all examples of a police tendency to distrust minority groups.

Interpol's charter limits it no more than the CIA's charter successfully prevented it from engaging in domestic espionage. An American government enquiry found that some forty percent of Interpol's dossiers related to non-criminal matters.[35] A Canadian solicitor general revealed that Interpol had files on 6000 Canadians under surveillance but charged with no offense.[36]

In the Computer's Grip

Dr. Simon Wiesenthal, the famous Nazi hunter, once observed that documents gathered in good faith by a democratic regime could readily be put to evil use by nondemocratic powers.[37] For years, the Canadian government has been centralizing data on all Canadian citizens through social insurance number (SIN) indexes, and this policy will continue: "Canadians should expect their social insurance numbers to be more widely used as identification in the computer banks of Government and private industry, Health and Welfare Minister Monique Begin told the House of Commons . . . [This is] a policy of common sense . . . 'I'm responsible for a budget of $14 billion,' an agitated Miss Begin told the House . . . 'I don't want any loss of control.' "[38] The possibilities of such central control being used as the basis of a police state are quite real in an age of "big government."

One of the great historical problems of those who have sought to establish totalitarian or police states is that there are rarely enough police to go around. The police can't watch everyone all the time. George Orwell suggested the answer to this problem in his prophetic novel, *1984*: electronic technology. Through modern computer systems connected to electronic surveillance techniques, each policeman becomes four or twenty or forty, as the occasion demands.

The multiplier effect of technology begins at the simplest levels. For example, a two-way radio carried by each policeman on the beat enables a police force to scatter its men thinly over a city, but to concentrate forces of sufficient number at any trouble point within a few minutes of the alarm. The radio also enables a constable to check out any citizen with the central computer file within minutes.

The next step is the permanent installation of television cameras at all important locations—banks, post offices, railways. One man may thus "police" several dozen locations. Electronic ears, in the form of matchhead-sized microphones and undetectable telephone taps, may feed into a central tape-recording system which can monitor hundreds of sources. Tapes are activated only when voices are heard. The newest systems can even detect a specific individual through a voice print, and central files of voice prints are now being collected.[39]

In a study of the use of electronic bugging by Canadian police, Jeff Sallot reported that police applications to use these devices secretly were turned down by judges only thirteen times out of 2499 requests. For each court authorization, an average of two or more wiretaps or microphones were planted. Allowing for differences in population size, Canadian police are seven times more likely to use electronic surveillance than police in the twenty-four American states where police can get a court order to bug people secretly. The Canadian wiretaps also run much longer on the average than those used in the United States.[40] Ironically, Canadian police get their authorizations to wiretap and bug under a Canadian law called the Protection of Privacy Act!

Indiscriminate use of electronic surveillance scoops up everyone in its net. Sallot reported that in 1977, 3623 Canadians were arrested who weren't even named in the original police applications for authority to wiretap. Yet in the same year, wiretap evidence was used in court in only 504 cases, of which only 275 led to convictions. All the conversations of everyone telephoning or visiting a bugged "suspect" are taped, and the resulting information can eventually find its way into the central computers. An unsuspecting citizen may be stopped by police for a simple traffic offense, and the policeman gets a computer report on the spot, by radio. This is an effective way to catch criminals, but what about the innocent citizen who is arrested? Canadians can be held for six days while a charge is investigated for which there is no evidence other than a computer report. Several Canadians have been held this way, then released with an apology, but no compensation.[41]

The RCMP has been eager to protect and extend its secret methods of getting information, while as stubbornly refusing to disclose its sources. In the Krever inquiry in Ontario, the RCMP has gone to appeal court to claim the right not to reveal the sources of confidential information it got from government medical files without the patients' consent.[42] Computers make it easier for secret bureaucracies to distribute information through police networks, but at the same time make it more difficult for citizens to catch up to the labels. One can hardly walk into a computer center and demand to see the files; only technicians know how to access the data. Even the possibility of a revealing leak is reduced.

The RCMP appears to be going to unusual lengths in the use of electronic surveillance. An Ontario Supreme Court judge recently condemned the Mounties for bugging a conversation between a Crown prosecutor and defense lawyer.

The RCMP claimed that the bugging was legal because an RCMP officer also present at the meeting consented to it—although none of the other participants were aware of it.[43]

A few years ago, sociological experts on bureaucratic secrecy were willing to admit that it had its "dysfunctional effects" on society. Secrecy reduced intelligent and informed discussion of organizational options. It enabled those in the know to enhance their own importance. It led to the production of useless, unreliable and unchecked information. Sociologists such as R. P. Lowry noted all these aspects of secrecy in dispassionate articles in scholarly journals.[44] If Lowry, himself a former military intelligence man, knew of more heinous effects of secrecy, these were not discussed.

What would be the use of revealing the truly horrifying work of secret intelligence services? Would anyone believe the allegations? To most people *The Manchurian Candidate* could only be fiction, not reality. But now we know otherwise. The CIA really did spend $25 million over twenty years to brainwash unsuspecting subjects. Some of the incredible experiments allegedly took place in Canada, at McGill University.[45] We had encountered hearsay of such "mind war" research, but had dismissed it as the product of someone's overworked imagination.

It seems impossible to believe that the RCMP have been involved in, or even informed about, mind-warping experiments or similar secret activities. Yet we must face the ugly fact that the RCMP has preserved its secrecy extremely effectively. The code of honor of "not ratting on the organization" has held firmly. Of course it is possible that the RCMP, unlike the CIA and the FBI and British DI5 and DI6, simply has no secrets to hide. But it is also possible that under the cover of scarlet tunics, scarlet deeds are hidden. As the Rockefeller commission reminded the American public, we must always keep in mind that tight secrecy may indicate that there is much to hide from public scrutiny.[46]

The Secret Purse

Since the earliest use of spies in affairs of state, their numbers and payment have been the privileged secret of rulers. In Britain today, "every MP knows the Secret Vote is only a fraction of the money needed to run [DI5 and 6]—the rest is hidden in other estimates, particularly those on defense."[47] The cost of intelligence services in the United States has been estimated at $12 billion a year by Senate committees,[48] but even this august body has no real idea how much the government spends on its secret police. American democracy has long since forgotten the warning of one of its founding fathers that "the purse and the sword must not be in the same hands."

Perusal of annual RCMP reports will provide the reader with an inevitable two pages devoted to the Mounties' Musical Ride and the RCMP Band, but hardly a word about security. Aside from a box in an organization chart, the Security Service would seem to be nonexistent.

The reader will understand, then, that most of what follows is based on estimates and guesstimates, made as carefully as possible and relying on many sources, but without hope of substantive verification until Canadians begin to demand a firm accounting of secret police spending. Even our best-placed informants inside the Ottawa bureaucracy were unable to provide us with more than a few clues to the closely-guarded secrets of federal security services spending.

The official statistics are available in *Public Accounts in Canada*, the *Parliamentary Estimates*, and the annual *Solicitor General's Report*. These show that the RCMP cost Canadians about $220 million in 1971, and about two and a half times as much—$550 million—in 1978. Obviously *official* RCMP costs grew at a much faster pace (150 percent) during these years than inflation (about 65 percent). The difference reflects not a spectacular increase in Mountie salaries (though these certainly improved generously over the decade) but rather a disproportionate increase in the size of the force.

From 1971 to 1977 Canada's population increased by about 6 percent (from 21.6 to 23 million). In the same period, the RCMP mushroomed from 13,500 members to at least 19,000.[49] This is a growth rate of 41 percent, or more than six times the growth rate of the population. Nor are these statistics derived from a carefully chosen base year. If we take

1961 as the base year, the rate is the same: between 1961 and 1977 Canada's population grew by 26 percent (from 18.2 to 23 million), while the RCMP grew from 7,500 to 19,000 or about 153 percent—again, about six times the population growth rate. Since 1951 the Canadian population has grown by about 60 percent, but the RCMP has expanded by more than 300 percent. In short, no "troubled sixties" or October Crisis accounts for the growth rate; rather it reflects a long-term government policy of steady expansion well ahead of population growth.

In comparison with present needs, the RCMP Security Service, at about 2000 men, is considerably overstaffed. This fact was repeated by several of our informants. One Security Service man put it baldly: "Once your files are done, you're done. You have to try and look busy." The fact has also been stated publicly by other RCMP informants.[50] The expansion of the RCMP in peacetime can only be understood as a policy of government preparedness for unwelcome eventualities. Should Canadians begin to grow restive and troublesome under an increasing burden of government control the RCMP can be relied on to keep the peace. The two earlier periods when the RCMP expanded well ahead of population growth were the years just following World War I, when the force was doubled in six months to meet the anticipated trouble from returning war heroes "infected by Bolshevism," and during the Depression.[51]

Almost any police force may be expected to complain that it lacks enough manpower to carry out its responsibilities. Hoover was famous for manipulating crime statistics at budget time to wangle more money from a dubious Congress. The RCMP has not been ashamed to exploit moments of good publicity. For example, during the media orgy over the expulsion of thirteen Soviet embassy staff in February 1978, Mounties complained they lacked the men and the legal power to control the Soviet presence in Canada. Thus far, no commission of inquiry has had the courage to carefully analyze RCMP claims for more men and more power.

There is no reason to believe that the official but rarely publicized data on costs and manpower are true, since here as in England and the United States many secret security costs may be hidden in defense spending. Parliamentary questions about Security Service manpower and costs have always gone unanswered.[52] However, one of our informants began work in the Security Service in the early sixties and kept abreast of developments up to the present. Though not privy to all the relevant data, he assured us that the Service had grown at least 400 percent over the past decade alone. This would put its growth rate during the period well ahead of that of the RCMP as a whole. He reported that one result was that men who began in the Security Service in the sixties had a much better chance of promotion into higher ranks of the force than those serving on the criminal investigation side. Thus Security men have risen to many important positions of power in the RCMP.

During a major political crisis, the RCMP could call not only on about 2000 men in the Security Service, but also on at least a portion of its contracted-out force (especially those familiar, as a result of past service, with Security Service procedures). It might also call on a significant number of its "alumni," now organized into an RCMP veterans' association and numbering more than 3600. Many of these men, retired after twenty years of service with good pensions, are still only in their late forties or fifties. (It was an ex-Mountie who arranged to copy the computer tapes for the Montreal team in Operation Ham.)

Some indication of where Ottawa expects a crisis is evident in the current distribution of RCMP forces across Canada. As of July 1977, the RCMP had 1275 men stationed in Quebec. This is about ten percent of the total force, excluding the Ottawa headquarters administrative staff, Musical Ride, RCMP Band, etc. At the same time, the force had 1078 men stationed in Manitoba and 1247 stationed in Saskatchewan.

This looks like a reasonable distribution, considering that Quebec has a much larger population than Manitoba or Saskatchewan. But in the prairie provinces the RCMP is the provincial police force as well as many municipal forces. In Quebec, the RCMP provides neither service, for Quebec has its own provincial and municipal forces. Even when Quebec RCMP forces are compared to those in Ontario, there is an imbalance. There were 1150 Mounties in Ontario (Toronto headquarters); less than those in Quebec even though Ontario has one million more people.

Police as Growth Industry

In almost any society today, citizens may tremble at the steady growth in police forces. The British secret services have doubled and redoubled since the war.[53] The CIA and FBI have become vast corporations dispensing billions of dollars. Federal, state and municipal police forces in the United States grew from 339,000 to 445,000 between 1967 and 1974. American police growth rates have averaged 5 to 6 percent a year while the U.S. population has grown about 2.5 percent a year.[54]

Para-police forces have also burgeoned during the past decade. No one seems to know exactly how many "rent-a-cops" there are, but one informant in the business estimated 30,000 private security men in Ontario alone. Various police powers are being delegated to para-police forces, such as parking-ticket officers and building superintendents. By freeing regular police for other work, all these developments add to total police power.

The growth of police forces in Canada, and particularly the RCMP, should cause those who cherish civil rights even more concern than in America, because of the structure of Canadian policing and the absence of constitutional safeguards. A police state would be more difficult to institute in the United States because of the multiplicity of police forces at every level, and the high degree of rivalry and jealousy among some of these forces. In Canada, the RCMP controls provincial policing in eight provinces and the two territories, as well as having a considerable base in municipal policing. The RCMP constitutes one quarter of all police in Canada.[55] It also operates under much weaker political, court and constitutional checks than American police forces. The RCMP's quasi-military structure would prove eminently adaptable to a police state's functioning.

No less an experienced authority than Allen Dulles, former director of the CIA, observed that the ideal organization to stage a coup d'état in a modern state is its secret intelligence service. Dulles made the comment in reference to the Soviet secret police, not his own CIA.[56] Occasionally Canadian members of Parliament have referred half-jokingly to the possibility of a coup d'état by the RCMP. We may well wish it to remain a joke, for surely no other organization in Canada is so well placed, so well equipped, with so little countervailing control.

The maple leaf on Canada's flag is not an entirely appropriate symbol, as any westerner knows; there are no maples growing naturally west of Manitoba. Perhaps the scarlet and gold of the RCMP would make a better national symbol. The RCMP, unlike the maple, does extend from coast to coast. And already their coat of arms is emblazoned on our paper money!

11

Recruiting Judas

All major intelligence services in the modern world (such as the KGB, CIA, British DI5, Israeli Mossad, South African BOSS, Iranian SAVAK, and the RCMP) rely heavily on informers. Regular members of a security service are only infrequently used as "agents" to ferret out secret information in the country or subculture being spied upon. Regular intelligence officers act mainly as recruiters and handlers of informers. This reliance on informers means that the recruitment of new "human sources" is a major concern of intelligence services, and their continued effective handling a high priority.[1]

"To recruit a new human source is a cause for celebration," one Mountie informant observed. Another explained, "Informers are essential to corroborate electronic or physical surveillance." Informers are particularly important when regular policemen are unable to "pass" as indigenous members of the subculture being watched. Certain RCMP wrongdoings, such as the break-in at the APLQ, may be viewed as the outcome of failure to recruit a human source inside the target group.

Police forces have achieved some success in passing in the drug subculture by wearing long hair and dirty jeans, but the North American drug subculture is in many ways a reflection of the mainstream culture. It includes university students, middle class people and even professionals.[2] A "straight-looking" cop can readily alter his appearance to look like a pusher. Aside from a certain special jargon, members of the drug subculture speak mainstream English. Whites are as acceptable as blacks, and a small-town boy from the Prairies would excite no more suspicion than a slum-dweller from Vancouver or Montreal.

Entry into black militant organizations is quite another matter. In *Black Like Me*, J. H. Griffin showed that a change of skin color was not enough to enable him to pass easily in the black subcultures of American cities.³ Since the vast majority of FBI, CIA and RCMP members are white, these forces have experienced considerable difficulty in penetrating black militant movements as undercover agents. The RCMP has been in an even worse situation than the FBI and CIA, which could at least recruit blacks among American college graduates. The proportion of blacks in Canadian cities, until recent years, has been small. When a militant black subculture developed in Montreal and Toronto in the sixties, the RCMP faced a new problem in intelligence gathering.

Apparently the problem was solved by importing at least one American black. The case of Warren Hart has received great publicity. Described as an "FBI informer," Hart was allegedly allowed to reside legally in Canada for five years (1971-76) even though he was officially deported by our immigration officials in 1971. It is reported that his immigration file was "red-flagged" so that whenever he came to the attention of officials for being in the country illegally an explanation would be supplied by the RCMP, who were using his services. Member of Parliament Elmer MacKay has information that the original deportation was at the RCMP's instigation to give them a "club to hold over Hart's head."⁴

Consideration of RCMP dirty tricks used in attempts to recruit informers in Quebec must be set against the above observations. The desperate measures used by the force to find informers suggests they were having great difficulty in finding Mounties who could pass as agents in the militant separatist underground. The FLQ situation resembles the RCMP problem with the black militant subculture.

Compare, for example, the success of an "RCMP officer who bought heroin worth $600,000 on the illicit market" which led to the arrest of three drug traffickers in London,

Ontario,[5] with the apparent failure of a single RCMP agent to successfully penetrate the FLQ during the early seventies. The RCMP seemed no more able to "pass" its regular men as separatist Québécois than it was able to pass them off as black militants. Indeed, one of our ex-RCMP informants suggested that most Mounties "stick out too much" to pass in politically subversive roles. This notion was confirmed publicly by an agent's comment on CBC's *Fifth Estate* (February 1, 1978) that Mounties are "too obvious—they look like cops."

A Necessary Loathing

In medieval England, if a man charged as a result of an informer's tip was not found guilty, the informer was hanged in his place. In modern police work, informers are generally necessary but still loathed. No one loves a Judas. Though the police reap considerable benefit from the informer's betrayal of the trust of his peers, most police cannot bring themselves to admire the informer's role. The informer violates an essential condition of civilized society—the expectation that one can trust one's friends. Once an individual becomes an informer, there is no way he can avoid eventually betraying those who trust him, for he must protect his "discrepant role."[6]

Informers come in several types, ranging from the money-grubber who will sell out his best friends, to the adventurer who enjoys undercover work as an agent provocateur and thrives on the self-importance of "working with the police," to the idealist who believes in an unpopular cause. But in almost every case, the relationship of informer to handler becomes one of mutual parasitism. This social symbiosis has rarely been examined by sociologists, and there is unfortunately no space to analyze it here. But there is ample evidence that the use of informers by the RCMP has been corrupting not only to the informers, but also to the Mountie handlers. There is much that has not been revealed, for instance, in the case of Warren Hart. He has continued to allege a "raw deal" from the RCMP, while admitting to many dirty tricks conducted in his years of service with the Mounties.

One of America's first spies set the tone for informers. "Every kind of service becomes honorable by being necessary," Nathan Hale claimed. The informer's handler is inevitably corrupted because he can only continue to garner information from the informer if the latter's "cover" is protected. This often requires illegal acts, or at least complicity in illegal acts, by the handler.

But whatever the handler does for the informer, the latter will never be fully able to trust the handler. For the handler has the power to destroy the informer at any time, merely by tipping off others in his circle or group. This is known as "burning" the informer. RCMP Commissioner Robert Simmonds stonewalled some questions by MPs about the RCMP's use of burning when an informer is of no further use and they want to stop paying him.[7] Since the informer knows that the handler will protect his cover only as long as he remains useful, there is immense pressure on the informer to keep producing information, whether or not it is valid. If the informer is financially reliant on the handler he may manufacture information, regardless of the consequences.

The informer is completely dependent on police assurances that when his role is finished his identity will be protected. If the informer must be identified and act as a witness, he may even need a new identity in a new locale, perhaps for the rest of his life. A fascinating story of one informant provided with RCMP protection is found in a book, *Under Protective Surveillance*.[8]

In short, the business of recruiting and handling informers—to say nothing of being one—is a messy activity. Philip Agee said, in a *Playboy* interview about the CIA:

> Don't think it's all excitement. A CIA officer . . . spends hours in musty little basement rooms waiting for agents [informers] to show up and make reports. Then he spends more hours listening to agents' problems—how their girlfriends are pregnant, how their cars need new transmissions, how their brothers-in-law would make good spies. When he isn't mothering agents . . . a CIA officer is . . . sucking up to a corrupt politician in the hope of corrupting him still further.[9]

Ideological Informers

It is most unlikely that the ordinary civilian, fairly content with his work, family life and friends, will become an informer for the police. Having to pretend to a role, and deceive those who trust you, is an exhausting experience.[10] Thus the security services are most likely to recruit the marginal and frustrated members of society: people who need money and are willing to do almost anything to get it, and people with a desire for vengeance or ambitions which cannot be legitimately achieved.

Only under certain special conditions is it likely that respected, intelligent, well-balanced individuals can be recruited by a security service as informers. These special conditions are ideological. The ideologically motivated informer is the best possible kind.[11] He will be the easiest to handle, and will require the least mothering. He will probably demand no payment, only the assurance that in case of detection he will find friendly political asylum in the country of his handlers.

The relative collapse of the Soviet KGB as an effective intelligence system may be partially explained by the disappearance of ideological informers in other countries willing to serve the Russian cause. During the twenties and thirties, a number of well-educated and even upper-class English, French, American and Canadian professionals, scientists and government officials felt an ideological kinship with the Russian experiment. They hoped for the eventual advance of socialist ideology in their own countries, and were therefore willing to betray their capitalist employers and governments, and aid the fledgling Soviet state. They became willing cooperators with the growing international Soviet intelligence system, which they viewed as a major bulwark against Fascism.[12]

The Soviet non-aggression treaty with Hitler in 1939 troubled many of these ideological informers, but most succeeded in rationalizing the treaty as a necessary though desperate act of self-defense by the USSR. When Hitler attacked Russia in 1941 and the Russians became allies of the free French, the British and Americans, the KGB's ideological spies in the western world could rest their consciences. During the Cold War period, they continued to sympathize with the Soviets, feeling that the western allies were now betraying a wartime ally who had paid a high cost for the defeat of Nazism. But the Twentieth Congress of the Soviet Communist Party in 1956, at which Khruschev revealed the extent of Stalin's terrorism, was followed by the Hungarian and later the Czechoslovak revolts, which were put down harshly by Soviet armed might. These actions disenchanted almost all of the ideological friends of the Soviets in the west, and the KGB lost its best possible source of motivation for the recruitment of spies.

The KGB example is by no means irrelevant to an understanding of the RCMP problem in recruiting informers in Quebec before and after the October Crisis. It is clear from the RCMP's clumsy tactics that they were as inept as the contemporary KGB in their effort to recruit ideological friends in French Canada. Thus, when the War Measures Act was declared in October 1970, the RCMP had to throw its net absurdly wide in the hope of arresting anyone who might be a separatist troublemaker. "We had to rush into action poorly prepared," an ex-Security Service member told us. In fact, more than 400 Québécois were detained. Only in sixteen cases was the RCMP eventually able to muster enough evidence to go to court.[13]

Effective police handling of informers does not consist entirely of threats and bullying. "Honey draws more flies than vinegar," the old saying goes. The handler may give the appearance of being non-judgmental of the informer's criminal activities, or at least take the stance that they are none of his business. For example, narcotics investigators may overlook ordinary thefts by informers who are providing them with useful information on the drug subculture. Competent handlers of informers will teach them which kind of information is desired, and which "we don't want to know about."[14]

The informer system is more relevant to some types of police work than others. In criminal investigations, it is among the "non-complainant" or so-called victimless crimes that informers are most useful. These are crimes where

members of the public involved with criminals, (e.g. drug
pushers and loan sharks) are unlikely to go to the police and
lay a complaint. Few complaints concerning national security
are made by members of the public to the RCMP, so the
situation parallels that of non-complainant crimes. Operations are usually generated by police action following an informer's tip. The Security Service handler will draw on many
of the techniques used to handle informers in criminal investigations, having learned such techniques prior to a
transfer to the Security Service.

Recruiting in Enemy Territory

When a security service such as the CIA needs informers in
an enemy country recruitment becomes problematic. Unless
the agency can find ideologically disgruntled informers, it is
reduced, as Philip Agee reports, to grubby deals in base-
ments, mothering an informer or blackmailing him.

The RCMP effort to recruit informers against the
separatists in Quebec may be viewed as a problem of operating in a sort of enemy territory. The operations had to be
carried out largely by outsiders—non-Québécois Mounties. It
was basically a WASP operation directed against an indigenous movement whose violent methods were not supported by
most Québécois, but whose political platform did express the
aspirations of many in the province. English Canada, out of
touch with Québécois attitudes, was profoundly shocked by
the degree of support for the FLQ manifesto when it was read
on television and at mass meetings in October 1970.

The RCMP has been extremely reluctant to let details of its
attempts to recruit informers in Quebec become public
knowledge. The argument used by RCMP lawyers was
naturally that disclosure was not "in the public interest."[15]
But perhaps it was not in the Mounties' interest, and not for
the obvious reason that illegal RCMP activity would be exposed. More important for this study, disclosure might reveal
how ineffectual the force was in handling Quebec informers.
The extent of the RCMP's problem of getting information in
Quebec is underlined by the fact that at the time, even a large

proportion of the French-speaking government bureaucracy in Ottawa came from *outside Quebec*.[16]

The techniques used in Quebec usually began with the "soft sell."[17] "We let him [the potential informer] know he was being watched, tried to talk him into cooperating, worked on his weaknesses," a Security Service member told us. One officer in the G section in Montreal told the McDonald inquiry that he had prepared a policy "approving the use of disruption, coercion and compromise, as well as infiltration, undercover operations, buggings and paying informers." What is missing in this catalog is any effort to recruit ideologically, or through shared loyalties. Instead, the RCMP methods show a striking similarity to the methods they accuse the communists of using: "compromise and duress."[18]

An RCMP document on "source development" signed by the deputy director of the Security Service describes the methods used.[19] They were labeled by the RCMP as "psychological pressure." The handlers collected information on a potential informer's love affairs, power struggles between factions, fraudulent use of funds, drug abuse, and any other information with which the handler could blackmail an individual into becoming an informer. Even the misuse of unemployment insurance might provide leverage.

The RCMP considered it necessary to use such tactics because "security service members in the field were becoming too reliant on technical sources such as wiretaps and electronic bugs."[20] This admission certainly corroborates our argument that the RCMP were operating in difficult, if not hostile, territory.

In "friendly territory" (such as Regina or Winnipeg) the RCMP would not have had to resort to such methods. They would have been able to rely on more traditional tactics, of which a favorite is the "noisy investigation." An RCMP officer simply visits the target's friends, neighbors and employer to "make some enquiries" and perhaps hint that the target is a "Red." The very fact of such a visit from a Mountie, in friendly territory, can compromise and embarrass the target. The threat of such an enquiry may persuade an individual to cooperate with the RCMP.

In hostile Quebec, such soft-sell techniques were generally ineffective, yet the RCMP's official position was that orthodox police methods were used. Inspector Donald Cobb claimed that the RCMP "sought informers among the idealist nationalists by trying to persuade them that violence hurt their cause."[21] This alleged reliance on ideological recruitment contrasts with the report of Dennis Finlay that "each handler had his own methods of dealing with informants . . . the RCMP kept files on individuals with their sexual tendencies, criminal records, psychological problems . . . as much information as possible."[22]

Even threats apparently failed to recruit enough human sources among the separatists. The Toronto *Star* reported that rougher techniques became necessary. For example, when the RCMP failed to persuade one Québécois to inform on his fellows, they decided to make an example of him which might encourage others to be more cooperative. They informed his employer that he was a member of a terrorist underground, and that he was booking off sick and using company cars to transport terrorists. None of these charges was true, but the man lost his job.[23]

The treatment got rougher still. The McDonald commission was told of one fifteen-hour "interrogation session" to attempt recruitment of an informer.[24] The intimidation began when RCMP officers "boxed a car in with three unmarked police cars . . . frisked the driver and then 'invited' him to come along for an uninterrupted session that ended fifteen hours later in an isolated motel." RCMP witnesses maintained that the victim was free to leave at any time, but also admitted that "he stood for a while facing a blank wall in the corner." One commissioner remarked, "I personally find it hard to believe that a thirty-year-old man would say 'I want to voluntarily stand facing a wall.' "[25] The Mounties also tried without success to buy his cooperation with $5000. Similar tactics were reported in other attempted recruitments of human sources.

The Public as Enemy

The notion that the RCMP in Quebec were for all practical

purposes operating in enemy country is by no means outlandish, especially in the context of conventional sociological studies of the police. Evidence that the regular police view the general public as something less than friendly supporters is abundant. The policeman's attitude may range from cynical doubt of public appreciation for his work to a feeling that many citizens are positively anti-police.[26] One police handbook argues: "The police are inclined to assume that unfriendly citizens are their natural enemies and that all citizens are unfriendly. Unfortunately, the police frequently act accordingly."[27]

The sales brochures of industries manufacturing police equipment often read like war weapon catalogs. In recent years, the police have emphasized the development of "tactical squads" armed as menacingly as any occupation troops.

The police definition of the public as enemy is to some extent a part of the trend toward professionalism. Under the old system of policing, recruitment was largely from the working class, and everyone kept the system going by tolerating a fairly high level of deviance both within the police force and from members of the public. Policemen learned early in their careers to "look the other way."

In the old system, the tendency was toward under-enforcement of the law. Policemen took a pragmatic approach to everything from a little prostitution to a little illegal bookmaking. The increased "professionalization" of police duties, and parallel factors such as increase in impersonality and size of police forces, and a breakdown in urban neighborhood solidarity, have produced a tendency among the public to let the police enforce the law: "They're the experts." "That's what we pay them for."

The general citizenry often appears to feel no responsibility to help maintain the law, and a gap grows between "the people" and "the law." The police become a paid group of "dirty-workers"—sometimes little more respected than those we pay to do other dirty work, such as collecting our garbage.[28]

Labeling of clients as enemies is a fairly typical response of those forced to do dirty work.[29] Professional police develop a kind of "perceptual shorthand to identify certain kinds of people as symbolic assailants."[30] They come to expect antagonism from certain groups, who are treated as "police property"—that is, fair game for police harassment whether or not a criminal offense has taken place.[31] In western Canada, for example, Indians have been RCMP property for decades.

When the police come up against an apathetic or critical public, their sense of isolation grows. It is well established that most experienced police, perhaps in self-protection, prefer the company of other policemen.[32] When working among an apathetic or hostile public, the police know they will get fewer "breaks" to carry out their duties. Informers will be difficult to recruit, and useful tips fewer and less helpful. The police will find themselves more and more reliant on their own intuitions and suspicions, but if these are acted on and prove ill-founded, the vicious circle of public hostility is augmented.

When the Security Service is left with the dirty work of watching potential subversives and recruiting informers, the rest of us can keep our hands clean. As sociologist Everett Hughes notes, the symbiotic relationship between "good people" and dirty-workers can often produce unfortunate consequences.[33] One outcome is the desire of the "good people" not to know about the dirty work. Thus the RCMP's rough tactics in recruiting informers reinforce the desire of top officers, political masters, and the general public not to know what the RCMP is doing.

Matters probably got further out of hand in Quebec than in other provinces because the RCMP there felt isolated not only from the public, but from fellow dirty-workers, the local and provincial police forces. Several police informants in Ontario informed us that there are often tensions and rivalries between local forces and the RCMP, similar to those between American municipal and state police and the FBI. But in Quebec there were added strains, indicated in the "falling out of thieves" after Bricole was revealed, but extending to a much earlier time. A Quebec RCMP informant explained that poor cooperation between the RCMP and Quebec police was rooted in the Duplessis era, when Quebec police were extensively corrupted. The Mounties considered themselves free from the taint of political corruption, and wanted to keep it that way.

Recruiting Judas on Campus

For centuries, university campuses have been somewhat privileged enclaves where social dissent has been less risky than in other settings. Out of unrestricted scholarship grew the doctrine of academic freedom. Faculty and students have been allowed to espouse unpopular and even heretical teachings. Thus universities have continued to be centers of radical political activity. Many universities also have their own police forces, and regular police enter the campus only when called upon.

It is obvious that the RCMP Security Service considers university campuses important places in which to conduct surveillance as well as recruit future members of the service. The conformist student shows his colors in contrast with his more questioning peers. He or she may be approached as a likely recruit—if not for service in the RCMP, then at least as an informer. The informer role is often begun on campus, but may continue thereafter, as the student graduates and enters his working life.[34] American campuses were favorite sources of CIA recruits.[35]

The university is also an easy place for most security men to penetrate. They can acquire a legitimate cover on campus as "mature students." They can mix readily with the middle class, mainstream culture of the campus. At least this has been true of the CIA and British intelligence.

However, the RCMP has been rather less successful than other security forces in infiltrating classrooms. Perhaps the social origin of many Mounties has some relevance here. On Quebec campuses the RCMP has operated in doubly hostile territory, for it is especially among the faculty and students of francophone universities that separatism has found strong support.

RCMP attempts to recruit campus informers have been embarrassed by both students and faculty blowing the whistle. A well-publicized example was that of a Laval student leader who was asked to inform on fellow student leaders. Instead, she went to the press. In another instance, just one month after an unequivocal denial of undercover campus operations in the House of Commons, the RCMP was revealed in an attempt to get information from top faculty members of Huntingdon College in Sudbury, Ontario.[36] In Regina, the participation of university students in a nuclear disarmament demonstration led to Mountie visits to parents, who were warned their children would get into trouble by associating with such demonstrations. In one incredible case, two Mounties from the Security Service visited the school of a fifteen-year-old boy after he wrote a satirical letter to a local newspaper. The letter suggested Santa Claus might be a communist, because he wore red and gave away free goods!

There is a conviction among many educators that the typical Security Service handler is incapable of distinguishing sufficiently between various shades of dissent in the information he gets from informers. The result has been a stubborn distrust of the whole RCMP Security Service. Mark MacGuigan, Liberal MP and former professor of law, suggested that many officers were not expert enough to distinguish between those "just shooting off their mouth and those intent on overthrowing the system."[37] The Canadian Association of University Teachers (CAUT) has urged its members "not to answer [RCMP] questions, even when they are part of the security investigation of persons seeking government employment."[38]

The RCMP's surveillance of university campuses is especially disturbing because it reflects a profound naiveté about student life. On the one hand, the RCMP seems to expect university students to swallow any radical utterance made by a professor as if it were gospel truth, when in fact most students have quite a skeptical attitude toward their teachers. On the other hand, the RCMP expects everyone, faculty and students, to swallow the bland assurance that they are "just collecting facts." RCMP Commissioner Harvison claimed, "At no time do we say that a person should or should not be employed" when collecting facts for a security clearance[39]—as if students and professors weren't aware that a report can be written so that the conclusion is obvious, though never explicit. There is also the fact that the mere act of making enquiries may prejudice an individual's case. Likewise, a professor's refusal to answer a Mountie's questions might reflect badly on the persons concerned.

In 1961, CAUT obtained assurances from the then commissioner of the RCMP, G. B. McClellan, "that there was no general surveillance on university campuses . . . that the RCMP would be pleased to inform university presidents when security investigations were made . . . that the RCMP did not ask . . . either faculty or students to act as informers . . . or to enroll in particular organizations to provide information for the RCMP."[40] By 1963, CAUT succeeded in getting a written assurance from Prime Minister Lester Pearson that "the RCMP would not engage in undercover activity or general surveillance on Canadian university campuses."[41]

Yet the recruitment of informers continued, along with instances of electronic surveillance. At the very time RCMP top brass were assuring CAUT that it was not policy to put undercover Mounties on campus, Corporal Jack Ramsay was taking an RCMP course in Ottawa where some men were warned they must accept campus operations or be transferred out of the security service.[42]

When electronic surveillance of classes at the francophone University of Ottawa was reported[43] CAUT again swung into action, with letters to the prime minister and a brief to the McDonald commission. The gist of the prime minister's replies was that all Canadians should be treated alike and none exempted from RCMP surveillance. With nice irony, Mr. Trudeau wrote, "It would seem to me that your members would regard any 'special' treatment in this area as inappropriate to their positions and status."[44]

The Spy Game

In February 1978 the newspaper headlines screamed: "RUSSIAN SPY RING SMASHED BY RCMP. OTTAWA EXPELS 11 RUSSIANS FOR TRYING TO INFILTRATE RCMP." A few weeks later the headlines read: "Canada spy-trap rapped by Soviets." All this occurred while the McDonald and Keable enquiries were looking into RCMP dirty tricks. What was going on?

The story behind the news was that employees of the Soviet embassy in Ottawa had been accused of attempting to recruit an informer among the RCMP: to "turn around" a Mountie, in the spy jargon. All of the Russians involved were in Canada legally, under their own identities, as embassy staff ("legals" in the jargon). They were not spies as such, but it is well known that the embassy staff of many nations act as handlers of informers. Embassies have served as cover for espionage since diplomatic privilege was first enacted by a British Law of 1708. All American embassies, for example, are required to provide cover for CIA members.[45]

It is standard procedure for modern security services to keep an eye on the embassy staffs of other nations within their borders. It is also standard procedure for embassy staff to try to turn around one or more of the security men assigned to watch them—that is, to recruit the watchers as informers.

In short, everyone in Ottawa was playing an orthodox game of intrigue when the Canadian government decided to blow the whistle. However, this time not merely one legal was sent to the penalty box, but eleven. The Soviet embassy staff were accused of attempting to bribe an RCMP officer, as they have successfully done in the past.[46] This time the officer pretended to accept an informer role, but told his superiors. He received $30,500 in payments, for which he provided the Soviets with "disinformation" (useless or misleading information). When the Soviets released their side of the story, they claimed that the affair had begun with the RCMP approaching Soviet embassy employees trying to recruit informers.[47]

For our purposes it doesn't really matter how the affair began. What is interesting is the claims made for the RCMP when External Affairs Minister Don Jamieson broke the news to Canadians. The "Soviet spy ring" (itself a misnomer since the Russians were in the country legally, and employees of the Soviet embassy) was labeled a "massive spy network" by the press and their exposure called "the biggest antiespionage coup the force has ever had."[48]

If this is taken at face value, then the RCMP's achievements in spy detection are reduced to the unimpressive feat of watching embassy officials. What of all the (much more dangerous) illegals operating in Canada under assumed identities? External Affairs also admitted that only a few of the expelled embassy officials were really involved in the attempted recruitment of the Mountie. The rest were "used only for giving signals for meetings."[49]

An unidentified RCMP spychaser was quoted by the press at the time as considering the expelled embassy staff "just the tip" of real Soviet subversion in Canada. But the RCMP never seems to get much below this tip. Igor Gouzenko came to them. Gordon Lonsdale operated here with impunity and was not detected until he went to England, where MI6 got him. There are various theories about the RCMP's undistinguished record of spy-catching. The most dramatic is that of Ian Adams (author of *S—Portrait of a Spy*) that the KGB for many years controlled the RCMP spy-chasing activities by having one of their own spies (a double agent) in a command position inside the Security Service.[50]

But what might be the real meaning of this much-publicized spy caper? One clue is offered in a comment by an unidentified source in External Affairs. "Other diplomatic employees have been expelled for spying, but there has been no public announcement." If the government was willing to take the risk of Soviet displeasure over a public announcement, it must have been because the RCMP needed the "good publicity" of an apparently successful operation so badly that a "drop in wheat sales" was worth it.[51]

A second clue is offered by the fact that the RCMP declined to identify the Mountie allegedly approached by the Soviets. The reason given was to protect the officer *from the Canadian public*. "You never know how the Canadian public will react to this," an RCMP inspector explained.[52] Was the RCMP really afraid the Canadian public would disapprove of a Mountie spy-catcher? Or were they just unwilling to allow the press to interview him, and then possibly cast doubt on the story?

The most obvious clue might be staring everyone in the face. Only eight times in the previous ten years has the Canadian government actually expelled a Russian embassy employee for spying; yet it is likely that far more than that were involved in gathering intelligence in Canada. (If not, we would have to believe that the Soviets were less assiduous in using their embassy staff for intelligence work than the Americans admit to being.) Why expel so many employees this time; especially those only tangentially involved?

As explained by an ex-Security Service informant, the standard counter-espionage procedure when a legal is detected in spy activity is to watch him especially carefully. The hope is not to catch him—he is *expected* to attempt to recruit Canadian informers.[53] The aim is to detect the natives whom he recruits. The RCMP has been dismally unsuccessful in this activity; since the 1946 cases exposed by Gouzenko, the RCMP can claim only three Canadians detected for spying for the Russians.[54]

Espionage is normally a quiet activity, the silent surveillance of little fish in the hope that they will lead to big ones. The embassy employees were not only little fish, but obvious ones. Their expulsion was like spearfishing in a barrel, and probably had more to do with publicity in the media than with national security.

The theory that the spy caper was a publicity grab is strengthened by the timing. The RCMP had known of the attempted recruitment of their member since April 1977 (i.e. before the government was forced by parliamentary pressure and the Keable inquiry to appoint the McDonald commission). Since no Canadians had been arrested at the time of the expulsions in February 1978, we conclude that the delay of ten months had not succeeded in locating any important Canadian contacts of the KGB. Arrests of a few Canadians, after all, would have been something for the RCMP to crow about.

While the Mounties may have wanted publicity they were not prepared to tell the journalists everything. For instance, how did alleged KGB operatives from the Soviet embassy approach the RCMP man *at his home* (as alleged by the RCMP) without the RCMP embassy-watchers being aware of it—unless they were actually seduced into doing so, as the Soviet story suggests? Of course, this is still an orthodox counter-espionage tactic, but if used, why isn't it admitted? How could the embassy employees, if they were in fact experienced handlers of informers, continue contacts with an RCMP man without watching and protecting such contacts, and thus guessing what the RCMP was up to? And finally, why did it require thirteen employees in all to service one potential Mountie informer? The RCMP may be supercops, but this is ridiculous!

One is led to conclude that the episode was indeed a publicity stunt. If a genuine spy ring had been involved, the sensible procedure would have been to keep tabs on the alleged spies, and encourage them to develop their activities (under RCMP surveillance, of course), until some important big fish in the Soviet espionage system in Canada was uncovered.

12

Feasting with Panthers

Many Canadians, even those with a reputation for civil libertarianism, would rather trust the cops than the politicians: "The RCMP is an institution that Canadians have come to trust. It has recognized procedures; its own sense of honor and propriety; a highly refined sense of duty."

These words are from a *Globe and Mail* editorial of June 30, 1973, arguing against political control of the RCMP. How times change! Since the revelations of 1977-78, the *Globe and Mail* editors are not quite so ready to trust the Mounties' "refined sense of duty." Though the opinion of many Canadians has *not* changed in spite of the RCMP's "dirty tricks," we must ask, "who's in charge here?"

If one wishes to feast with powerful pets one should have a weapon handy at the dinner table. Many Canadians apparently prefer to feast unarmed with panthers. They are not alone in this; the tendency in many modern nations has been to keep a powerful police force, with no means to control it in an emergency. To neutralize fears of what an unchecked police force might do, we tend to sanctify the police role. The chief of police becomes a chief priest, even offering absolution to his political masters, just as the high priests of old wielded sacred power over monarchs.

The "sacred" in society is socially set apart because it is both important *and* dangerous.[1] The United Kingdom has for many years sanctified its bobbies as a sacred institution.[2] Hoover's FBI, until recently, symbolized everything good

196

and powerful in the United States.[3] The RCMP has readily embraced the same role in Canada. As the RCMP lectures for recruits put it, "The policeman is in very truth a guardian of democracy."[4]

The role of sacred guardian enables the police to combine the honor of moral crusader with the power to interpret the law at their own discretion.[5] A policeman thus sanctified may transcend the laws governing mere mortals, for he symbolizes the fundamental order and harmony of society. The role provides all the traditional priestly powers: hearing confessions, excommunication (imprisonment), and granting absolution:

> Speaking to the Commons Justice Committee in November, [RCMP Commissioner R. H.] Simmonds virtually absolved the government of interfering with the RCMP.[6]

> Who gave absolution?
> The new commissioner of the RCMP.
> Who did he give it to?
> The present prime minister and recent solicitors-general.[7]

The traditional priesthood was responsible to powers higher than the king. The modern police force claims the same transcendence by its responsibility to "the law." Ex-deputy commissioner W. H. Kelly argued: "The first priority is to the law . . . if the Minister was to be made responsible for police operations, it would tend to make the RCMP a political force."[8]

It is essential to distinguish between *partisan* and *political* control of the police. The myth that a politically responsible police force would be undemocratic and even totalitarian has been reinforced in recent decades by a misunderstanding of the power of the Gestapo, the KGB, and the CIA. All became most dangerous when they got beyond the political control of civilian authorities. Himmler and Beria were essentially rulers of states within states.[9] Even before Watergate, the CIA was recognized as "virtually a separate U.S. government with many of its activities unknown to the legitimate authorities."[10]

Yet many Canadians have swallowed the mythical desirability of a police force independent of politics, which means, in effect, *civilian control*. They prefer a police which may be trusted on its own reputation. In 1975, 67 percent of the population felt there was still *too much* political control of the RCMP,[11] at the same time when the solicitor general seemed to be exercising very little control, or at least claimed that he didn't know what the RCMP was doing.

Taming the Panther

How effective is Canada's constitutional structure as a control upon our police forces? A weak leash may be a sign of danger, and in police matters, poor control is the harbinger of failure of democratic liberty.[12] Poor political control of police leads to partisan control. When the legislature has no effective voice in police matters, the police become an arm of the executive alone (as in police states such as Nicaragua), or take over the executive role themselves, usually in alliance with the military (as in Brazil).

Canada's "constitution," the British North America Act (a law of the British Parliament which may only be amended in London), makes no provision for a federal police force. The administration of justice is given to the provinces. The question of whether the federal government even has the right to prosecute criminal cases is now before the Supreme Court.[13] However, the Supreme Court, holding to its traditional support of the federal power, has confirmed the right of the federal government to organize its own police force.[14]

The RCMP Act and regulations under it, first passed in 1873 and since revised, provide (1970 version, Section 18) that the RCMP shall "perform all duties that are assigned to peace officers in relation to the preservation of the peace, the prevention of crime, and of offences against the laws of Canada and the laws enforced in any province in which they may be employed . . ."

Section 44 provides the Security Service with its power to "maintain and operate such security and intelligence services as may be required by the Minister." Thus, the ultimate control ought to reside with the federal solicitor general.

However, he has no access to the RCMP except through the commissioner, and the director-general of the Security Service, who ranks below the commissioner. In the case of the army, the Minister of National Defence can reach down through the generals to the lower ranks to fire a troublesome officer. In several cases he has done so, the most recent being a commander of paratroops who publicly opposed the minister's policies. But the solicitor general has never reached into the lower ranks of the RCMP. Would such intervention be considered "political interference" of the sort most Canadians apparently disapprove of in police matters, while expecting the army to be firmly under government control?

The comparative independence of the RCMP from responsibility to a representative civilian authority (such as Parliament) is by no means unique. Much the same is true of the CIA and FBI, both of which are barely responsible to the president, and certainly beyond effective control of Congress. The British situation is very similar.[15]

The Trudeau government's position has been that they exert all necessary control over the RCMP. Solicitor General Francis Fox claimed:

> In 1971 the government set up the police and security planning group . . . designed to help provide a more sophisticated analysis. . . . In 1974 we had the Official Secrets Act in which Parliament for the first time defined the term "subversion." Within the Act, an obligation was put on the RCMP Security Service to obtain the authorization of the Solicitor General of the day in any matters requiring wiretapping or electronic eavesdropping . . . In 1975 the government gave a new and clear mandate to the RCMP . . . In 1976 we had the Marin Commission . . . In the spring of 1977 within the Security Service there was established an operations review committee . . .[16]

But the picture emerging from Fox's recitation of government efforts to control the RCMP is not the one he tried to convey: the reining-in of a reluctant police force. Instead we see the opposite: repeatedly futile tugs on a straining leash. George Bain concludes: "We had all these Mountie watchers and no real control.'' Bain goes further back than Fox, to Prime Minister Trudeau's statement of October 24, 1969, on the McKenzie commission report:

> This government will control and restrict within its competence any state activity that interferes unduly with individual liberty. . . . The law enforcement agencies are instruments of government. They are responsible to the government and answerable for their activities.[17]

In pursuit of this policy, the Trudeau government appointed a civilian director general to the Security Service; established the security planning group mentioned above by Fox, and set up independent security committees in various departments as well as a cabinet committee on security. On the surface these look like coherent efforts at asserting control, not unlike recent efforts in Washington to rein in the CIA. But the government emphasized its control of the RCMP on some occasions, and the independence of the force from ''political influence'' on others. For example, the prime minister argued that it would be folly to pretend that the minister should be accountable and must resign because someone at the end of the corridor did something illegal. But when it suited the government to oppose freedom of information legislation, it argued the opposite: ''Ministers are responsible for the actions taken by them or by public servants represented by them.''[18]

The government has spoken out of both sides of its mouth because, to some extent, its structure leaves no alternative. Parliamentary democracy, as developed over the centuries in Britain, demands that ministers of the Crown be responsible to the legislature. At the same time, ministers come and go, sometimes with startling frequency. It is the deputy ministers (permanent civil servants) who really run the departments and know what is going on. How can a minister who is this year's postmaster general and next year's solicitor general know either department effectively? Ministers are compelled to argue, ''I cannot be responsible for something I don't know,'' while, in effect, the parliamentary system demands that they be responsible.

As one former deputy commissioner put it in a public debate (attended by one of the authors), "the problem was not so much keeping information from the solicitor general, but finding the time in his schedule to keep him abreast of developments. It was difficult to persuade him to give us two or three hours a month to tell him what was going on." Many ministers, given the choice between the nearly impossible task of keeping check on most things of importance in their department (and thus becoming more and more implicated in everyday events), or ruling with majestic detachment and the need not to know, will often lean to the latter course.

Health and Welfare Minister Monique Bégin, in a rare flash of political candor, admitted to Carleton journalism students that the solicitor general had become little more than a messenger between the RCMP and Parliament.[19] Of course she "clarified" these candid remarks later under pressure of parliamentary questioning. The picture that emerges is one which historian Hannah Arendt depicted as arising in many modern western democracies: "rule by nobody."[20] No decision or action can be traced directly to any responsible person. Naturally it is in the interest of political oppositions to insist on ministerial responsibility—while they remain the opposition. When they become the government, the situation mysteriously changes.

Wrestling With the Panther

A theory has emerged that the government not only fails in its parliamentary responsibility for the RCMP, but in fact, can barely keep it under control at all. This theory argues that a kind of cold war has existed between the Liberal cabinet and the RCMP, and earlier—when the Conservatives were in power—between the Diefenbaker cabinet and the force: "The Liberal government seems to be the friend, protector and boss of the Mounties, but in fact the Liberals and the Mounties have been carrying on a quiet war since the Munsinger scandal was exposed in 1966."[21]

There is no need here to go into the sordid details of the Gerda Munsinger bed-hopping spy scandal, its impact on the

Diefenbaker and Pearson governments, and its finale in a royal commission report. Certainly the fallout was more severe for Canadian politics than it was for national security. The upshot was that the Mounties were made to look bad, and they retaliated:

> The Liberals for the first time in history appointed outsiders (first John Starnes, then Michael Dare) to run the security service. . . . But instead of subduing the Mounties, these government moves made them more intransigent. . . . In the Sky Shops investigation the RCMP interrogated Jean Marchand (a Liberal minister) so thoroughly that he publicly complained of harassment.[22]

For a Liberal cabinet member to accuse the RCMP of harassment was certainly a new turn of events. And ironically, it was not an NDP or Conservative opposition member, but a Liberal, Mark MacGuigan, who eventually made the most candid admission about a "quiet war" between RCMP and Liberal government. Mr. MacGuigan admits that RCMP wrongdoing is more serious than Watergate because it was by police, not merely civilians, and concludes: "We want a government prepared to respect the police but also prepared to clamp down on them if they exceed their mandate."[23]

Several of our Mountie informants confirmed that at least some members of the RCMP feared that a state of hostility (if not quiet war) existed with the Trudeau government. One referred to "a prime minister who for reasons best known to himself has closer relations to Castro than any other leader in the western world," and asked rhetorically, "Have we got a government we can trust?" The Mounties' distrust of federal ministers responsible for controlling the RCMP has repeatedly surfaced in the press. Warren Allmand in particular seems to have been suspected as an undercover communist. RCMP informer Warren Hart has even charged that he secretly bugged Mr. Allmand on RCMP orders.[24]

The alleged cold war between the Trudeau government and the RCMP grows hotter on any occasion when the Mounties find their precious image under attack. Ex-commissioner William Higgitt attempted to turn the heat away from the

RCMP over illegal mail opening by testifying at the McDonald inquiry that cabinet ministers knew about mail openings and did nothing to stop them. Mr. Trudeau immediately retorted that Higgitt was contradicting his own testimony at the earlier Keable inquiry.[25]

It was one of Trudeau's favorite ministers, Solicitor General Francis Fox, who caught much of the shrapnel in the quiet war. He found himself using affidavits to prevent the Keable commission from exposing more of the RCMP dirty tricks after the APLQ revelations opened the Pandora's box. The more the RCMP was exposed, the more Fox defended them in Parliament. The Liberal cabinet had every reason to be afraid of the RCMP; as journalist Charles Lynch observed, every political leader must have been wondering what the RCMP had on him.[26] "After all, even Trudeau admits that his file goes back to 1951 when he was banned from entry to the United States on suspicion that he was a communist sympathizer."

As for Fox, he was forced to resign when a hospital document on which he signed another man's name to allow a woman with whom he was having an affair to obtain an abortion came to light.[27] It remains unclear to this day exactly where this document came from, and why it popped up just when Fox was having the most difficulty with the RCMP. We are bound to ask whether the timing was more than mere coincidence.

A political power which attempts to maintain an image of legitimacy is always more susceptible to political blackmail than an unabashed tyranny. When the powerful wear no halo and mask none of their ruthlessness, a mere sexual peccadillo won't cause a downfall. But when governments suggest that their hands (and slates!) are clean, they make themselves perennially vulnerable to those who "have something on the leadership."[28]

After the fall of Fox, the government made its bare-faced attempt to rehabilitate the RCMP by the sensational "spy plot" announcement (see chapter 11). This seemed to confirm the extent to which the politicians were afraid of the RCMP, as Douglas Fisher earlier warned: "Sure they're scared. Wouldn't you be scared of the guys who have the files

204 The RCMP vs The People

and the dope about God knows what, all held internally, while out in the country they're honoured and glorified in song, story and TV scripts?''[29]

Among our informants, various journalists with contacts inside the RCMP and several ex-Mounties have referred darkly to the "Featherbed file," with its alleged information on the private sins of Canada's highest political figures. "We've got to keep an eye on those guys," one ex-Mountie with years in the Security Service assured us. Occasionally a reference to Featherbed slips into print, with the merest hints of its juicy details. For example, Morton Shulman, a former Ontario MPP and then a hard-hitting journalist, wrote in December 1977:

> Three years ago when I was working as an MPP on organized crime I was told the story of the Featherbed operation by a member of the Justice Department. The SS . . . file on Trudeau bulged with evidence of his visits to Communist countries and sympathy with socialist causes. The file contained other material, far more delicate, which indicated he conceivably might become the subject of blackmail.[30]

Shulman described how the RCMP attempted to use some of the contents of the Featherbed file to prevent Trudeau's election as Liberal leader. He alleged that the Mounties leaked the information to a right-wing organization, which then attempted to distribute it at the Liberal convention. However, its source was disreputable and the information was discredited. Later, Shulman claimed, the CIA got confirmation on the Mountie leaks when a Soviet agent came over to the CIA side, and brought with him, among other things, data from the Canadian Featherbed file!

Was that a purr or a growl?

When a police force enjoys the public reputation of the RCMP, and has in its hands all the usual weapons of the law, it may not have to use more than the merest suggestion of coercion, or of political blackmail, to have its way with any government whose concern for legitimacy is paramount.[31] Its officers need only hint that unacceptable attempts to leash them will precipitate trouble. The friendliest purr is pregnant with a menacing growl. As journalist John Gray put it:

> A quite simple technique which was guaranteed to make almost any politician gun-shy. . . . If the Solicitor General suggested any change which did not meet the favour of the Force, senior RCMP officers would say, "You've got to be careful there, Sir. There might be criticism of that." And sure enough, within a few days the Conservative party would have information about the change . . . For example, the government wanted the RCMP to reflect something of the bilingual nature of the country. Should flashes and police station signs be bilingualized? . . . The Conservatives, led by John Diefenbaker, went to town on that one.[32]

Another pressure technique is playing the role of frustrated guardians of law and security in Canada when appearing before public inquiries. Thus ex-commissioner William Higgitt appeared at the McDonald inquiry as a righteous super-cop prevented from doing his duty by bungling politicians. The government was told repeatedly that the Mounties were required "to put themselves at risk" to carry out its policies.[33]

Over the years, the Liberal government has shown the utmost reluctance to tame the RCMP. Whenever the opposition, or organizations such as the Canadian Civil Liberties Association, have urged that those in the RCMP already known to have been involved in illegalities should be charged in court, the government has replied that everything must be left to the McDonald commission and its report, which is tantamount to delaying action for several years.

The RCMP's reluctance to accept criticism and change is by no means unusual; it is a familiar characteristic of every police establishment.[34] Sociologist James Wilson's evidence is the most persuasive. He found that when the Chicago press was very critical of the city's corrupt police force, 79 percent of the police sergeants felt the criticisms unwarranted and unfair. Four years later, after the inauguration of a new police chief and a departmental clean-up, the press became quite favorable to the city's "new police force." Yet 65 percent of the police sergeants still felt the press was too critical of the police![35] Similarly, those who have written from the inside, such as ex-Mountie William Kelly, have found it almost impossible to fundamentally criticize anything about the force.

It is not unusual for people in power to decide that they know best, and to consider themselves indispensable. The result is revealed in testimony like that of ex-Commissioner William Higgitt and ex-director general of the Security Service John Starnes, at the McDonald inquiry. Mr. Higgitt argued that there are times when the law can be set aside because of the urgent tasks facing the police.[36] Mr. Starnes was even more forthright; he argued that only idiots would not have realized that the "tough responsibilities" of the RCMP would necessitate the risk of violating the law.[37] In what might be taken as near-contempt for such "idiots" he said that "a security service isn't run like a dairy farm."

It is not easy for most police to break the law. They have been trained and disciplined in the maintenance of the law, and the belief that they represent the personal embodiment of legal morality. The police role breeds love of the conventional.[38] Thus, the policeman experiences "cognitive dissonance," or inner mental contradiction,[39] when he goes beyond the law to enforce the law. The resulting anxiety is reduced by appeal to a higher morality, such as controlling organized crime or the drug traffic, or defending national security. Appeals to "higher loyalties" are a form of neutralization of deviance-provoked anxiety.[40] To put it in plainer English, they are high-level excuses intended to divert public attention from the fact that the police are breaking the law.

Cognitive dissonance will be further reduced if the police believe that a "silent majority" of the population supports them, even if the press or government does not. The rejection of criticism is not merely a refusal to concede errors; it is a claim to righteousness. "The fact is that the CIA has never carried out any action of a political nature . . . without appropriate approval (from) the government," Allen Dulles insisted, even while personally aware (as later events demonstrated) that this was not true.[41] In the face of any criticism, the reaction is to deny, deny, deny. Thus for many years the CIA denied its domestic surveillance activities, while devoting huge resources to them.

Apparently politicians, like policemen, can feel anxious about the contradiction of putting themselves above the democratic principles they have sworn to uphold. When John Turner was minister of justice he sponsored the Federal Court Act of 1969, Section 41 of which gave him and his successors such absolute powers. In August 1976, now a private citizen, he told the Bar Association at a meeting in Winnipeg that he opposed this section of the Act. "I have always found it unsettling when anyone claims to be a judge in his own cause," he conceded.

"Official order proclaimed that the police were above the common law," Jacques de la Rue writes of the Gestapo in Nazi Germany. "And no one dared to say that this was a sign of the moral decomposition of the state, the end of true justice and legality."[42]

In Canada many police believe, according to police informants, that they are above the law and can break the law when necessary. When the police take such a view, robing themselves in righteousness and rejecting all criticism, they are well on the way to being in charge. Can we trust the panthers to run the house?

The Supremacy of Parliament

Canadians have traditionally put their hope for the continuation of democratic freedoms in the "supremacy of Parliament." In this we follow the British tradition of the unwritten constitution, rather than the American institution of "entrenched" constitutional rights. (Conferences of first ministers have been divided between those who continue to trust Parliament and those favoring a Canadian bill of rights entrenched in a new constitution.)

With no constitutional or judicial weapons of the sort prominent in the American system, Canadians who hope to keep the RCMP properly leashed to its duties must rely on five institutional structures: the government (cabinet and supporting apparatus); the opposition in Parliament; royal

208 The RCMP vs The People

commissions; the courts; and the press. (We will discuss courts and commissions in the following chapter, the press in the final chapter.)

We have already demonstrated that during the ten years of Trudeau rule, attempts to improve government control of the RCMP were not outstanding in their efficacy. Generally, the Trudeau cabinet relied on the RCMP's self-restraint, rather than on any system of accountability or checks and balances.

The most determined effort in the Trudeau years to get a tighter rein on the RCMP was the creation of the Security Planning, Analysis, and Research Group in the solicitor general's department, under Colonel Robin Bourne. A former army career officer, Bourne was expected to bring to his job a different perspective than that of a career Mountie, but there is little evidence that he was any more concerned with the preservation of an open society against the expansion of secret police forces than any RCMP officer. A second noteworthy appointment of the Trudeau regime was that of John Starnes, the first civilian to rule the Security Service as director general. There is no evidence that his appointment has brought greater government control of the RCMP.

A third and very mysterious attempt by the Trudeau government to tighten the RCMP leash was the appointment, in September 1978, of Marcel Cadieux as an "adviser" to the top officers of the Security Service. Cadieux is a leading diplomat and recently our ambassador to the European Economic Community in Brussels. He has also been a chief negotiator in the difficult maritime boundary dispute of 1978 with the United States. Suddenly, without explanation, he was appointed to advise the commissioner of the RCMP and the director general of the Security Service.

Ottawa's Mountie watchers speculated that the Liberal government was growing increasingly worried about the steady (but painfully slow) advance of the McDonald commission toward the men at the top. The government was also worried, speculated journalist Douglas Fisher, that the top RCMP witnesses would prove unhelpful to the Liberal cause.[43] The contemporary commissioner, Simmonds, was viewed as an honest cop, but no canny politician. Ex-RCMP officers Higgitt and Starnes proved to be even less useful to the Liberal cause. An experienced diplomat like Cadieux might be able to save the Liberals some embarrassment by counseling the RCMP in diplomatic finesse. The government also assigned two other diplomats, Peter Johnston, ambassador to Czechoslovakia, and C. F. W. Hopper, high commissioner to Jamaica, to "help" the McDonald commission with its investigations.[44]

The Privileges of Sovereignty

We can't be sure who's really in control of the Security Service, but one thing is certain: the Trudeau government doesn't intend to let us see the documents which might give us a firm answer. When the RCMP wrongdoings were first being exposed in Parliament and the press, the Trudeau government used every possible device to evade responsibility or full discussion. The ruling of the speaker of the House of Commons that former ministers (such as ex-Solicitors General Allmand and Goyer) could not be called on to explain events in their former departments once they had left them, was frequently invoked to prevent probing questions. When the heat is on a minister, an easy solution is to move him to a new portfolio, promptly frustrating investigative inquiries.

The Trudeau government also invoked its powers of executive privilege to prevent the disclosure of evidence. President Nixon attempted to promulgate this doctrine for his own use by referring to the presidency as "sovereign," but did not succeed. The American constitution clearly makes the people sovereign. If Nixon had had Section 41 of Canada's Federal Court Act to rely on, he probably would have remained president. This section enshrines as effectively as divine right the principle that the sovereign federal government is beyond the people's reproach. Section 41 reads:

> When a Minister of the Crown certifies to any court by affidavit that the production or discovery of a document or its contents would be injurious to international relations, national defence or security, or to federal-provincial relations, or that it would disclose a confidence of the Queen's Privy Council for Canada,

discovery and production shall be refused without any examination of the document by the court.

With this, the minister has ample grounds for the refusal of *any* document and his affidavit may not be appealed. The court has no opportunity to examine the document in order to validate the affidavit. The minister's word is enough. Louis XIV (*"La loi, c'est moi"*) could not have asked for more!

The doctrine of executive privilege has never established a firm foothold in American jurisprudence, and its exercise is only recent. Lincoln kept nothing from Congress, even in wartime. Executive privilege was claimed fifty times by American presidents from 1952 to the Watergate tapes, twice as many times as in the previous two centuries, and half of these claims were made by Nixon. Nevertheless, his claims were effectively overruled, and the White House tapes became public knowledge.

Executive privilege has an ancient pedigree in Britain. Despite the centuries of battle between Parliament and the Crown, the Queen's Privy Council (the cabinet) remains largely unaccountable to the legislature and people. Only at election time, and in the event of a rare vote of non-confidence in the House of Commons, must the government account for itself. Even then it need not disclose its secrets. Voltaire said, "The English are free for a day, once every five years."

In 1968 a British appeal court ruled that a cabinet minister could not arbitrarily withhold a document from the court. The judge claimed the right to see it, at least to decide whether it was as sensitive to national security as the minister claimed, or was merely part of a cover-up. This breach in crown privilege was short-lived, but sufficiently worrisome to provoke the Canadian government to immediately enact the Federal Court Act of 1969 to prevent a similar right of access developing in this country.

The "discovery" of documents (the opportunity for parties in a court case to examine them) is of vital concern to anyone involved in a legal action against the government. Yet the Crown is able to rely on its own interpretation of documents as a reason to refuse to disclose them, even when the Crown is itself a party to the action.[45]

The Role of the Opposition

If the government is at least as concerned to cover up its own activities as it is to provide any effective control of the RCMP, what of the opposition? The New Democratic Party, and a few individual members of the Conservative Party deeply concerned with civil liberties, have maintained a long standing tradition of demanding accountability of the RCMP to Parliament. Former NDP leader Tommy Douglas repeatedly argued for strong civilian control of the RCMP: "The time has come to take the security and intelligence branch out of the RCMP, to staff it with highly trained people . . . who know the difference between nonconformity and espionage."[46] Ed Broadbent, current leader of the NDP, has also vigorously attacked the government's lack of adequate supervision of the RCMP, concentrating on the principles of cabinet responsibility and the rule of law.[47]

Among the Conservatives, attacks on government RCMP policy have come from two contradictory sets of assumptions. On the one side are members such as Elmer MacKay, who have been concerned for the rights of individual Mounties as well as civil liberties. From the other flank have come demands, like those of Tom Cossitt, that the government beef up the Security Service and increase its role as a security force against alleged Cuban, French and Soviet subversion in Canada.[48]

Members of Parliament such as Mr. Cossitt appear to function as cats' paws for the RCMP, being supplied with leaked documents by disgruntled Mounties. Their concern is apparently to embarrass the government rather than defend civil liberties against the impact of a secret police apparently out of government control. Indeed, their object seems to be *less* government control. Mr. Cossitt told *The Globe and Mail* his impression was "that there is a great deal of discontent in the RCMP and they feel the security service has been maligned, that they're doing an excellent job and that

212 The RCMP vs The People

government inquiries into them aren't doing them any
good."[49]

To be entirely fair it must be noted that the NDP, while
maintaining a posture of civil libertarianism in Parliament,
has also cast a worried eye backward to its constituencies,
since much of the public resents political criticism of the
RCMP. Thus it is not unusual to find an NDP critic of the
force wrapping himself in scarlet and gold by pretending to
be "on the Mountie side" against the government. For example, Stuart Leggatt, NDP, held forth: "I want to say, Mr.
Speaker, that I am proud of the RCMP. . . . They are one of
the finest police forces in the world. I want to say one other
thing. It is the opposition that is protecting the reputation of
the RCMP."[50]

The Magic Cloak

In the comic strip *Little Orphan Annie*, one of Daddy War-
buck's sidekicks casts a magic cloak over evil characters, and
they simply disappear. For the Canadian cabinet, Section 41
of the Federal Court Act fulfills much the same purpose.
Annie sometimes asks where the villains went. We are never
told—but we can guess where the embarrassing facts hidden
by cabinet ministers eventually collect: in the files of the
RCMP, especially the Featherbed files. Since anyone appointed to the cabinet must be cleared by the Security Service, every minister may be assured that the RCMP "knows
where the bodies are buried." The similar power of British
intelligence has provoked crises in several British governments.[51]

The government must constantly choose between trying to
tame the panther by imposing rules on it, and trying to
placate it with kindness. It doesn't help the taming process to
know that most of the Canadian population is on the panther's side. Thus the government has usually tempered any
criticisms it may have of the RCMP by more frequently coming to its defense—as well as feeding it an ever more generous
budget.

When the government defends the RCMP, and refuses to
discipline its dirty tricks, it reaches for a more powerful cloak

than Orphan Annie ever knew—the cloak of national security. This cloak will hide just about anything. Of course it may be used for good purposes. There *is* a need to defend our democratic rights against any group or foreign power seeking to undermine them. The problem is that we are rarely allowed to see exactly what, or whom, the cloak has been used to cover. We have to take the assurances of politicians, and of security police who openly admit that they have been "trained in deception," that the cloak has been used for our good, and not theirs.

13

The Commission Game

When Parliament proves an unsuitable theater for the performance of a ritual investigation into political controversy, the issue is often turned over to an ad hoc troupe of nonprofessionals styled a royal commission. The government may use a commission to bury its errors and scandals effectively—or at least postpone full revelations until safely after the next election. In the United States, the device is called a presidential commission but the outcome is usually the same—months of hearings during which the issue cools off and is buried in a mountain of transcripts and documents.

In the United Kingdom, royal commissions have had little impact on the police. They don't even shed much light on what transpires behind closed doors.[1] A major problem, in our opinion, revolves around the appointment of a judge to chair a commission. Judges are accustomed to going along with the Crown in court refusals of documents.[2] They have often been seduced by what sociologist C. W. Mills called the higher immorality. "Judges become openly executive-minded, interpreting the law (whenever room for doubt exists) in what they conceive to be the 'national interest,' "[3] that is, the interests of the ruling groups.

Winston Churchill argued strongly that the appointment of judges to royal commissions which carry out essentially political tasks (often for the purpose of whitewashing a government in trouble), does no good for the public or the judiciary:

The principle of the complete independence of the judiciary from the executive is the foundation of many things in our island life. It has been widely imitated in varying degree throughout the world. It is perhaps one of the deepest gulfs between us and all forms of totalitarian rule.[4]

There would be little difficulty in persuading most American readers that Churchill's gulf, the separation of powers of judiciary and executive, should not be filled in. Nevertheless, judges are repeatedly appointed to commissions on politically controversial issues in the United States; the Warren Commission on the death of President John Kennedy being the most obvious example. When judges are appointed to inquire into police affairs (especially the secret police such as the FBI and the CIA), it is questionable whether public accountability will be achieved. Morton Halperin, one-time assistant to Henry Kissinger, writes: "When the courts did receive a rare case involving the covert agencies, they usually accorded the bureaus extreme deference. Thus, the Supreme Court refused to allow a citizen to bring suit against the CIA's secret budget, even though the Constitution explicitly requires a regular accounting of expenditures."[5]

Inquiries organized within the parliamentary framework may be no more effective than those given the apparent independence of a royal (or presidential) commission. A few Senate committees in the United States (such as the Kefauver committee on organized crime) have succeeded in achieving vigorous investigation, revealing hearings, and a legislative response. But as journalist Jack Anderson observes from his own experiences, "getting a senate committee or a government inquiry is a mixed blessing. . . . The targets are often asked friendly questions, while honest witnesses are hounded."[6]

If the committee is chaired by a determined legislator, as in the case of Otis Pike's congressional committee on the CIA, the result may be the unearthing of hidden documents and investigation of "activities that the agencies prefer to keep secret. . . . But its subpoenas were resisted, its investigators frustrated, and in the end, its report suppressed by Congress itself."[7] Other committees, such as Senator Frank Church's inquiry into the CIA, have made gains by treading softly, but Halperin notes that this committee only achieved publication of its report by allowing the CIA to censor the final version! The inescapable conclusion is that commissions of inquiry are often "a part of the elite's way of defining social reality."[8]

There are other, often overlooked, structural reasons why commissions, especially those headed by judges and lawyers, tend to attenuate the potential impact of a public inquiry. These reasons have to do with the structure of courtroom justice.

It is conventional wisdom that anyone charged by the police with a violation of law will "have his day in court." Justice will be done openly, and will be seen to be done. Nothing could be further from the facts. A very small proportion of criminal charges actually go to trial—in fact, barely ten percent in most types of offenses.[9] Our judicial system would collapse from overload if even half of those charged went to trial.

Our present system works because more than ninety percent of defendants plead guilty, and are sentenced largely through a process known as plea bargaining. This saves everyone's time, and usually results in a lighter sentence for the defendant than if he or she insisted on a trial. The typical attitude of judges is that a defendant who puts society to great expense with an actual trial, and is still found guilty, should pay more dearly for his offense.[10]

The most salient feature of the plea bargaining system is that it is conducted *in camera* (behind closed doors). The defendant, the press and the public are not present when the judge, prosecutor and defense lawyer make their deal. The defendant must approve the deal before it takes effect, but only the outcome (the sentence) is public information. No court clerk records the discussion, argument, evidence cited, or evidence ignored, in the judge's chambers.

It is not unreasonable, then, to conclude that when a lawyer or judge moves from his courtroom world to that of a commission inquiry, he will carry with him implicit, if not explicit, assumptions about the nature of secret and open inquiry. Hence the issue of holding hearings in camera will be recognized as one of strategic significance.

We are not overlooking the fact that judges and lawyers appointed to enquire into police wrongdoing will probably bring with them other important attitudes from their courtroom experience. Few readers will need persuading that when a judge's decision must rely mainly on the credibility of witnesses rather than on material evidence, a policeman's word and a civilian's rarely have equal weight. Nor will most readers question the argument that Canadian courts have generally supported the status quo rather than social movements of dissent and change. There is also a fairly common attitude among judges and lawyers (with the exception of the rare "civil rights" lawyer) that the police should generally be allowed to get on with the job of controlling crime without too much interference. The police, after all, are the experts—and successful practitioners in the field of law are among the elite whose property and prestige the police are expected to serve and protect. All these and other factors suggest that if members of any royal commission enquiring into police misbehavior have a bias, it will most likely go in the direction of sympathy with the police, not with their accusers. We do not have space to examine the likely impact of all these factors on the structure and action of such commissions. In what follows, we consider the most important factor: the secrecy of commission proceedings.

Clash at the McDonald Commission

An apparent battle over secret hearings occurred at the McDonald inquiry into RCMP wrongdoing. Two lawyers for government ministers argued that key government documents should be discussed only in secret. First we should note what *Maclean's* magazine reported about these lawyers: "Back in June, 1976, two prominent Montreal attorneys, Joseph Nuss and Michel Robert, concluded in a study for the Quebec Bar on commissions of inquiry, that they should 'as a general rule sit in public.' "[11]

These lawyers now presented 314 pages of legal argument to the McDonald commission in October 1978. Their main point: the commission should hold its hearings in camera whenever the government requested.

The Nuss-Robert arguments went even beyond the claims of executive privilege enacted in Section 41 of the Federal Court Act. The government wanted closed hearings at the inquiry whenever "cabinet confidences" were contained in documents, whether or not national security was involved. This position was reinforced by statements of the prime minister. Mr. Trudeau told an Ottawa meeting that the commission "should not have the right to tell the public what certain ministers and I have said about the operation of the RCMP."[12]

The position of the government was that *all* cabinet proceedings—related to national security or not—were confidential. Mr. Trudeau rejected the possibility that the commission could go searching through cabinet documents in pursuit of evidence that the RCMP wrongdoings were originally ordered by ministers of the crown:

> We don't feel the public has a right to know everything.[13] We shall not let the RCMP or the commission or the opposition or the country have access to all cabinet minutes . . . in the possibility that they are going to find some illegality.[14]

The commission would be given the documents it asked for, to examine in camera. "How can the commission ask for files it doesn't know about?" retorted Stuart Leggatt, an NDP member of Parliament. The government maintained it was not covering up and had not revised its stance since setting up the commission, at which time the solicitor general had assured Parliament:

> The terms of reference [of the commission] are quite clear that if, in the opinion of the commission, there is a matter of national security which is at stake, it has the power and indeed is directed to sit in camera. However, if matters do not relate to the national security . . . there would be no obligation to sit in camera . . . whether or not the commission would do it in camera or in public depends on the decision of the commission itself in conformity with its terms of reference and powers.[15]

Now that government documents were about to see the light of day, the ministers concerned wanted to "cover their asses." "If ministers or senior police officials know that their orders will be made public, they'll stop giving orders," Mr. Trudeau insisted.[16] In short, government by the informed consent of the governed was impossible. The McDonald commission, as events developed, did not agree that the government would collapse in the light of publicity. But in order to oppose the government, and insist on its own right to decide when to meet secretly and when in public, the commission had to come up with a better argument than the government's.

Whose side are they on?

There is a problem to resolve before we consider how the McDonald commission argued for its right to decide when to hold public hearings. The problem is: why did the commission bother? Why didn't it go along with the government?

When the commissioners were first appointed there was a good deal of suspicion that they were intended to whitewash the government and cover up RCMP wrongdoings. Mr. Justice McDonald was an old friend of the Liberal government; in fact he was at one time president of the Alberta Liberals. The other commissioners had close personal connections with the Liberals, it was alleged. The Law Union of Ontario even went to court to have the McDonald commission disqualified because of its apparent bias.[17]

Judge Alex Cattanach of the Federal Court ruled on the Law Union's charges. He did not determine whether the McDonald commission was biased, but settled the issue on legal grounds. He held that the commission was only a fact-finding body, so possible bias was irrelevant. The commission's report would go to the federal cabinet, he pointed out, and the cabinet could do what it liked. It could publish the report, or part of it, or "consign the report to oblivion."[18]

The court refused to decide whose side the commission was on, but instead played along with the commission game: royal commissions don't really matter much because they are only fact-finding bodies—presumably with no political effect. However, the *structure* of the McDonald commission, like most other royal commissions, is instructive. The commissioners all share a legal and/or bureaucratic background, and would be thoroughly accustomed to secret discussions and decisions. Therefore they ought to have agreed to in camera hearings when these were requested by the government. Why didn't they?

Some journalists answer this question by presuming a sort of "conversion" of the commissioners. Having become involved in their work, the argument goes, the commissioners wanted to find out the truth. The snail-paced progress of the commission's first year may have been designed to give the government time to get re-elected, but "something happened on the way to the report," and the commission declared its independence of the government which created it. Douglas Fisher puts it this way: "The commission may be slow but the work of its lawyers is sharpening, and the three commissioners . . . are clearly after the truth and not covering up for the Liberals."[19]

Mr. Fisher and other analysts of the commission's apparent declaration of independence from the government seem to assume that the commission had only two alternatives: cover up for the Liberals or go after the truth. But there is a third alternative: cover up for the RCMP at the expense of the Liberals *and* the truth. Only the final report will tell which alternative has been chosen.

The commission needed a better argument than the government's executive privilege in order to declare its independent right to hold public hearings. What better argument could there be than a mission to save the RCMP's reputation? There should be public hearings "so as to maintain public trust . . . and public support for the work of the Security Service," the commission claimed.[20] Privately, one commissioner expressed to the authors his concern "not to hurt the people in the Security Service and their families."

However, it would not do for the commission to take a public stance which seemed ready to forgive the Security Service its wrongdoings long in advance of a final report. It was the abstract reputation of a security service which had to be protected. Legitimation for this course of action was found, ironically enough, in the principles of an open society! In fact, it was found in the very principle which the RCMP Security Service and any secret security service most often violates and contradicts. "The cardinal principle must be the principle of publicity," Mr. Justice McDonald proclaimed.[21]

But what was the actual structural situation? Was publicity really the operating principle of the commission? Not necessarily. The whole affair could be a game of "let's pretend." Joseph Nuss, the government lawyer, reminded the commission that they already had in their possession the documents which the government did not want made public. He invited the commission to play games: "We say, you have the documents and now, when it comes to considering whether they will be produced as exhibits, we really start afresh; we, in a sense, pretend that you haven't had them until now, and say: No objection is made to their production in camera."[22]

The Structure of Investigation

While the public is diverted by games of "let's pretend" and apparent battles for independence from government, the structure of investigational procedure which the commission has established to do its work may eventually prove more influential than any argument. The most significant aspect of this structure is its overwhelming dependence on the RCMP's goodwill.

In late 1978, the commission had forty people on staff, including consultants and per diem contracts. Besides a regular investigating staff of two, under Professor Peter Russell as director of research, the commission had the full-time assistance of seven Mounties (some officers, some NCOs). It is an understatement to observe that the commission has shown no propensity to hire independent civilian troubleshooters of the Ralph Nader variety. Our informants have said there is little sense of anxiety about exposure among RCMP members. Small wonder—the investigation of RCMP wrongdoing seems cosily arranged so as to prevent matters getting out of hand.

The working procedure of the commission provided for the chief counsel to consult with RCMP lawyers about all new incoming data gathered by the investigators. Any complaints coming to the commission from other sources—such as the general public or organizations—were referred first to the RCMP. The seven RCMP investigators worked together, forming a tight faction among the commission's otherwise heterogeneous staff. They selected those documents from among the RCMP's vast files which they considered relevant to the commission's purposes. The commission's legal counsel had the power to go through the RCMP files, but rarely did so. The rationale was that the Mounties' "magnificent seven" knew better where to look for RCMP files relevant to the inquiry.

The genteel manner in which the McDonald commission is investigating the RCMP stands in sharp contrast to the federal government's methods when the postal workers went on an illegal strike in 1978. Allegedly to get the documents to prove that union officials had violated the law (which every Canadian knew anyway when their mail didn't arrive, to say nothing of the union's president admitting the strike on television!) the government ordered the Mounties to swoop down on union offices across the country and seize their documents. We can be sure that no McDonald investigators have swooped down on any RCMP offices to seize the files!

Another question which should trouble those who expect the McDonald commission to reveal what goes on inside the Security Service is the reliability of Mountie testimony. We have already demonstrated the great skill of high-ranking officers in stonewalling interrogators. How much faith can we put in the statements made by ordinary Mounties, when they have repeatedly admitted that they are "trained in deception"? Some of the Mounties we interviewed are so convinced that the Trudeau government are communists anyway (or at least "soft on communism") that they could very well see themselves as lone guardians of Canadian freedom.

Though a number of independent complaints have come to the commission, there was little indication that these will be investigated thoroughly, or take up much commission time in public hearings. We have noted a tendency among commission staff, speaking privately and off the record, to dismiss many of the complaints as biased or "troublemaking," and some complainants were dismissed as "extremists." For example, the Native Indian Brotherhood has publicly complained about RCMP break-ins of their premises, but little has come of such complaints. Commission staff argued that public hearings of many such complaints would be a waste of time and "counterproductive." "If you have hearings, people want to see the relevant files," it was suggested, and of course, that would be troublesome.

It is worth noting that the bulk of commission hearing time has been devoted to the perpetrators of RCMP wrongdoing or those tangentially involved, with extremely little time given to the victims. It would doubtless be difficult for many victims to bring themselves to testify. Their appearance before the commission as "certified targets" of RCMP surveillance might rebound to their misfortune in employment or the community. Many would probably prefer to keep a low profile. The commission could, of course, protect such victims by in camera hearings, and surely the victims have more right to secrecy than the government. But secret hearings have more to do with power than with getting at the truth, in our opinion.

The commission staff have privately acknowledged their acceptance of various forms of the doctrine of the public's "right not to know." While objecting to that simplified formula, one commission member argued with us that some things are best kept hidden. "No good would come of knowing about that now . . ." The RCMP do not even have to make public the reasons why they want to keep certain matters secret. Indeed, the greatest concern of the commission seems to be to help restore the Security Service's reputation. "The Security Service is expecting a lot from us. We won't let them down,'' one major commission official assured us.

The Keable Commission

Much of the flavor of proceedings at the Keable inquiry has already been provided (chapters 2, 3, 4). The commission has distinguished itself from the McDonald inquiry by its aggressive investigations, its probing questioning of witnesses, and its much more rapid pace. A sense of rivalry developed between the two commissions. In February 1978 there was competition for major witnesses just before the federal government succeeded in closing down the Keable commission. (It has since reopened.) The Keable inquiry's lawyers even suggested the McDonald inquiry was "pirating witnesses."[23]

The Keable inquiry has earned the respect and praise of various groups concerned with aggressive defense of civil rights in Quebec, such as La Ligue des droits de l'homme, and the Quebec Bar Association.[24] Again, it is not a question of good guys versus bad guys, but differences in structure. If the Keable commission has been more aggressive, the explanation lies in the background of its members and in its investigative procedures. Jean Keable is a former Parti Québécois member, and was appointed by the Parti Québécois government. Fortunately for the Canadian public, this background tends to work to uncover federal government secrets. Of course, the opposite would probably be true if the Keable commission were investigating Parti Québécois secrets!

In contrast to the McDonald commission, the Keable inquiry has relied on its own investigators. Far from depending on the RCMP, the Keable staff were concerned to protect their documents from them. After aggressively subpoenaing evidence from the RCMP and QPP, the inquiry protected it with a guard dog. "We couldn't very well ask the Mounties or the Quebec Police force to protect our documents," commission staff laughingly observed. The Keable staff have also taken advantage of the structural conflict between the RCMP in Quebec, and the Quebec provincial and municipal forces.

The commission has obtained numerous useful documents about the RCMP by getting file copies from the Quebec forces.

The smooth, efficient and impressive machinery of the Keable hearings, featuring hard-hitting Michel Decary as counsel, contrasts sharply with the desultory questioning of witnesses at the McDonald hearings. The Keable people are all at least a decade younger than the McDonald key staff; the latter's major counsel, Jake Howard, is over seventy. Journalists have frequently and disapprovingly noted the way Mr. Howard failed to follow up a line of questioning and left reporters with more questions than answers for their readers.

Nevertheless, Jean Keable is a lawyer schooled in the gentlemanly art of courtroom politics, and he has "played the game" by not pressing the federal government as much as his evidence would have allowed. He already had copies of many of the documents Francis Fox wanted to prevent him from making public as exhibits, but he was apparently reluctant to push his luck against the Official Secrets Act.

By October 1978, the McDonald commission had become emboldened enough on behalf of the RCMP's reputation to tweak the federal government's nose. The October statement by the McDonald commissioners more or less dares the government to use the Official Secrets Act against them. The McDonald commissioners wisely appealed to the "higher public interest":

> It would be a nice legal question whether, in a particular case, receiving a certain document or information in evidence in public would be in the interest of the State . . . in that the State has an interest in the public having confidence in the proceedings of a commission of inquiry before which there are questions of the conduct of persons holding high public office.[25]

The language here is the restrained, formal language of the courtroom, but it could be interpreted as saying to the federal ministers, "Be careful, your reputation may be on trial here!" Keable might have been politically astute to have taken the same stance, counting on the reluctance of the federal government to use the Act against him. As it was, he allowed them to defeat his inquiry with a lower-profile weapon—that of federal-provincial jurisdictions.

Francis Fox and his successors were able to take Keable to court for violating the constitutional division of powers between the federal and provincial governments through his investigation of the activities and procedures of a federal police force. The federal ministers obviously felt they could count on the Supreme Court to come down firmly on their side. It did, on October 31, 1978:

> The court ruled unanimously that . . . Mr. Keable or any provincial inquiry has no constitutional authority to investigate the RCMP policies and internal investigative procedures. Nor do they have the power to force the federal Solicitor General to produce papers from the Mounties' files.[26]

The Supreme Court action is especially interesting because the British North America Act gives jurisdiction over the establishment of criminal law to the federal government, but the administration of law to the provinces. Yet the Supreme Court in the Keable decision ruled that the federal ministers had a constitutional right to "withhold documents by affidavits or otherwise" even when the documents relate to the commission of allegedly criminal acts. The constitutional issues involved were of great import to both sides, and six provinces (New Brunswick, Ontario, Manitoba, Saskatchewan, Alberta and British Columbia) allied themselves to the Quebec side of the case with the RCMP. The Keable decision also confirmed the constitutional right of the federal government to establish and manage the RCMP.[27]

Thus the federal government succeeded in temporarily hobbling an inquiry which threatened to get out of hand, and perhaps proceed much further than apprehended RCMP wrongdoing in Quebec. It was apparently feared that Keable would use his mandate to open up an investigation of the October Crisis of 1970 and the federal government's use of massive armed force in Quebec at that time. Federal ministers have opposed any such inquiry, saying they have nothing to hide!

The McKenzie and Marin Commissions

A brief review of two earlier commissions on the RCMP will help to set the McDonald commission in perspective and, perhaps, provide some clues as to what we might expect of its final report.

During the sixties—a period of profound social changes in Canada tending in the direction of more open government—a great swell of criticism rose against the RCMP Security and Intelligence service. The Toronto *Telegram* headlined Tommy Douglas' characterization of the security service as "ham-handed."[28] The Toronto *Star* asked, "What has happened to the Mountie image?"[29] The Canadian Association of University Teachers called for an inquiry.[30] In an attempt to shore up Mountie morale, Commissioner C. W. Harvison published an article, "Why the Police Are Losing Prestige," in *Weekend* magazine.[31] Later, Commissioner George Mc-Clellan charged that criticism was "part of a sinister plot to destroy the force."[32] In Parliament, critics such as NDP deputy leader Doug Fisher spoke of RCMP bungling of its security responsibilities.

The federal government came to the rescue by appointing in 1966 a commission of inquiry into the RCMP security role—the McKenzie commission. Maxwell McKenzie, chairman, was president of Chemcell Company of Montreal and former deputy minister of trade and commerce. Yves Pratt was a Quebec lawyer who was later, in Peter Worthington's words, "awarded the plum of heading Air Canada."[33] (He is now a judge in the Supreme Court of Canada.) M. J. Coldwell was former national leader of the CCF. In 1969, when the federal government published a carefully censored version of the McKenzie commission's report, James Eayrs, professor of international relations at the University of Toronto, characterized the commission as follows:

> What manner of men have produced a report so deficient in understanding, so mean in spirit? M. W.

> McKenzie provides the insights one would expect of a part-time mandarin and manager of a firm whose fortunes depend to a degree on industrial espionage. . . . It is sad that the name of M. J. Coldwell, that grand old man of Canadian social democracy . . . should be associated with this report simply to . . . provide a progressive gloss.[34]

The commissioners were admirers of state secrecy and security, and their report frequently comments on the need of government to protect its secrets.[35] Eayrs notes that at the very time other countries were developing freedom of information concepts the McKenzie commissioners were arguing that where there are doubts about the loyalty of an individual, "such doubts must be resolved in favour of the state."[36]

The report won no more praise from the right than it did from the left. Peter Worthington wrote:

> As a thorough investigation of security and espionage it is a disgrace. It belabours the obvious; its suggestions are mediocre. . . . One cannot avoid the feeling that the three commissioners failed to do their homework.[37]

Worthington joined with the left in reacting strongly against the suggestion that Canada should have a CIA: "Surely no freedom-loving Canadian would advocate a secret police system, independent and controlled by a security secretariat such as the report recommends."

Prime Minster Trudeau swiftly rejected the suggestion of a civilian security agency. His reasons undoubtedly reflected the horrified reaction of the RCMP itself, which would have lost that special prestigious function which makes it more than a mere police force. As an ex-Security Service informant reminded us (years later), the federal government would have had to staff a new agency largely with men from the RCMP security branch anyway. There was no alternative Canadian source of experienced personnel. But most Security Service men would not have left the force, at least "not unless they could take their pensions with them."

Despite the "gloss" of an aging Mr. Coldwell, the report demonstrated none of the sensitivity to individual liberty in an open society which might have been expected at the end of the sixties. Instead it breathed all the anxieties of the Cold War period of the fifties. Two years of commission hearings (175 of them), 250 secret witnesses including Richard Helm, director of the CIA, months of writing, and nearly a year of government censoring, brought forth a report which "staked out a stronger position for the state, a tighter and more disciplined approach."[38]

For example, it was recommended that potential civil servants be subjected to thirteen specific security checks, including criminal record, credit rating and membership in organizations over the previous ten years. Recognizing the damage such Draconian measures might do to the wrongfully charged citizen, the commission recommended appointment of a review board independent of government or the RMCP. The board would function as a court of last resort for appeal against Security Service actions. The Liberal government announced that it would act on this recommendation, but it has never done so.

Instead, the government has created new committee structures which make it all the more difficult for anyone (probably including those on the inside!) to tell who's in charge. The organization chart (see appendix) indeed suggests Hannah Arendt's "rule by nobody." The Security Planning, Analysis, and Research Group (SPARG) was created under Colonel Robin Bourne. (It was originally called the Police and Security Planning and Analysis Group). SPARG is not a review board at all, nor in any way open to civilian participation. It acts to collect and analyze intelligence information and make overall decisions on security policy. If anything, it is more clandestine than the Security Service.

The Marin commission, appointed in 1974, advanced the cause of an open society no further than the McKenzie commission. Its report acknowledged the excessively rigid, centralized and formal system of internal discipline concentrated in the hands of RCMP officers, and commented: "The attention of the commission was called to a disturbing number of instances . . . where the full weight of a highly formalized system of investigation and punishment was invoked in response to seemingly minor, and sometimes petty, breaches of standing orders . . ."[39]

The commission observed that the result of officer zeal was "resentment and bitterness" among the lower ranks, and an undermining of general morale. Nevertheless, it concluded that its recommendation of an appeal procedure, including a federal ombudsman, "is not based on any discovery of a history of abuse or neglect. On the contrary, we have not found many cases where the force was not both thorough in its investigation and fair in its disposition of complaints." As is evident, the commission swallowed its own contradictions easily. It was also able to believe: "The fact that the Force serves as the police force in eight of the ten provinces . . . gives credence to the claim that it has provided a satisfactory response to public complaints."[40]

Solicitor General Warren Allmand commented on receiving the Marin report that he "liked its general thrust." An ombudsman to protect RCMP members from irrational and excessive internal discipline could be created immediately by a cabinet order, he said. It was not. His successor, Francis Fox, promised "the creation of the review authority [ombudsman] in proposed changes to the RCMP Act to be presented in parliament in January 1978."[41] As we go to press the ombudsman has not been created. According to our RCMP informants, an appeal procedure is still very much needed. So far, the Marin commission has proved to be little more than another costly, time-consuming method for postponing effective action behind the facade of a commission of inquiry.

Commissions as Educational Games

There seems very little evidence that royal or presidential commissions are effective tools of political action. When their findings support the government, they are superfluous; when they oppose the government, their recommendations are left unimplemented. In the USA the President's Commission on Obscenity and Pornography spent millions of dollars and several years on elaborate surveys, but President Nixon didn't like the report and buried it. The Canadian Commission on Bilingualism and Biculturalism funded numerous scientific projects, but failed utterly to blunt the advance of Quebec separatism. The LeDain Commission on Drug Use recommended the decriminalization of marijuana use, basing its findings on exhaustive research. The government found the proposals politically unpalatable, and continued the policy of prosecuting more than 40,000 Canadians a year on marijuana charges, while deliberately under-reporting convictions by at least seventeen percent to avoid arousing public criticism.[42]

However, royal and presidential commissions do serve as useful educational games for the academic and scientific establishments, and to a lesser extent, the general public. They fund a great deal of valuable research which would otherwise fail to find financial support. Indeed, the relative independence of commissions allows research which would be entirely hamstrung by the bureaucratic regulations of the civil service. Commissions also involve academics in socially useful projects, when they might otherwise fritter away their time on esoteric articles for obscure academic journals.

Since most commissions hold at least some public hearings, they afford an opportunity for the press to communicate some of the issues and data to the public as "news." The submissions of researchers become regarded as news when the same data, published in an academic journal, would be ignored by the press. Likewise, the final reports of the commissions, including supporting research documents, may find their way into the news media.

But games are games, for all that. Spectators at wrestling matches may choose to assume that a real battle is going on, rather than a form of theater. If there is more fun that way, little harm is done. But a great deal of harm may be done to Canadian democracy by postponing effective government action—and effective opposition criticism—through sweeping official deviance under the rug for several years or more while a royal commission investigates. By the time most commissions report the heat is off, and the findings are more entertainment than news.

14

The Phony Dilemma

Every study of police power, whether from a pro-police or civil-libertarian point of view, eventually deals with the "dilemma" of police in a free society.[1] The question is usually put this way: How can the police be given enough power to do their job effectively, while at the same time the citizens are protected from abuse of their democratic rights? The greater the citizens' freedom, the more difficult the work of the police. For example, if a citizen's home cannot be searched without advance notice, then anyone hiding stolen goods may have time to move them. A few moments delay of the police at the front door may allow time to flush contraband down the toilet!

Opinions on this dilemma range from one extreme to the other. There are those who would rather allow ten guilty persons to go free than abuse the rights of one innocent citizen. And there are those who would allow the police to use the same methods as the people they are trying to catch—beating up suspects, entering homes without warning, and stealing evidence if necessary. Since unchecked police power would eventually add to the total amount of crime in society (as police and criminals waged an ever-escalating war against each other), most Canadians want definite limits on police power. We generally insist that the police should stay inside the law while chasing outlaws.

But in the area of national security, the tendency has been in the other direction. More and more, we hear the argument that the end justifies any "necessary" means. Usually the argument is made with patently obvious (and therefore ridiculous) examples. Ex-Solicitor General Francis Fox spoke of the security police dilemma in Parliament: "It is quite a dilemma, because after all, what we say . . . is that a Security Service is expected to carry out its operations strictly within the law. I totally agree, [but] some situations are completely nonsensical. For instance . . . a security officer who would try to secure a code from a foreign country might be accused of burglary."[2]

An example such as this obscures the fact that the RCMP Security Service has directed much of its illegal action against the very Canadian citizens whose freedoms it is supposed to protect. In totalitarian countries, police face no dilemma between effective action and citizens' rights, because police forces are given license to use whatever means are deemed necessary. But in a democratic society the benefit of the doubt is supposed to go to the citizen, not the police. This has long been the basis of criminal law enforcement. Should it not also be the basis of security enforcement?

The heads of most security services apparently think not. They argue that security police should have the same unchecked powers in a democratic society as their counterparts in a totalitarian society. Our Security Service argues that the same means are not evil or at least not *as* evil, when used to protect democracy as they are when used to protect a dictatorship.

Former CIA staff chief James Angleton put the argument bluntly: "I find it inconceivable that a covert agency is expected to obey all the overt orders of the government."[3] The Hoover Commission held:

> Hitherto accepted norms of human conduct do not apply . . . We must learn to subvert, sabotage and destroy our enemies by more clever, more sophisticated and more effective methods than those used against us.[4]

William Stevenson, biographer of the famous spy called Intrepid, warned Canadian members of Parliament in 1978 that our secret police must have the same powers to fight communism as the communists use to fight us. He warned

Canadians not to "play into the hands of people who want to discredit security agencies. . . . People's mail is opened in totalitarian countries, and they vastly outnumber us. . . . A certain amount of freedom has to be given up to protect Canada against communism."[5]

RCMP leaders have tended to be less blunt, but the argument goes in the same direction. Ex-Commissioner William Higgitt felt the RCMP should be able to break the law in the pursuit of a "noble purpose."[6] Former Security Service director John Starnes suggested anyone was an idiot to think the service could carry out its responsibilities without breaking the law.[7] He was able to cite in his defense the McKenzie commission report, which said:

> A security service will inevitably be involved in actions that may contravene the spirit if not the letter of the law, and with clandestine and other activities which may sometimes seem to infringe on an individual's rights.[8]

But if the need to protect Canadians against communism justifies giving unlawful and anti-democratic powers to the security police, then what rights will Canadians have left to protect? The McKenzie commissioners concluded that the methods used by the Security Service were not "appropriate police functions."[9] Did they therefore recommend avoidance of such unlawful methods? Not at all! They simply recommended that the security police job be taken away from the RCMP (thus protecting the Mounties' reputation) and given to a new CIA-style agency. The commission, and others like it, have invariably ignored the effect of undemocratic police methods on organized protest in a free society. If unions, native rights groups, the women's movement, and other groups working for social change find themselves "disrupted" by secret police, the citizens' belief in the possibility of peaceful social change is eroded. Cynicism about Canadian democracy sets in, paving the way for extremism, communism and terrorism.

The most honest argument for giving our security police whatever power is necessary to do their job comes from those who make no pretense about what the security police are protecting. For example, the Institute for the Study of Conflict

(London, England) states frankly: "Traditional Canadian complacency *and the open society* [our italics] have created a threat to the security of the North American heartland."[10] While still in office in 1965, RCMP Commissioner Harvison said, "If we make any errors it is better to err on the side of the security of the state."[11]

The New Demonology

During the Middle Ages, the Inquisition was given almost unlimited power to root out heresy and witchcraft. In the end, it was the Inquisition itself which proved to be the greatest evil. But for many decades the inquisitors were able to discredit all critics of their power by accusing them of being heretics, *or* sympathizers and tools of heretics.

Whether a citizen is in league with the devil or in league with Moscow, the same rationale is now advanced: the evil is so great that we must suspend the everyday rules of a peaceful society. The evil is "dramatized"[12] and critics of the inquisitors are all tarred with the same brush. For instance, Canada's parliamentarians have been warned that criticism of the RCMP is engineered by communists who see intelligence operations as the first line of defense against them.[13]

The new demonology is well established in the RCMP Security Service. One ex-Mountie informant who did *not* share its views told us that the service was "always giving the government dire warnings of some big commie plot on Canada." Those who do share the demonology deeply resent those who do not. Ex-Deputy Commissioner William Kelly complains: "It seems that on the one hand espionage by foreign intelligence officers is tolerated for the sake of good foreign relations, and on the other hand the Security Service is expected to control it."[14]

A Mountie informant who shared the demonology argued: "It's plain history. For example, the London School of Economics was the main breeding ground of communism in England, so we'd be remiss not to keep an eye on any leftist professor." (The London School of Economics is the alma mater of many prestigious Canadian economists who would be amazed indeed to learn that they were communists or tools of communism.) RCMP recruits have been taught that sedition includes "acts which are designed to create discontent among the citizens."[15] By that definition, almost any criticism of the government in power or any movement of protest or social change could be labeled seditious.

The demonologists have difficulty in believing that their own people (family, friends, workmates, students) could become heretics (or protestors) on their own motivation. They have to be "corrupted." Neither Nixon nor Hoover could believe American youth had grown discontented with the war in Vietnam all on their own. Likewise they refused to believe America's blacks would protest unless they were being duped and misled by communists; so Martin Luther King must be a communist, or at least a communist tool.[16] The RCMP naively traced demonstrations at the University of British Columbia and McGill to visits by foreign leftists.[17]

People who deliberately choose to support a dramatized evil can be explained away on demonological grounds. They "can't help it," they have been "possessed." Henry Kissinger refused to "stand by and watch a country go communist due to the irresponsibility of its own people" after Salvador Allende was elected president in Chile.[18] In other words, the Chileans couldn't be trusted to govern themselves once Allende had bewitched them.

Facing the Real Dilemma

The end-justifies-means argument, the dramatization of evil, and the association of critics with the demons, are all familiar tactics of those who want security police to have much greater powers than ordinary police. These powers may be justified whether or not they are legal. The government may simply change the laws (as has been proposed in the case of mail-opening) to legalize what the security police want to do. Or it may overlook their illegal acts—or defend them on national security grounds.

The Gestapo in Nazi Germany never faced a dilemma. Neither does the Soviet KGB today. In totalitarian societies it is openly admitted that the responsibility of the security police is to keep the existing power elites in control of society. When the end-justifies-means argument is used in a democratic society, we may reasonably wonder whether the objective is not the same. That is, the task of the security police is not to protect the security of all citizens, or the security of the democratic system. Its task is to protect the power of financial, political and military elites, or what President Eisenhower first labeled "the military-industrial complex."

The argument that the security police exist to protect the power elites is obviously controversial and cannot be examined in detail here, much less proved. But the possibility exists that the "dilemma" of the RCMP Security Service—protecting Canadian democracy while themselves having to obey the law—is not the real dilemma at all. It may be a phony issue—and a red herring!

Suppose that the real task of the Security Service is to protect Canada's elites. There would be no dilemma then, because those in power would simply alter the laws—or overlook violations of the law—as much as necessary to allow the SS to protect them effectively. Any hand-wringing by the government or RCMP about the police "dilemma" would be strictly propaganda to mislead the public.

If this thesis is valid, then the power elite and the secret police face a different dilemma: *How can the secret police be given all the power necessary to protect the elites without this situation becoming obvious to ordinary citizens?* Or, how can secret police operations be as effective as they are in totalitarian countries without Canadians realizing that they do not live in a true democracy? How can the pretense of democratic laws and freedoms be maintained while the reality of a secret police in the service of the power elites is also effectively maintained?

This is a dilemma which openly dictatorial governments do not face. Nicaragua's President Somozo makes no pretense about whose laws his police enforce, and the Shah made no pretense about who governed Iran. The white South African government makes no pretense that its security police (BOSS) is protecting the security of all citizens of the country, or even the majority of citizens—since the vast majority are black, and openly excluded from democratic power.

The possibility that the RCMP Security Service has much the same role as Iran's SAVAK or South Africa's BOSS or the Soviety Union's KGB is a very unpalatable notion for most Canadians. But Miles Copeland, a former CIA agent and still an admirer of the agency, writes that security services generally tend to become alike, since their task is the same—the preservation of the power of the ruling group. "Whether staffed by leftists or rightists, intelligence and security services tend to be . . . firmly part of the establishment."[19] When Sir Harold Wilson resigned as prime minister of Britain, he indicated to reporters that he felt certain activities of Britain's own intelligence service could be the greatest threat to his country's democracy.[20]

It is conceivable that the most dangerous subversives in a democracy are the secret police allegedly assigned to protect national security. Professor Arthur Lower of Queen's University warned in 1957 that "it is hard to see how [the RCMP] can be distinguished from the secret police in other countries," and added, "we would be poor citizens indeed" if we were not aware of the direction in which a secret police force leads.[21] Even the RCMP did not dare to suggest that this renowned professor was a communist or fellow-traveller. Likewise no one has suggested that the conservative American journalist, Joseph Kraft, is a subversive. Yet he concluded, like many other Americans, that the FBI-CIA-Watergate excesses brought America "a hell of a lot closer to a police state than I thought possible."[22]

Whose Law? Whose Order?

It is impossible in a study focusing on the RCMP Security Service to deal adequately with the larger social and political background in which the service operates. But Canadians should at least be prepared to ask probing questions about whose "national security" the Security Service is protecting. There is a growing body of social science literature to demonstrate that the "law and order" which powerful political leaders refer to on the campaign platform is not necessarily the law and order most ordinary citizens have in mind.

The law and order sought by the typical Canadian voter consists of freedom to walk the streets safely, day or night; to leave one's home without worrying about burglars; to ride a bus or subway without fear of violence, etc. But an increasing proportion of our laws are calculated to label certain elements in society as dissidents, while protecting the rights of the powerful.

For example, many laws are directed against users of drugs, those involved in allegedly immoral activities such as pornography, and the like. Recent proposals for revisions to the Canadian criminal code are largely concerned with petty crimes. But as the President's Commission on Law Enforcement (United States, 1967) reported, the cost to society of everyday, unorganized crime is far less than the cost of white collar and organized crime. Tax evasion, fraud and forgery account for three times the property losses accounted for by automobile theft, burglary and mugging. Yet our police forces concentrate on the latter, while largely ignoring white collar crime. Almost nothing effective has been done in Canada to combat organized crime, and some police deny it even exists!

Not only are police resources directed away from the types of crime likely to be committed by the powerful (such as tax evasion); the penalties meted out by the courts for lower-class crimes are often much stiffer than those for middle- or upper-class crime. Likewise, the penalties for the same crime will vary according to the social class of the offender. Slum youths who commit vandalism or theft are likely to go to jail, while youth from affluent districts will probably be taken home by the police with nothing more than a stiff warning to parents.[23] The unemployed youth's crime is no more serious than the university student's hijinks—but the penalties usually differ. Likewise, when corporations are found guilty of combining to monopolize industries and fix prices, or of selling faulty or dangerous products, they are usually fined—and sometimes the fines are substantial.[24] But the responsible executives are almost never sent to jail. And who eventually pays the fines? The consumers, of course, as they continue to buy the guilty corporations' products.

The Politics of Power

In its heyday the CIA dispensed with the luxury of phony dilemmas about lawfulness, and adopted the *real politik* of Machiavelli. Morals were used only as tricks of the trade. The first objective was always power.[25] Even when security services act within the law, they can exploit the law as a weapon of power.[26]

In both the United States and Canada, conspiracy laws have been developed as weapons of power. Conspiracy laws do not require an overt criminal act for a conviction. Once the accused is linked with others through discussion of an offense, conspiracy law allows evidence applicable to only some of the accused to be used against all—even those who did nothing but talk.[27]

In recent years, "the nation state is everywhere in trouble . . . and the legitimacy of official truth [is] radically challenged," American sociologist R. P. Wolff remarks. As a result, many officials have "preferred order to justice and make no apologies for sacrificing one to the other."[28] But as other sociologists such as Richard Quinney and William Chambliss have noted,[29] the "order" to which justice is sacrificed is not the everyday harmonious life of the citizen at work or on the street or asleep in bed. It is a notion of national security distorted to the point of presenting a frightening "threat to those who, like the blacks, the native peoples and the immigrants . . . are among the most powerless and vulnerable members of Canadian society." And these are not the words of communists or fellow-travelers, but of the editors of *The Globe and Mail*![30]

Because of the laws which the power elites of Canada[31] have established to protect themselves—laws such as the Official Secrets Act and Section 41 of the Federal Court Act—Canadians may never know the extent to which high officials have used the Security Service and the notion of national security to maintain their positions of power. But there is certainly some evidence among RCMP informants of resentment at being used by the elite. By no means all members of the Security Service are willing collaborators with the high and mighty of Canada. Quite a number still believe in the democratic principles they absorbed in school.

It is conceivable that much of the "bungling" in RCMP dirty tricks is accounted for by a certain resistance to Machiavellian politics. Bungling may be evidence not of stupidity or lack of expertise, but rather of a profound ambivalence about one's work. Some Mounties are deeply torn between their training to obey orders and their wish to retain the democratic traditions of our society. A guilt-ridden involvement with dirty tricks leads to errors and misjudgments, as well as leaks to MPs and journalists.

There is growing evidence of a lack of effective political, legal, civilian or parliamentary restraint on the RCMP Security Service. In the absence or weakness of external controls on secretive police power, the survival of such democratic freedoms as Canadians enjoy is largely dependent on the self-restraint of the police. If this is the case, then the outlook for continuing freedom in Canada is bleak. Self-restraint is a frail foundation, since those in power will be more concerned with *what works*. The CIA has shown us the road to the higher immorality: "Is it legal, is it ethical or moral? We never gave any thought to this line of reasoning, because we were just naturally pragmatist. . . . Will this course of action work, will it get us what we want?"[32]

Political pragmatism, or *real politik*, is the ultimate philosophy of "higher immorality" of those in power. Canadian sociologist John Hagan observed, using Watergate as an example: "Unfortunately, the first line of defense, inner constraint, is problematic in a society whose conception of upperworld morality is badly defined. In lieu of a public morality which harshly condemns upperworld crime, the occurrence of such behavior will depend largely on the risks and rewards."[33] But we can hardly expect our upperworld leaders to be candid about their political motives. The pretense of democracy remains important, if for no other reason than that it reduces the need to impose government policy by force. Fewer men and resources are required to enforce obedience to government policy when ordinary citizens remain under the illusion that the majority governs, and that power is exercised with the consent of the governed. Thus pragmatism must continue to be clothed in righteousness.

Canadian history and sociology demonstrate that when Canadians must choose between freedom and order, they almost always choose order.[34] The *Globe and Mail* editors put it this way: "We Canadians seem to have concluded at about the time of Confederation that whatever the authorities do must somehow be good for us or they wouldn't do it."[35] But if Canadians continue to choose security and order, rather than facing the challenge of free criticism and individual liberty, they will have to keep in mind Benjamin Franklin's warning: The citizen who chooses safety over liberty deserves neither!

15

The Road Ahead

The McKenzie commission in 1969 defined subversion as a "threat to the fundamental nature of the state"[1] not, it must be noted, as a threat to the government or ruling elite of the state. The McDonald commission has answered the question, "What is security for?"—it is for the preservation of a democratic society "where the coercive powers of government are subject to the rule of law."[2] Over the centuries, the citizens of western nations have struggled to improve the democratic nature of the parliamentary state. It is easy to forget that our right to vote, our right of habeus corpus, and our free press emerged very slowly and against great resistance by the ruling elites. It is easy to forget that two centuries ago only the prosecution, not the defense, could call witnesses in court. It is easy to forget that women became persons in Canadian law only fifty years ago.

Our democratic state is a fragile human achievement. It could be undermined by the very guardians established to defend it. The sorcerer who unleashed the CIA, President Truman, later regretted the apprentices:

> These fellows don't just report on wars and the like, they go out and make their own, and there's nobody to keep track of what they're up to. They spend billions on stirring up trouble so they'll have something to report on . . . They've become a government on its own and all secret. They don't have to account to anybody.[3]

After several decades of service in the CIA, John Stockwell, author of *In Search of Enemies*, finally concluded, "Our survival as a free people has obviously not been dependent on the fumbling activities of the clandestine services . . . but on the dynamism . . . and competitive energies of our people."[4] Where does Canada's strength lie—in its Security Service, or in its political, legal, educational and professional institutions, its voluntary organizations and minority groups, its free press and media? Does our strength lie in a secretive bureaucracy which resists the publication of its documents, or in an accessible, honest and respected public service? Does our strength lie in suppression of dissenting opinion, or in a lively public discussion of all the issues affecting our welfare and future?

The McDonald commission seems to be preparing to sidestep a key problem of any secret service—its very *secrecy*. In a letter of November 9, 1978, the commission indicated that it will preoccupy itself with the same "phony dilemma" of previous inquiries: "Recent activities suggest that a member of the RCMP may be faced with a serious dilemma when asked to carry out an order which he perceives to involve a transgression of law. . . . How can the balance best be struck between the need for responsible and sensitive members and the need for discipline and efficiency?"[5]

Sociologist Amitai Etzioni has argued that in an open and democratic society, the most important form of social criticism is fundamental criticism—that is, criticism which goes beyond the "community of assumptions" or the "taken for granted."[6] Useful sociological criticism must get at the assumptions which are so widely held that no one notices they are still *assumptions*, not necessarily facts.

The structural analysis of official deviance in the RCMP leads us to challenge the assumption that Canada needs a *secret* security service at all—or that we are better off with one than without one. To put the problem by analogy, suppose it were assumed that our society needed places where socially undesirable people could be detained, while doing useful work. We could call such places labor camps. Or we could speak of protecting society by concentrating the socially undesirable in these work camps, and call them concentration camps.

The point is that the term "concentration camp" began as a euphemism, a laundered label. Now a dilemma emerges. How can we have concentration camps which are efficient (so that people don't escape) but also sensitive to the needs of the inmates? (Perhaps we will launder that term too, and call them "clients"?) No doubt a royal commission could be appointed to resolve this dilemma, and show us how to manage humane but effective concentration camps.

Our example is not outlandish. Scholars such as Michel Foucault and Thomas Szasz have argued that we make much the same set of assumptions about "humane treatment" of those labeled mentally ill.[7] The Soviets use mental hospitals for the "treatment" of political dissidents. Many Germans were persuaded, *in only a decade*, to make the unquestioned assumption that concentration camps were necessary. In Canada many are persuaded that a secret security service is necessary.

Challenging the Taken-for-Granted

The British royal commission on the police (1962) came as close as any official body could to grasping the nettle of police power in a free society when it concluded: "British liberty does not depend, and never has depended, upon any particular form of police organization. It depends upon the supremacy of Parliament and the rule of law."[8]

Nothing came of these fine words, and a section of the British secret service is now regarded by former Prime Minister Harold Wilson as potentially a very grave threat to British liberty.[9] In the United States, analysts of the CIA have worried that it has become a "state within a state," but few have been prepared to say that America would be better off without it. In Canada, the RCMP has been roundly criticized in some of the media for its illegalities, but the assumption remains that we need a secret security service. Most Canadians still believe that it is possible to have a secret police which can be structurally organized to act in accordance with the theme of the RCMP handbook: "The state is the servant of the individual, and not the individual the servant of the state."

We have to question this assumption. We cannot avoid concluding from an analysis of the characteristic structure of secret police forces, *that a secret police can never remain the servant of the people*. History demonstrates that secret police forces eventually become the most fearsome of sorcerer's apprentices. Professor Brian Chapman concludes from his study of police history that a secret police by its very nature "tries to work toward self-government, setting its own norms and controlling its own operations."[10] The lesson John Stockwell learned from years of service in the CIA was that a powerful and secret bureaucracy "takes on its own momentum," fails to learn from disaster and instead "casts about for the next war."[11]

Our usual response to discovery of wrongdoings by our security services has been an attempt to strengthen our control over these dangerous forces without really changing their structure. Analyst John Bullock goes so far as to argue of the British DI5: "It is far better to record a few failures [in the work of our] intelligence services . . . than to diminish any further the right of the citizen to conduct his own life as he sees fit."[12] But Bullock does not propose to abolish the secret service altogether.

Perhaps a proposal so radical as abolition of the Secret Service will appear hopelessly naive to many Canadians. We live in a world of terrorism and hijacking, espionage and subversion, nationalist passions and international tensions. People are bound to ask: How could we possibly survive without a secret service?

Looking at Alternatives

The present study is only a beginning in the fundamental sociological analysis of the RCMP and the wider problem of a security service for Canada. We are not in possession of all the relevant information on which to propose changes. No Canadian will have this information until enough citizens demand that the officials who govern us release the documents. However, we do have enough data to suggest some alternative structures. We begin with the assumption that Canada does need a security service. This is probably the minimum assumption on which most Canadians would proceed, but note that it is still an assumption. There is no conclusive evidence that Canadian society would collapse if we had no security service at all. Indeed, the most trenchant critics of the Security Service would argue that Canada has been in that situation for some years anyway, since the SS has caught so few spies.

A second assumption, which we have defended but certainly not proved, is that a *secret* security service is by its very nature subversive to democratic liberties. Thus we need a security service which is not organized around the model of a secretive bureaucracy. The question is, what other effective intelligence-gathering models are available which don't rely on secretive bureaucracy?

Our third assumption is that a democratic security service must be limited to the task of gathering, correlating and analyzing intelligence. It should not have police powers (law enforcement powers). These powers must remain vested in an entirely separate police structure. Many will not find this a controversial assumption, since it is already the case in many other security services. The CIA has no police powers in its charter, though it did appropriate such powers to itself illegally.[13] The British secret service has no police powers, and Lord Denning, a prominent jurist, has argued, "They have managed very well without them. We would rather have it so, than have anything in the nature of a secret police."[14]

However we do not make the assumption that denial of law enforcement powers to the security service will prevent it from becoming a secret police. We have demonstrated that an intelligence service does not need law enforcement powers to subvert democracy. Aside from arrogating police powers to itself illegally, a secret security service can exercise law enforcement powers quite easily merely by using ordinary police who accept official definitions of the nature of "national security."

Our fourth assumption is that a change in the structure of the Security Service alone will not protect our liberties. There must be concomitant changes in other law-enforcement institutions. The ordinary police forces must be under more effective civilian control than they are now. Should a security service official attempt to use provincial and municipal police for illegal activity in the name of national security (as in the case of the Montreal and Quebec police in Operation Bricole), a civilian commission should learn of such attempts promptly, and abort them. Important changes in other institutions such as the courts are also needed. For example, judges must have the power to subpoena "security documents" to decide for themselves (as Judge John Sirica did in the Watergate scandal) whether political leaders should have the privilege of withholding evidence.

But if such changes are to be considered, Canadians must first be convinced that a feasible alternative to a *secret* security service exists. We suggest that there *are* models of intelligence-gathering which are not based on secretive bureaucracies.

Investigative Journalism

The authors of this study hold no rosy view of the press as a bulwark of freedom in North America. Sociologists are all too aware of the extent of corporate control of the press and electronic media, their tendencies toward monopoly, and their willingness to cater to the lowest common denominators in public taste. We hold no illusion about the free press as adequate guardians of truth. William Colby is not unfair in stating that the press began a full criticism of the CIA only after its reputation was damaged at the Bay of Pigs.[15]

However, the organizational structure of the free press in North America does create social conditions favoring the collection and dissemination of important information. The news media are competitive, and thrive on "scoops." It tends to be to the advantage of at least some media to collect and reveal, rather than ignore and cover up, information likely to be of great public interest. William Colby describes how he was able to persuade newsmen not to publish certain stories about the CIA. (Sometimes such tactics hid news of vital importance from the public for several years.) But Colby had to promise each cooperating newsman who stumbled onto a good exposé and who agreed not to use it, that if he discovered he couldn't persuade any one newsman to withhold the story, he would let them all know that they were free to go with their stories.[16] In one case it was the aggressively inquisitive journalist Jack Anderson who blew the cover on a story, thus releasing all the other newsmen from their promises. At this point in the process, one individual becomes important as a catalyst or precipitator of events. But Anderson no more "caused" an exposé of the CIA than a Serbian assassin "caused" World War I by killing the Austrian Archduke.

The role of one or more investigative journalists in restoring the public's right to know has been dramatized in recent years, the most exciting case being the Watergate break-in. It is no accident that those determined to prevent the public from knowing what's going on are bitterly antagonistic toward investigative journalists. When the CBC staff of "Fifth Estate" broke new revelations of RCMP wrongdoing, a cabinet minister publicly criticized the CBC for "wasting taxpayers' money" and threatened to reduce its budget. Later, a federal government spokesman warned that "too much news media attention to the operations of Canadian intelligence agencies can endanger national security."[17] Even the prime minister accused the press of "Watergate envy."

Former CIA director Allen Dulles wrote: "I always considered first, how the operation could be kept secret from the opponent and second, how it could be kept secret from the press. Often the priority was reversed."[18] Many years and errors later, his successor William Colby showed a change of heart. He rejected the argument that "the public must take it on faith that we too are honorable men devoted to the nation's service." Instead, he argued for a new openness in intelligence.

William Colby noted the resemblance between journalism and intelligence gathering.[19] The journalist collects information and makes it available, but *protects his sources*. A democratic intelligence service could do the same. Even more convincing is the argument of Jack Anderson, who notes that reporters manage to pry information from the most powerful and secretive opponents (such as a White House staff determined to reveal nothing). Generally speaking, journalists get their information without breaking the law—without burglarizing files or intercepting mail—Anderson claims.[20] Consider the number of sensational exposés American, British and Canadian investigative media have achieved in the past few years, compared to the unimpressive record of the RCMP even though it has frequently broken the law. Colby argues that the products of espionage do not have to remain secret; on the contrary, they would be more effective if published. "Most of the important conclusions and assessments of intelligence today do reach the citizenry" anyway, "through official releases and unofficial leaks."[21]

An open approach to security would resolve one of the problems repeatedly touched on by insiders now writing on the CIA, FBI and RCMP—namely, the fact that secrecy prevents adequate discussion of alternative policies. Many of the errors of secret bureaucracies arise from the simple fact that those who could point out the error—or contribute corrective information—are not allowed to know what is going on.

The Sociologist as Model

A tradition of thorough investigation into off-beat and hidden worlds within society has developed in North American sociology. It ranges from studies of juvenile gangs to the criminal underworld, to secret sexual byways to the drug subculture.[22] The data have been collected by ethical techniques conducted within the law. They have provided at least as reliable a basis for social policy as the undercover operations of the CIA or RCMP. They have also been available for criticism and the process of self-correction built into the scientific method.

"The sociologist as detective"[23] usually has far less funds to work with than a secret service agent, and certainly a less elaborate back-up organization. The sociologist has less power to collect data than the journalist, since the latter is more likely to be able to protect sources through assurances of confidentiality. A newspaper or television network will usually come to the moral and financial support of a reporter under pressure to reveal his sources, but the sociologist is protected by neither privilege nor influence. The journalist can also use the power of the press to persuade informants to make a statement; the sociologist has no such leverage. In spite of these handicaps, sociologists have demonstrated many times over that it is possible to *find out* without intimidation or bribery.

Many aspects of an open and accountable security service will require further detailed consideration. For instance, to what extent should the service be allowed to use deception and infiltration? Successful reporters and sociologists sometimes gather information through mild forms of deception and infiltration, for example, by attending meetings without revealing their status.[24] Does a reporter have the right to sneak into a meeting which has been closed to the press? Certainly some of the best stories are obtained in this manner. However, the agent provocateur role which many Mounties have been guilty of is clearly outside the limits of an open and lawful security service.

The legitimate place to draw the line on deception can be illustrated by two recent and much-publicized Canadian examples. In the first instance, the RCMP planted an informer inside the Western Guard, a white-supremacy group in Toronto. At the trial of Guard members, the RCMP informer admitted participating in 200 incidents, ranging from painting swastikas on buildings to driving a car while Guard members threw bricks through windows. "I knew I was breaking the law with every incident," the informer admitted, but the RCMP justified its methods: "The more active you were, the more information you got." But there was little evidence at the trial that the Mounties needed fourteen months and 200 admitted criminal actions to get the necessary information. On the contrary, such agent-provocateur techniques raise the suspicion that the RCMP surreptitiously directs right-wing groups to illegally harass left-wing groups, thus killing two birds with one stone.

The contrasting instance is that of the CBC television production, *Connections, The Second Series.* A fifteen-person research team headed by investigative reporter Jim Dubros conducted 1200 interviews and shot a total of 90 hours of film, to produce this sensational three-program revelation of Mafia activities in Canada. Deception was certainly used to gather some of the information and film footage. Underworld leaders were captured in conversation by hidden body microphones, and filmed without their knowledge even at night by the use of hidden cameras and special light-gathering lenses. All CBC employees except those with a "need to know" were deceived about the research team's subject of investigation. However, there was no participation in or provocation of criminal acts. More important, secrecy was not used by the CBC to protect its own image or to withhold information from the public. On the contrary, secrecy was used to enable the *gathering of intelligence intended for the fullest possible publication, while at the same time protecting innocent sources of information.* The CBC instance clearly comes closer than the RCMP-Western Guard instance to an illustration of an open intelligence service.

In general, it may be concluded that deception and infiltration should be severely limited within ethical boundaries of the same sort that govern journalists and sociologists, who nevertheless manage to uncover many hidden worlds. The products of deception and infiltration should always be made public as soon as possible. It is up to the whole population—not merely to a government or police elite—to decide if the threat to our security is real or imagined. Only such open publicity will force elites to distinguish between threats to their power, and real threats to democratic society.

It is essential that Canada's Security Service be responsible to Canada's citizens. It is our freedom they are supposed to guard! But this is not simply to endorse a civilian security agency. The McKenzie commission proposed to replace the Security Service with a clandestine security force modeled on the CIA. Fortunately for Canada this proposal was never implemented. Nor is the appointment of civilian directors over the SS a solution.[25] Events since the appointment of a civilian director in 1971 have certainly proved that.

The McKenzie commission proposed a civilian review board to which Canadians with grievances against the Security Service (for example, losing a job as a result of designation as a security risk) could appeal. While well intentioned, such a proposal has the same failing as current Freedom of Information legislation in Canada. It puts the citizen in the adversary position of having to take initiative against a powerful (and under the McKenzie proposal, entirely secretive) bureaucracy. Few citizens have the confidence or resources to fight and win such an appeal.

"No taxation without representation" has long been a basic principle of parliamentary democracy. Why should this principle be abandoned in the case of a security service? The public has a right to know both the amount of funds voted each year to Canada's Security Service, and the general disposition of those funds. The specific uses of security funds should be under the close supervision of a civilian body which would help prevent any spending for illegal purposes. (Recall that the Mounties involved in the barn-burning were told not to put transmission repairs on the expense account!) Close regulation of Security Service spending would help prevent unethical infiltration and recruitment of informers by cutting off funds for bribes and payoffs.

The need for public accountability, adequate redress of grievances, and tight financial control require us to look for working models in other Canadian institutions which might be modified and adapted to a new security service. Such models must also have an important additional ingredient: the capacity to resist the trend in police organizations to claim professional status. What Canada does *not* need is a more "professional" security service—though we expect this is what the McDonald commission will call for.

We have tried to show that appeals to professionalism in policing and security work—as in any other occupation—are really claims for *independence from public accountability*. When an occupation asserts its "professional rights" it is asserting the right to set its own fees, monitor its own skills, qualify its own members, and set its own penalties for malpractice.

When the claim of professionalism is advanced in any public service, the public can give up hope of demanding accountability. We simply have to trust the profession's ethical autonomy. This is precisely the argument made by those who have called on the McDonald commission to give the RCMP

Security Service professional freedom. For instance, the corporate secretary of the Montreal office of a huge multinational corporation told the commission to trust the SS as "honest and true Canadians" who should be "left to their own discretion in clandestine operations."[26] He condemned the "pathetic desire" of democracies to have everything controlled by the rule of law. If more executives spoke so candidly, the argument that the Security Service and the rule of law exist to protect not democracy, but only the ruling elites of corporate and political power, would soon be proved.

Several existing models of public control of vital bureaucratic and police powers suggest themselves as starting points for reconstructing the Security Service. One model is the police commission. The police forces of numerous Canadian municipalities are not independent of public accountability, but are not directly under the control of politicians either. Municipal police commissions often include appointed civilians who act (or at least are supposed to act) as watchdogs on behalf of the civil liberties of all citizens.

Another relevant model is that of the auditor general's department in the federal government. The auditor general reports directly to Parliament, and has considerable independence from the government bureaucracy. This department's investigative methods—which are well within the law—have exposed numerous malpractices which bureaucrats tried to cover up.

No doubt other models would suggest themselves during any informed public discussion of the most effective structure for a democratic security service. The shortcomings of existing models (such as those of certain municipal commissions which have become rubber stamps for local police chiefs) must be taken into account.

Certainly one of the most important control mechanisms is publicity. Whenever *any* public body—a court, a police commission, a welfare agency, a labor board, a workmen's compensation board, or any body which is financed by public taxation and is responsible for administration of public policy—goes into secret session, we should become suspicious. Our reaction should not be "trust them" but rather "what do they have to hide?" Such is the typical reaction of the investigative journalist or sociologist, and usually it turns out that there *is* something to hide. This is not because certain members of the organization are "bad apples." Rather it is in the very nature of vested interests of officials in bureaucratic structures. If all the officials in all the bureaucracies in Canada were suddenly fired and replaced by new people, the new people would be behaving in much the same ways as their predecessors in very short order, as long as they were allowed—and encouraged—by the structure of the organizations.

A Democratic Security Service

The formation of a democratically structured security service for Canada will require much more research and consideration than we have been able to provide in this limited study. The work should probably begin with proposals for a charter for the new organization. This charter should set out the ideals for the service so as to meet the basic requirements of respect for human rights already written into comparable charters—such as the Canadian Bill of Rights, the American Bill of Rights, and the United Nations Declaration of Human Rights.

Our suggestions for a democratic security service would include the following:

1. a civilian controlling body representative of the wide diversity of Canadians. This body would include representatives from major organizations of business, labor, farmers, consumers, women, native peoples, etc. The nominating mechanism would insure that the parliamentary opposition had as much voice as the government in the final selection.

2. an internal structure providing members of the security service with the same rights and freedoms as all Canadians. The military form of organization of the present SS would be abandoned. Employees would be hired through an open and competitive system like that of the best civil service departments. They would be free to organize for collective bargaining. The recommendation of the Marin commission for an ombudsman would be implemented.[27]

3. The actual operations of the service would be patterned on the ethics and procedures of investigative journalism and sociology. The products of intelligence gathering would become public knowledge as rapidly as possible. *We would defend our open society by becoming an even more open society.* Bureaucratic secrecy is not only corrosive of liberty, it is ultimately inefficient. Bruce Lockhart's exhaustive study of government secrecy concludes that covert operations are "expensive, difficult, unreliable."[28]

4. The legal and political contexts in which the new security service operated would have to be changed, or the old structures would soon corrupt the new policies. Specifically, the Official Secrets Act should be entirely repealed. The United States has survived without one. Section 41 of the Federal Court Act should also be repealed. And perhaps most important would be the revocation of the War Measures Act. This legislation allows a hysterical or venal government to claim or manufacture an apprehended insurrection and then imprison hundreds or thousands of citizens in violation of their rights. Even leaders of the Conservative party who voted for the Act's declaration in 1970 have since publicly regretted it. Members of the Liberal party have promised that it would be withdrawn and replaced by less easily abused legislation.

The process of constructing a new body of legislation in which a democratic security service can operate will require a variety of other legal reforms, such as abolition of the infamous "writs of assistance" which still permit Mounties to enter and search without a warrant.

5. New legislation will be required to enable citizens to assess the operations of the security service as these are made public through its controlling body. The public has a right to know, without having to repeatedly prove that right. The existing Freedom of Information legislation must be replaced by procedures which put the burden of proof on bureaucratic officials to show why any requested information or document should *not* be disclosed.

6. Every Canadian, and every Canadian organization, has the right to know which activities the security service considers potentially subversive to Canadian democracy. (In the jargon of the intelligence community this is called "tar-

geting.'') The charter of the security service should clearly state what kinds of activities will be targeted for surveillance. The specific targets should be approved by the controlling body, not merely by officials of the service, and certainly not by low-echelon personnel on the basis of personal suspicions (as was done in Quebec).

Thus far, our approach to targeting would have the support of parliamentary RCMP reformers and some critics within the intelligence community itself. As civil libertarians, we further propose that the targeted individuals and groups have a right to know they are suspected, and a right to appeal this status. One of the most consistent abuses of the secret powers of the Security Service has been the covert, and publicly denied, targeting of groups and individuals who rightly resent being labeled subversive. Several legal and democratic trade union organizations, for example, have strongly condemned the RCMP for its covert infiltration and surveillance.

The whispered charge that a citizen is subversive can be a very damaging form of slander. In a democratic society each citizen deserves the opportunity to challenge such charges, if he or she believes there is evidence to combat the allegations. The worst excesses and abuses may occur when the citizen doesn't even know that suspicions exist.

The claim that public knowledge of targeting will vitiate the work of the security service by letting real spies know they are being watched is naive and unfounded. Any spy or saboteur assumes automatically that he is being watched— and once the security service is aware of the spy, the spy will usually be aware of the security service. The irony is that the KGB knows far more about the inside of the RCMP than the best-informed Canadians!

Obviously safeguards would have to be established to prevent damaging allegations which prove to be false, but which cannot be fully wiped from the public consciousness. The truth usually has a difficult time catching up to a smear. Thus the procedure should probably be one of requiring the controlling body of the security service first to inform a citizen or organization that it is to be targeted. A right of appeal would apply immediately, and the first stage should have the same protection as "discovery" in libel and slander suits. That is, it should not be open to the press. But once the decision was made to continue the target (by the service) or appeal the allegation (by the citizen or group) the process should be open to the media, like any libel or slander trial. Obviously the media would be governed by normal respect for ethics and legal liabilities.

Openness Essential to an Open Society

Canadians cannot hope to enjoy the liberties of an open and democratic society unless they are prepared to practice openness to the greatest possible degree. Our analysis and proposals are based on this belief. We are not consciously underestimating the problems to be faced. The task of constructing a democratic security force is daunting. Robin Bourne, one of Canada's mandarins of national security, has admitted that "getting an institution like the Force [RCMP] . . . to change directions is like trying to turn around a jumbo oil tanker."[29] But the alternatives to not trying are fearful to contemplate.

There was never a time when participation in the defense of liberty offered more exciting and challenging prospects. The task of maintaining freedom has usually fallen to the vigilant and energetic few; we can hardly rely on the government to protect our rights. "Liberty has always come from the subjects of it, and never from governments," President Woodrow Wilson warned. "The history of liberty is a history of resistance."

When Quebec Justice James Hugessen tried to prevent the federal government from closing down the Keable commission on RCMP wrongdoing, he supported his decision with these words:

> Much has been made, in the present case, of national security and state secrets, but we must not forget that in principle we live in an open and democratic society. Even the security of the state can and must be the subject of informed debate among all citizens.[30]

But Justice Hugessen wasn't able to solve our problems for us; his decision was soon overturned by the Supreme Court and the Keable inquiry was temporarily silenced. There may be many such setbacks, and few easy victories, in the effort to achieve a democratic security service in Canada.

Selected Bibliography

Adams, Ian. *S, Portrait of a Spy*. Toronto: Gage, 1977.

Agee, Philip. *Inside the Company, A CIA Diary*. London: Penguin, 1975.

Anderson, Jack. *The Anderson Papers*. New York: Random House, 1973.

Arendt, Hannah. *Crises of the Republic*. New York: Harcourt Brace, 1969.

Armstrong, T. R., and Cinnamon, K. M., eds. *Power and Authority in Law Enforcement*. Springfield, Illinois: Thomas, 1976.

Banton, Michael. *The Policeman in the Community*. London: Tavistock, 1964.

Becker, Howard. *The Other Side*. New York: Free Press, 1964.

Bent, Alan. *The Politics of Law Enforcement*. Toronto: Lexington Books, 1974.

Bercuson, David. *Confrontation at Winnipeg*. Montreal: McGill University Press, 1974.

Berger, Peter. *Invitation to Sociology*. New York: Doubleday, 1963.

Berkley, George. *The Democratic Policeman*. Boston: Beacon, 1969.

Bittner, Egan. *The Functions of the Police in Modern Society*. Washington: National Institute for Mental Health, 1970.

Blau, Peter, and Meyer, M. *Bureaucracy in Modern Society*. New York: Random House, 1971.

Blishen, Bernard; Jones, F.; Naegle, K.; and Porter, J. *Canadian Society, Sociological Perspectives*. Toronto: Macmillan, 1964, 1968.

Bordua, David, and Reiss, Albert. "Command, Control and Charisma; Reflections on Police Bureaucracy." In Quinney, 1969.

Bowes, Stuart. *The Police and Civil Liberties*. London: Lawrence and Wishart, 1966.

Breton, Raymond. "The socio-political dynamics of the October events." In *Aspects of Canadian Society*. Montreal: Canadian Sociology and Anthropology Association, 1974.

Brown, Lorne, and Brown, Caroline. *An Unauthorized History of the RCMP*. Toronto: James Lorimer, 1973.

Buckner, Taylor. "Police Culture." Paper presented to the Canadian Sociology and Anthropology Association annual meetings, 1972. Department of Sociology, Concordia University, Montreal.

Bunyan, Tony. *Political Police in Britain*. London: Freedman, 1976.

Burdman, Milton. "The Conflict Between Freedom and Order." *Crime and Delinquency*, vol. 15, no. 3 (July 1969), pp. 371-76.

Bush, Gary. "Status inconsistency and right wingism." *American Sociological Review* 32 (February 1967): 86-92.

Centre for Crime Research. *The Iron Fist and the Velvet Glove*. 1975. 2490 Channing Way, Room 507, Berkeley, California.

Chambliss, William J. "The Saints and the Roughnecks." *Society*, November 1973, pp. 24-31.

Chambliss, William J. *Whose Law? Whose Order?* New York: Wiley, 1976.

Chapman, Brian. *Police State*. New York: Praeger, 1970.

Chwast, J. "Value conflicts in law enforcement." *Crime and Delinquency* 11 (April 1965): 151-61.

Clark, J. P. "Isolation of the Police." *Journal of Criminal Law, Criminology and Police Science* 56 (1965): 307-19.

Clement, Wallace. *The Canadian Corporate Elite*. Toronto: McClelland and Stewart, 1975.

Cloward, Richard, and Ohlin, Lloyd. *Delinquency and Opportunity*. New York: Free Press, 1960.

Colby, William. "The Playboy Interview." *Playboy*, July 1978.

Colby, William, and Forbath, Peter. *Honorable Men*. New York: Simon and Schuster, 1978.

Commager, Henry. "The banality of evil." *New York Review of Books*, September 30, 1976.

Conference on Government Secrecy. "None of Your Business." New York University, 1973.

Conquest, Robert. *The Soviet Police System*. London: Bodley Head, 1968.

Cook, Ramsay, "Canadian Freedom in Wartime," in *His Own Man*. Edited by W. H. Heick and Roger Graham. Montreal: McGill University Press, 1974.

Copeland, Miles. *The Game of Nations*. New York: Simon and Schuster, 1969.

Copeland, Miles. *Without Cloak and Dagger*. New York: Simon and Schuster, 1974.

Cox, B.; Shirley, J.; and Short, M. *Fall of Scotland Yard*. London: Penquin, 1977.

Cray, Ed. *The Enemy in the Streets, Police Malpractice in America*. New York: Doubleday, 1972.

Creighton, Donald. *Dominion of the North*. Toronto: University of Toronto Press, 1957.

Crozier, Michael. "The problem of power." In Armstrong and Cinnamon, 1976.

De Larue, Jacques. *The Gestapo*. New York: William Morrow, 1964.

Denning. *Lord Denning's Report* (The Profumo affair). His Majesty's Stationery Office, London, England, September 1963.

Douglas, Jack, and Johnson, John. *Official Deviance*. Toronto: Lippincott, 1977.

Dulles, Allen. *The Craft of Intelligence*. New York: Harper and Row, 1963.

Durkheim, Emile. *Elementary Forms of Religious Life*. New York: Free Press, 1954. (Orig. pub. 1912).

Earle, Howard. *Police-Community Relations*. Springfield, Illinois: Thomas, 1967.

Etzioni, Amitai. *The Active Society*. New York: Free Press, 1969.

Festinger, L. *A Theory of Cognitive Dissonance*. Stanford: Stanford University Press, 1957.

Fitzgibbon, C. *Secret Intelligence in the 20th Century*. New York: Stein and Day, 1976.

Foucault, Michel. *Madness and Civilization*. New York: Vintage, 1965.

Flemming, Marlis. *Under Protective Surveillance*. Toronto: McClelland and Stewart, 1976.

Freitag, Peter. "The Cabinet and Big Business, a study of interlocks." *Social Problems* 26 (1975): 137-62.

Galnoor, I. *Government Secrecy in Democracies*. New York: Harper and Row, 1977.

Garrison, Omar. *The Secret World of Interpol.* New York: Ralston-Pilot, 1976.

Goffman, Erving. *The Presentation of Self in Everyday Life.* New York: Doubleday, 1959.

Goffman, Erving. *Asylums.* Chicago: Aldine, 1961.

Goode, William. "A Theory of Role Strain." *American Sociological Review,* vol. 25, no. 4 (1960), pp. 483-96.

Greenaway, W. K., and Brickey, S. L. *Law and Social Control in Canada.* Toronto: Prentice-Hall, 1978.

Griffin, John. *Black Like Me.* New York: New American Library, 1961.

Haas, Jack, and Shaffir, Bill. *Decency and Deviance.* Toronto: McClelland and Stewart, 1974.

Hagan, John. "The philosophy and sociology of crime control." *Sociological Inquiry,* vol. 47, no. 3-4 (1977), pp. 181-208.

Hagan, John. *The Disreputable Pleasures.* Toronto: McGraw-Hill Ryerson, 1977.

Halperin, Morton; Berman J.; Borosage, R.; and Marwick, C. *The Lawless State.* London: Penquin, 1976.

Harney, M., and Cross, J. *The Informer in Law Enforcement.* Springfield, Illinois: Thomas, 1968.

Henschel, Richard. "Controlling the Police Power." *Canadian Forum,* November 1977.

Hogarth, John. *Sentencing as a Human Process.* Toronto: University of Toronto Press, 1971.

Hughes, E. C. "Good People and Dirty Work." *Social Problems* 10 (1962): 3-11.

Humphreys, Laud. *Tearoom Trade.* Chicago: Aldine, 1975.

Jackson, Elton. "Status Consistency and Symptoms of Stress." *American Sociological Review* 27 (1962): 469-80.

Jamieson, Stuart. *Times of Trouble; Labor Unrest and Industrial Conflict.* Study 22, Task Force on Labor Relations. Ottawa: Queen's Printer, 1971.

Johnson, Terence. *Professions and Power.* London: Macmillan, 1972.

Katz, Sidney. "Inside Canada's Secret Police." *Maclean's,* April 20, 1963.

Keable, Jean. Commission of inquiry into the RCMP. Montreal, Quebec.

Kelly, William, and Kelly, Nora. *The Royal Canadian Mounted Police.* Edmonton: Hurtig, 1973.

Kelly, William, and Kelly, Nora. *Policing in Canada.* Toronto: Macmillan, 1976.

Koenig, David. "RCMP views of themselves, their jobs and the public." Report 195, Attorney General's Department, British Columbia, 1975.

Koestler, Arthur. *Darkness at Noon*. London: Penguin, 1971.

Lauer, Robert. *Perspectives on Social Change*. Toronto: Allyn and Bacon, 1977.

Leighton, Barry. "Freedom of Information Legislation in Canada." Paper presented to the Canadian Sociology and Anthropology Association annual meetings, 1978. Department of Sociology, University of Toronto.

Lipset, Seymour. "Canada and the United States, a comparative view," *Canadian Review of Sociology and Anthropology*, 1964, pp. 173-85.

Lockhart, Bruce. "Relations between secret services and government in a modern state." *Journal of the Royal United Services Institute*, vol. 119, no. 2 (June 1974).

Lower, Arthur R. M. "Is the RCMP a threat to our liberty?" *Maclean's*, July 6, 1957.

Lowry, R. P. "Toward a sociology of secrecy and security systems." *Social Problems* 19 (1972): 439-50.

Macleod, R. C. *The NWMP and Law Enforcement, 1873-1905*. Toronto: University of Toronto Press, 1976.

Manning, P. K. "The Police." In *Crime and Justice in American Society*. Edited by Jack Douglas. New York: Bobbs Merrill, 1971.

Marchetti, Victor, and Marks, John. *The CIA and the Cult of Intelligence*. New York: Knopf, 1974.

Marin, Justice René. Report of the Commission of Inquiry relating to public complaints, internal discipline and grievance procedure in the RCMP. Ottawa: Information Canada, 1976.

Marshall, Geoffrey. *Police and Government*. London: Methuen, 1965.

Masters, D. C. *The Winnipeg General Strike*. Toronto: University of Toronto Press, 1950.

McDonald Commission of Inquiry into certain RCMP activities. "Freedom and Security, an analysis of policy issues." Ottawa: October 1978.

McKenzie, M. W. Report of the Royal Commission on Security. Ottawa: Queen's Printer, 1969.

McNaught, Kenneth. "Political Trials in Canada." In *Courts and Trials*. Edited by M. Friedland. Toronto: University of Toronto Press, 1975.

Merton, Robert. "Social conformity, deviation and opportunity structures." *American Sociological Review* 24 (1959): 177-89.

Miller, Walter. "Lower class culture as a generating milieu of gang delinquency." *Journal of Social Issues*, vol. 14, no. 3 (1958), pp. 5-19.

Mills, C. Wright. *The Power Elite*. Oxford University Press, 1959.

Moorhead, William. Report of the House Foreign Operations and Government Information Subcommittee, 1972. United States Congress.

Morand, Donald. Report of the Royal Commission into Metropolitan Toronto Police Practices. Toronto: Queen's Printer, 1976.

Morton, Desmond. "Aid to the Civil Power: The Canadian Militia in support of social order, 1867-1914." *Canadian Historical Review*, December 1970, p. 407.

Municipal Police, Chicago. "Municipal Police Administration." 1961.

Naegle, Kaspar. "Canadian Society, Some Reflections." In Blishen, 1964.

Neff, Franklin, and Lubin, Bernard. "Training program for police managers." In Armstrong and Cinnamon, 1976.

Newman, Graeme. *Comparative Deviance*. New York: Elsevier, 1976.

Niederhoffer, Arthur. *Behind the Shield; Police in Urban Society*. New York: Doubleday. 1969.

O'Toole, George. *The Private Sector*. New York: Norton, 1978.

Packer, Herbert. "Who can police the police?" *New York Review*, September 8, 1966.

Packer, Herbert. "Two models of the criminal process." *University of Pennsylvania Law Review* 113 (November 1964).

Penrose, Barry, and Courtiour, Roger. *The Pencourt File*. New York: Harper and Row, 1978.

Petras, James. "Police and Liberty." Mimeographed. Department of Political Science, New York State University, May 1978.

Porter, John. *The Vertical Mosaic*. Toronto: University of Toronto Press, 1965.

Quinney, Richard. *Crime, Justice and Society*. Boston: Little, Brown, 1969.

Quinney, Richard. *The Social Reality of Crime*. Boston: Little, Brown, 1970.

Radelet, L. A. *The Police and the Community*. Toronto: Collier Macmillan, 1973.

Ramsay, Jack. "My Case Against the RCMP." *Maclean's*, July 1972. Also reprinted in Haas, 1974.

Reasons, Charles, and Rich, Robert. *The Sociology of Law.* Toronto: Butterworth, 1978.

Reith, Charles. *British Police and the Democratic Ideal.* Oxford University Press, 1943.

Rhead, C.; Abrams, A.; Trosman, H.; and Margolis, P. "Psychological assessment of police candidates." *American Journal of Psychology*, vol. 124, no. 11 (1968), pp. 1575-80.

Robertson, Geoff. *Reluctant Judas.* London: Temple Smith, 1976.

Rockefeller Commission. Report of the Commission on CIA Activities in the United States. U.S. Government Printing Office, 1975. Also in Douglas and Johnson, 1977.

Sanders, William. *The Sociologist as Detective.* New York: Praeger, 1974.

Schrank, Jeffrey. *Snap, Crackle and Popular Taste.* New York: Delta, 1977.

Schur, Edwin. *Labelling Deviant Behavior.* New York: Harper and Row, 1971.

Skolnick, Jerome. *Justice Without Trial.* New York: Wiley, 1967.

Snider, Laureen. "Corporate Crime in Canada." Ph.D. thesis, Sociology, University of Toronto, 1978.

Steadman, Robert. *The Police and the Community.* Baltimore: Johns Hopkins University Press, 1972.

Stevenson, William. *A Man Called Intrepid.* New York: Ballantine, 1976.

Stockwell, John. *In Search of Enemies.* New York: Norton, 1978.

Sykes, Gresham, and Matza, David. "Techniques of Neutralization." *American Sociological Review*, vol. 22, no. 6 (December 1957), p. 664-70.

Szasz, Thomas. *The Manufacture of Madness.* New York: Delta, 1970.

Tannenbaum, Frank. *Crime and the Community.* Boston: Ginn, 1938.

Tardiff, Guy. *Police et Politique au Quebec.* Montreal: Aurore, 1974.

Task Force on Policing in Ontario. Report to the Solicitor General, 1974.

Taylor, Ian; Walton, Paul; and Young, Jock. *The New Criminology.* London: Routledge and Kegan Paul, 1973.

Thompson, Anthony. *Big Brother in Britain Today.* London: Michael Joseph, 1970.

Toch, Hans. "Psychological consequences of the police role." *Police* 10 (September 1965): 22-25.

Turk, Austin. *Criminality and the Legal Order.* Chicago: Rand McNally, 1969.

Turner, William. *The Police Establishment.* New York: G. P. Putnam's Sons, 1968.

United States National Commission on the Causes and Prevention of Violence: Reports. U.S. Government Printing Office, 1969.

Vallee, F. G., and Whyte, D. R. "Canadian society, trends and perspectives." In Blishen and others, 1964.

Vallières, Pierre. *The Assassination of Pierre Laporte.* Toronto: James Lorimer, 1977.

Vidich, Arthur. "Political legitimacy in bureaucratic society." *Social Research*, vol. 42, no. 4 (Winter 1975), pp. 778-811.

Watters, P., and Gillers, S. *Investigating the FBI.* New York: Doubleday, 1973.

Weber, Max. *Economy and Society.* New York: Bedminster Press, 1968. (Orig. pub. 1922).

Westley, William. "Secrecy and the Police." *Social Forces*, vol. 34, no. 1 (1956).

William, David. *Not in the Public Interest.* London: Hutchinson, 1965.

Wilson, James. "The police and their problems, a theory." *Public Policy* vol. 12, 1963. Cambridge: Harvard University Press.

Wilson, James. *Varieties of Police Behavior.* Cambridge: Harvard University Press, 1978.

Wise, David, and Ross, Thomas. *The Espionage Establishment.* New York: Random House, 1967.

Wise, David. *The Government Against the People.* New York: Random House, 1976.

Wolff, Kurt. *The Sociology of Georg Simmel.* New York: Free Press, 1950.

Wolff, R. P. *The Rule of Law.* New York: Simon and Schuster, 1971.

Notes

For complete entry on any author, see Selected Bibliography.

Chapter 1

1. Lower, 1957.
2. Katz, 1963.
3. Ramsay, 1972.
4. McDonald commission, October 1978, p. 3.
5. Douglas, 1977. For a detailed explanation of labeling theory in a Canadian context, see Hagan, 1977.
6. Wilson, 1963, p. 18.
7. Cox, Shirley, Short, 1977.
8. See Newman, 1976, for consensus support of law in six countries.
9. See Snider, 1978, for a detailed study of unequal enforcement of laws against upperworld and lowerworld offenses.
10. Chambliss, 1973.
11. Hogarth, 1971.
12. See Reasons and Rich, 1978 for a detailed consideration.
13. Brown and Brown, 1973.
14. Montreal *Gazette*, March 30, 1978.
15. Naegle, 1964, p. 501.
16. Vallee and Whyte, 1964, p. 10.

Chapter 2

1. RCMP testimony at the McDonald commission, reported by *Toronto Star*, July 18, 1978.
2. See Watters and Gillers, 1973; *Maclean's*, September 25, 1978, p. 22.

3. *Los Angeles Times*, September 26, 1975.
4. Neff and Lubin, 1976, p. 119.
5. Skolnick, 1967, p. 47.
6. Rhead et al., 1968.
7. *The Globe and Mail*, February 14, 1978.
8. *Toronto Star*, June 28, 1972; U.S. Senate Committee on the Judiciary, Subcommittee on Internal Security, Hearings, October 10, 1969.
9. *The Globe and Mail*, January 14, 1978.
10. Copeland, 1974.
11. *Toronto Star*, June 25, 1977.
12. Ibid., January 13, 1978.
13. From a typescript of "personal and confidential" draft letter "to CO's" by M. J. Nadon, commissioner, following conviction of Samson; supplied to the Keable commission (photocopy).
14. Ibid.
15. From a xerox copy of letter supplied to the Keable commission.
16. From a photocopy of a draft, typescript letter to the solicitor general from M. J. Nadon, commissioner; supplied to the Keable commission.
17. From a photocopy of a RCMP top secret telex from Donald Cobb, officer in charge of the Montreal section of the RCMP Security Service, to the deputy director general of the Security Service, April 5, 1976; supplied to the Keable commission.
18. Ibid.

Chapter 3

1. *Law and Order in Canadian Democracy*, King's Printer, Ottawa, 1949. This is a series of RCMP lectures for recruits.
2. "Logistics of a Bag Job," *Seven Days*, April 21, 1978, p. 18.
3. Hansard, October 31, 1977, p. 471.
4. *Toronto Star*, June 30, 1969.
5. *The Canadian*, September 23, 1978, p. 14.
6. *Toronto Star*, November 30, 1977.
7. *The Globe and Mail*, February 23, 1978.
8. Watters and Gillers, 1973, p. 351; Copeland, 1974, p. 76.
9. Keable commission, transcript of hearings, January 31, 1978.
10. Commager, 1976.
11. De Larue, 1964, p. 133.
12. *The Globe and Mail*, October 29, 1977.

13. Hansard, October 31, 1977, p. 458.
14. *The Globe and Mail,* November 2, 1977.
15. Ibid., September 11, 1978.
16. *Toronto Star,* November 30, 1977.
17. *The Globe and Mail,* April 28, 1978.
18. The following paragraphs are based on top secret RCMP telex reports supplied to the Keable commission, dating from August 11, 1972 to January 8, 1973.
19. Approval for Operation Ham at a high level was requested in a letter marked top secret of November 21, 1972, to the assistant deputy director general (ADDG), and subsequently to the deputy director general (DDG) with the note penned in (December 11, 1972); photocopies of letters were supplied to the Keable commission. News report on Parent's loss of memory: *The Globe and Mail,* November 24, 1977.
20. From a photocopy of a top secret telex of January 10, 1973, supplied to the Keable commission.
21. *The Globe and Mail,* November 10, 1978.
22. RCMP memorandum to the Officer in Charge of Automated Information Services, July 7, 1975; a photocopy was supplied to the Keable commission.
23. Top secret telex; a photocopy was supplied to the Keable commission.
24. *The Globe and Mail,* April 25, 1978.
25. *Toronto Star,* August 1, 1978.
26. Halperin, 1976. p. 8
27. Toronto *Sun,* October 30, 1977.
28. See Hugessen's judgment re Keable commission, December 9, 1977, pp. 27-29.
29. *Toronto Star,* November 4, 1977.

Chapter 4

1. *The Globe and Mail,* September 27, 1978.
2. Cray, 1972, p. 195.
3. Copeland, 1974, p. 275.
4. *The Globe and Mail,* November 24, 1977; *Maclean's,* November 20, 1977.
5. Kelly and Kelly, 1976, p. 95.
6. *The Globe and Mail, Toronto Star,* September 12, 1978.
7. *Toronto Star,* September 12, 1978.
8. *The Globe and Mail,* September 13, 1978.
9. Ibid.

10. Ibid., April 29, 1978.
11. Ibid., September 27, 1978.
12. *The Globe and Mail*, September 12, 1978.
13. *The Canadian*, February 3, 1979.
14. Festinger, 1957.
15. *Toronto Star*, September 12, 1978.
16. Ibid.
17. Ibid.
18. *The Globe and Mail*, September 12, 1978.
19. Ibid., September 19, 1978.
20. *Toronto Star*, September 13, 1978.
21. *The Globe and Mail, Toronto Star*, September 14 and 20, 1978; *Maclean's*, September 25, 1978; *Toronto Star*, October 5, 1978.
22. *The Globe and Mail*, September 27, 1978; CBC National News, September 26, 1978.
23. *The Globe and Mail*, September 27, 1978.
24. Hagan, 1977, p. 87.
25. *The Globe and Mail*, September 14, 1978.
26. Ibid., January 10, 1978.
27. Authors' translation of a photocopy supplied to the Keable commission.
28. The goal is to "destabilize" and is thus an admission of the stability of the situation. See Keable transcripts, vol. 38, p. 10-11. For classic examples of disinformation, see Stevenson, 1976.
29. *The Globe and Mail*, January 10, 1978.
30. Ibid.
31. Berger, 1963.
32. *Le Devoir*, December 13, 1971.
33. See Goffman, 1959.
34. *Toronto Star*, January 15, 1978.
35. *The Globe and Mail*, January 10, 1978.
36. *Maclean's*, October 2, 1978.
37. *Toronto Star*, January 15, 1978.
38. Ibid.
39. *The Globe and Mail*, July 19, 1978.
40. *Toronto Star*, July 19, 1978.
41. Ibid.
42. *The Globe and Mail*, September 23, 1978.
43. *Toronto Star*, November 11, 1977.
44. *Ontario Report*, August 1978, p. 7.
45. *The Globe and Mail*, March 18, 1978.

Chapter 5

1. Schrank, 1977, p. 97.
2. *The Globe and Mail*, March 7, 1978.
3. Ibid., April 12, 1978.
4. *Canadian Association of University Teachers Bulletin*, October 1978.
5. Halperin, 1976, p. 35.
6. *The Globe and Mail*, February 24, 1978.
7. Ibid., May 3, 1978.
8. Hansard, October 31, 1977, p. 454.
9. *The Globe and Mail*, May 10, 1978.
10. Cited by the Marin Report, 1976, p. 26.
11. *Toronto Star*, September 12, 1978.
12. Transcripts of the Keable commission, vol. 105, p. 40ff.
13. Keable transcript, vol. 105, p. 58.
14. Ibid., p. 63.
15. Ibid., p. 64.
16. Ibid., p. 68.
17. Ibid., p. 66.
18. Ibid., vol. 102, p. 36ff.
19. *Playboy*, July 1978.
20. Skolnick, 1967, p. 145.
21. *The Globe and Mail*, April 12, 1978.
22. From RCMP telex supplied to the Keable commission (photocopy).
23. From RCMP telex supplied to the Keable commission (photocopy).
24. A photocopy was supplied to the Keable commission.
25. Turk, 1969.
26. Hagan, 1977, p. 92.
27. Merton, 1959, p. 361.
28. Cloward and Ohlin, 1960.
29. Schur, 1971, p. 73.
30. Berger, 1963, p. 100.
31. *The Globe and Mail*, April 25, 1978.
32. Douglas Fisher, Toronto *Sun*, November 28, 1977.
33. *The Globe and Mail*, September 28, 1978.
34. Judgment by Judge R. Vincent, June 16, 1977, p. 5; authors' translation.
35. *The Globe and Mail*, September 29, 1978.

Chapter 6

1. See Blau and Meyer, 1971.
2. Weber, 1922/1968, p. 196.
3. Anderson, 1973, p. 65.
4. Ibid., p. 66.
5. Ibid., p. 67.
6. Hansard, October 31, 1977, p. 454.
7. Transcripts of the McDonald commission, October 5, 1978.
8. Ibid.
9. Ibid.
10. Ibid.
11. *The Globe and Mail*, January 10, 1978.
12. Ibid.
13. Ibid., September 11, 1978.
14. Transcripts of the Keable commission, vol. 102, p. 59.
15. Ibid., vol. 105, p. 49.
16. *The Globe and Mail*, November 24, 1977.
17. *Washington Star*, October 7, 1978.
18. See Schur, 1971, p. 82ff.
19. Keable transcript, vol. 102, p. 47.
20. *The Globe and Mail*, February 24, 1978.
21. Hansard, April 2, 1976.
22. CBC National News, November 8, 1977.
23. *The Globe and Mail*, February 16, 1978.
24. Ibid., November 2, 1978; *Maclean's*, November 8, 1978.
25. *The Globe and Mail*, November 2, 1978.
26. See Williams, 1965, for discussion of problems of parliamentary debate on security matters.
27. *The Globe and Mail*, April 14, 1978.
28. Hansard, October 31, 1977, p. 454.
29. *The Globe and Mail*, December 9, 1977.
30. *Toronto Star*, July 19, 1978.
31. *The Canadian*, September 16, 1978.
32. Ibid.

Chapter 7

1. Macleod, 1976, p. 144.
2. Ibid.
3. Ibid., p. 145.
4. Ibid., p. 150.

5. Quoted in Creighton, 1957, p. 292.
6. See Kelly and Kelly, 1973, p. 16.
7. Ibid., p. 21.
8. See Kelly and Kelly, 1973, p. 72 for an account of one such incident.
9. See Brown and Brown, 1973, p. 24, for an excellent account of this role of the NWMP.
10. Morton, 1970, p. 407; Jamieson, 1971, p. 1.
11. Kelly and Kelly, 1973, p. 151.
12. Bercuson, 1974, p. 173.
13. Masters, 1950, p. 107.
14. Hansard, March 9, 1920, p. 243. Charles Murphy, M.P. quoted a letter from Gouin dated February 4, 1920.
15. See footnote 14 above.
16. Hansard, June 7, 1920, p. 3209.
17. Mr. Cahill, M.P. in Hansard, June 7, 1920, p. 3203.
18. Hansard, April 10, 1922, p. 829.
19. The Hon. George P. Graham in Hansard, April 10, 1922, p. 831.
20. Hansard, April 10, 1922, p. 844.
21. See Kelly and Kelly, 1973, p. 156.
22. Hon. Ernest Lapointe in Hansard, June 19, 1936, p. 3897.
23. Quoted by Lapointe in Hansard, February 16, 1933, p. 2187.
24. J. S. Woodsworth, M.P. in Hansard, June 22, 1936, p. 4061.
25. Woodsworth in Hansard, May 6, 1932, p. 2683.
26. Hon. M. Dupré in Hansard, February 21, 1933, p. 2335.
27. Hon. W. A. Gordon in Hansard, May 23, 1932, p. 3249.
28. Letter to Grant McNeil, M.P. dated April 27, 1939.
29. Cook, 1974, p. 37.
30. Ibid., p. 38.
31. Ibid., p. 50.
32. Commissioner S. T. Wood, "Tools for Treachery," *The Canadian Spokesman*, February 1941.
33. Record group 18, RCMP Files, Public Archives of Canada, Vol. 3314.
34. Lower, 1957.
35. Hansard, June 11, 1940, p. 667.
36. Ibid., p. 676.
37. Ibid., April 4, 1922, p. 600.

Chapter 8

1. See the RCMP's series of lectures for new recruits, *Law and*

Order in Canadian Democracy, King's Printer, Ottawa, 1949, for their concept of the ideal policeman.

2. The Solicitor General's report for 1974-75, for example, showed seventy-eight persons on the waiting list.
3. See Kelly and Kelly, 1976, p. 109.
4. Ibid., p. 110.
5. *Toronto Telegram*, June 14, 1963.
6. See *The Varsity*, the University of Toronto newspaper, January 19 and following days of publication, 1979, for the most recent examples. The Canadian University Press decided at their fortieth annual conference (1978) to urge member student papers not to carry RCMP advertising.
7. Report of the McKenzie commission, 1969, p. 20.
8. The lack of training was not, of course, openly advertised at the Keable or McDonald hearings by the RCMP; it was evident in the reported activities of lower ranks already discussed in chapters 2, 3 and 4. See also the sharp criticism by an ex-Mountie in Hansard, Proceedings of the Justice and Legal Affairs Committee, May 18, 1978, Appendix.
9. See Watters and Gillers, 1973, chapter on the FBI by William Turner, 1968.
10. Hansard, Proceedings of the Justice and Legal Affairs Committee, May 18, 1978, Appendix, p. 7.
11. Toronto *Telegram*, June 2, 1965.
12. Ibid.
13. Kelly and Kelly, 1976, p. 120.
14. See Goffman, 1961.
15. Ramsay, 1972.
16. Niederhoffer, 1969, p. 95.
17. Ibid., p. 47.
18. Goffman, 1961, p. 167.
19. Wilson, 1978, p. 138.
20. Wilson, 1963, p. 18.
21. Ramsay, 1972.
22. Hansard, Proceedings of the Justice and Legal Affairs Committee, May 18, 1978, Appendix, p. 5.
23. Task Force on Policing in Ontario, Report to the Solicitor General, 1974, Conclusions.
24. See Kelly and Kelly, 1976; Task Force on Policing in Ontario, 1974; Marin, 1976; Morand, 1976.
25. Morand, 1976.
26. Marin, 1976.
27. Bent, 1974, p. 155.

28. See Wilson, 1978, p. 30, for arguments that police are not professionals.
29. See Johnson, 1972.
30. See Agee, 1975.
31. *The Globe and Mail*, February 10, 1978.
32. See Agee, 1975; Thompson, 1970.
33. *Toronto Telegram*, June 30, 1969.
34. See Jackson, 1962; Lauer, 1977, p. 239.
35. See also Hansard, Proceedings of the Justice and Legal Affairs Committee, May 18, 1978, Appendix, p. 7.
36. *The Globe and Mail*, February 2, 1978.
37. Toronto *Sun*, October 4, 1978.
38. Goffman, 1959.
39. Niederhoffer, 1969, p. 22.
40. Blishen et al., 1968, p. 741.
41. Solicitor General's estimates, March 31, 1978, p. 25.
42. See Hansard, Proceedings of the Justice and Legal Affairs Committee, May 18, 1978, Appendix.
43. Bush, 1967.
44. *The Globe and Mail*, January 10, 1978.
45. Colby, 1978.
46. Wise, 1967, p. 141.
47. Top CIA men are largely recruited from Ivy League colleges. See Dulles, 1963; Agee, 1975; Copeland, 1974.
48. Wise, 1967, p. 4.
49. Copeland, 1974, p. 8.
50. Most Mounties abroad are said to masquerade as immigration visa control officers, See *Toronto Sun*, October 1, 1978.

Chapter 9

1. *The Globe and Mail*, August 5, 1972.
2. Marin, 1976, p. 24.
3. Ibid., p. 23.
4. Ibid., p. 33.
5. Ramsay, 1972.
6. *The Globe and Mail*, May 10, 1978.
7. The opinion is that of Lord Goddard, former chief justice of England. Kelly and Kelly, 1976, p. 269.
8. See Koestler, 1971.
9. Ramsay, 1972.
10. *The Globe and Mail*, May 10, 1978.
11. Cray, 1972, p. 98.

12. Goode, 1960.
13. Lee, John Alan. "Equity in Student Petitions," *Canadian Journal of Higher Education*, Fall 1967, pp. 23-37.
14. See Niederhoffer, 1969, p. 78; Watters and Gillers, 1973, p. 95.
15. Hansard, Proceedings of the Justice and Legal Affairs Committee, May 18, 1978, Appendix.
16. Anderson, 1973, p. 15.
17. *Maclean's*, May 31, 1976.
18. Ibid.
19. Hansard. See footnote 15 above.
20. *Toronto Star*, January 27, 1973.
21. See Bowes, 1966, p. 18; Cray, 1972, p. 5.
22. *Law and Order in Canadian Democracy*, King's Printer, 1949, p. 34.
23. *The Globe and Mail*, October 15, 1974.
24. Ibid., October 26, 1978. See also Keable transcript, vol. 38, p. 72.
25. *The Globe and Mail*, October 20, 1978.
26. Ibid., November 8, 1978.
27. Ibid.
28. Ibid., November 1, 1978.
29. Ibid., November 8, 1978.
30. Henschel, 1977.
31. Jamieson, 1971.
32. *Law and Order in Canadian Democracy*, King's Printer, 1949, p. 154.
33. Miller, 1958.
34. See Toronto *Sun*, November 5, 1978.
35. Niederhoffer, 1969, p. 2, 185.
36. Berkley, 1969, p. 46.
37. Task Force on Policing in Ontario, Report to the Solicitor General, 1974, p. 22.
38. Berkley, 1969, p. 39.
39. Parliamentary Estimates, Solicitor General's department, 1971 to 1978.

Chapter 10

1. Wolff, 1950, p. 310.
2. Moorhead, 1972.
3. Mills, 1959, p. 355.
4. McKenzie, 1969.
5. Leighton, 1978, p. 14.

6. *The Canadian*, September 16, 1978.
7. *The Globe and Mail*, March 10, 1978.
8. Toronto *Sun*, March 7, 1978.
9. *Toronto Star*, March 15, 1978.
10. Ibid., December 15, 1978.
11. Williams, 1965, p. 92.
12. Ibid., p. 129.
13. *Saturday Night*, February 1978.
14. Wolff, 1950, p. 337.
15. See Leighton, 1978.
16. Dulles, 1963, p. 249.
17. Thompson, 1970, p. 31.
18. In Canada, Crown privilege is protected by Section 41 of the Federal Court Act.
19. Williams, 1965, p. 80; Wise, 1967, p. 124.
20. Weber, 1922, 1968.
21. Westley, 1956. See also Niederhoffer, 1969, p. 6.
22. Wolff, 1950, p. 332.
23. Thompson, 1970, p. 42.
24. Wolff, 1950, p. 333.
25. Halperin, 1976, p. 227.
26. *Toronto Star*, May 5, 1973. See Watters and Gillers, 1973.
27. Watters and Gillers, 1973, p. 93.
28. Centre for Crime Research, 1975, p. 119.
29. Watters and Gillers, 1973.
30. Robertson, 1976, p. 40.
31. *The Globe and Mail*, November 23, 1978; January 24, 1979.
32. Solicitor General's Annual Report, 1977, p. 45.
33. See footnote 32 above.
34. RCMP Annual Report, 1941, p. 15.
35. Report of the Comptroller General, United States, December 27, 1976.
36. Hansard, April 30, 1975, p. 5333.
37. Garrison, 1977, p. 79.
38. *The Globe and Mail*, October 28, 1978.
39. Solicitor General's Annual Report, 1975, p. 18.
40. *The Globe and Mail*, December 30, 31, 1978.
41. *Toronto Star*, September 17, 1974.
42. *The Globe and Mail*, Januray 13, 1979.
43. Ibid., February 16, 1979.
44. Lowry, 1972.
45. *Maclean's*, February 12, 1979.
46. Rockefeller Commission, 1975.

47. Bunyan, 1976, p. 174.
48. Wise, 1976, p. 399.
49. Solicitor General's Annual Reports, 1972, 1978.
50. CBC "Fifth Estate," February 21, 1978.
51. Brown and Brown, 1973, p. 45.
52. Hansard, Proceedings of the Justice and Legal Affairs Committee, May 18, 1978, p. 21.
53. Bunyan, 1976, p. 174.
54. Centre for Crime Research, 1975, p. 7.
55. *Maclean's*, May 31, 1976.
56. Dulles, 1963.

Chapter 11

1. Wise, 1976, p. 106.
2. Haas and Shaffir, 1974, p. 80.
3. Griffin, 1961.
4. *Toronto Star*, March 3, 4, 1978.
5. Ibid., July 21, 1978.
6. Goffman, 1959.
7. Commissioner Simmonds answered the question of Elmer MacKay, M.P., "Do you just burn them when they are no longer of any use to you?" with a lengthy statement which throws the blame on any informer who, when no longer of use, "is likely to say he was promised the moon, but nobody was in a position to make the promise and it is not made." Hansard, Proceedings of the Justice and Legal Affairs committee, May 18, 1978, pp. 15 and 17.
8. See Flemming, 1976, for an interesting example.
9. *Playboy*, August 1975. "The Playboy Interview," with Philip Agee.
10. See Berger, 1963.
11. Dulles, 1963, p. 183.
12. Ibid., p. 184.
13. See Kelly and Kelly, 1976, p. 153 for comments on War Measures Act, 1970.
14. Skolnick, 1967, p. 121.
15. *The Globe and Mail*, March 23, 1978.
16. See Breton, 1974 for an insightful analysis of the Quebec situation in which the RCMP operated.
17. Note that typical police interrogation methods usually employ two roles, the "sympathetic" or soft role, and the "tough guy." See Harney and Cross, 1968.

18. McKenzie, 1969, p. 6.
19. Signed June 11, 1971, and reported at the McDonald commission on March 6, 1978. In 1975, David MacDonald, M.P., revealed a 30-page RCMP interrogation manual which suggests that after soft and legal methods have failed to wring a statement from a suspect, "the interrogator must open up his bag of tricks and go for . . . any evidence which may be placed in court, regardlesss of the method employed to secure that evidence." *The Globe and Mail*, March 26, 1975.
20. *The Globe and Mail*, March 7, 1978.
21. Ibid., January 12, 1978.
22. *Ottawa Journal*, November 17, 1977.
23. *Toronto Star*, May 4, 1978.
24. *The Globe and Mail*, March 23, 1978.
25. Ibid., March 15, 1978.
26. Morand, 1976, p. 152.
27. Municipal Police Administration, 1961, p. 456.
28. See Hughes, 1962.
29. See Buckner, 1972; Manning, 1971.
30. Skolnick, 1967, p. 45.
31. See Cray, 1972.
32. Skolnick 1967, p. 50.
33. Hughes, 1962.
34. Bunyan, 1976, p. 175.
35. *Society* (previously called *Trans-action*), vol. 12, no. 3, April 1975.
36. Katz, 1963, p. 14.
37. *Canadian Press*, May 7, 1969.
38. *CAUT Bulletin*, April 1963.
39. *Maclean's*, April 1963.
40. Letter of CAUT President Gordon Jones to P. E. Trudeau, April 4, 1978; *CAUT Bulletin*, October 1978, p. 18.
41. *CAUT Bulletin*, April 1963.
42. Ramsay, in Haas, 1974, p. 91.
43. *The Globe and Mail*, November 25, 1977.
44. *CAUT Bulletin*, October, 1978, p. 18.
45. Agee, 1975; Wise, 1976.
46. Hansard, Proceedings of the Justice and Legal Affairs committee, November 29, 1977.
47. *The Globe and Mail*, March 16, 1978.
48. *Toronto Star*, February 9, 1978.
49. *The Globe and Mail*, February 10, 1978.
50. Adams, 1977.

51. *The Globe and Mail,* February 10, 1978.
52. Ibid.
53. Adams, 1977, p. 57.
54. House of Commons Justice and Legal Affairs Committee hearings, reported in *The Globe and Mail,* February 10, 1978.

Chapter 12

1. Durkheim, 1912, 1954.
2. Banton, 1964, p. 236.
3. Watters and Gillers, 1973.
4. *Law and Order in Canadian Democracy,* King's Printer, 1949, p. 40.
5. Becker, 1964, p. 122.
6. Mary Trueman, *The Globe and Mail,* January 1978.
7. Douglas Fisher, Toronto *Sun,* November 28, 1977.
8. *Ottawa Gazette,* July 6, 1977.
9. See Chapman, 1970, p. 90.
10. *The Globe and Mail,* June 28, 1969.
11. Marin, 1976, p. 46.
12. Armstrong, 1976, p. 57.
13. The case is Regina vs. Hauser.
14. In the judgment on the Keable commission, October 31, 1978.
15. See Wise, 1967, p. 84; Lord Denning's Report, Her Majesty's Stationery Office, September 1963.
16. Hansard, October 31, 1977, p. 460.
17. George Bain, *Toronto Star,* November 4, 1977.
18. Government paper, "Legislation on Public Access to Government Documents," June 1977, Ottawa.
19. *Ottawa Journal,* November 10, 1977.
20. Arendt, 1969, p. 127.
21. *Saturday Night,* January 1978, p. 3.
22. Ibid.
23. Hansard, October 31, 1977, p. 472.
24. *The Globe and Mail,* January 7, 1979.
25. *Toronto Star,* October 25, 1978.
26. *Ottawa Journal,* November 10, 1977.
27. See Douglas Fisher, *Toronto Sun,* January 31, 1978.
28. Crozier, 1976.
29. Toronto *Sun,* July 8, 1977.
30. Ibid., December 6, 1977.
31. See Crozier, 1976.
32. *Ottawa Citizen,* June 23, 1977.

33. *The Globe and Mail*, October 25, 1978.
34. See Niederhoffer, 1969; Cray, 1972; Wilson, 1978.
35. Wilson, 1978, p. 81.
36. *The Globe and Mail*, November 3, 1978.
37. Ibid., November 9, 1978.
38. Skolnick, 1967, p. 48.
39. Festinger, 1957.
40. Sykes and Matza, 1957.
41. Dulles, 1963, p. 9.
42. De Larue, 1964, p. 94.
43. *Toronto Sun*, October 1, 1978.
44. John Best, *Ottawa Journal*, September 27, 1978.
45. See Williams, 1965, p. 192.
46. Hansard, June 3, 1963.
47. Hansard, October 31, 1977, p. 456.
48. *The Globe and Mail*, February 16, 1978.
49. Ibid., March 3, 1978.
50. Hansard, October 31, 1977, p. 466.
51. See Penrose and Courtiour, 1978.

Chapter 13

1. Williams, 1965, p. 167.
2. Ibid., p. 193.
3. Mills, 1959, p. 341. See also Thompson, 1970.
4. Churchill, 1954, cited in Williams, 1965, p. 187.
5. Halperin, 1976, p. 224.
6. Anderson, 1973, p. 63.
7. Halperin, 1976, p. 220.
8. Quinney, 1970, p. 304.
9. Hagan, 1977, p. 41.
10. Skolnick, 1967, p. 13.
11. *Maclean's*, October 23, 1978.
12. *The Globe and Mail*, October 17, 1978.
13. *Toronto Star*, October 14, 1978.
14. Ibid., October 28, 1978.
15. Ibid., October 7, 1978.
16. *The Globe and Mail*, October 15, 1978.
17. Ibid., April 4, 1978; *Toronto Star*, June 10, 1978.
18. *The Globe and Mail*, August 5, 1978.
19. *Toronto Sun*, October 1, 1978.
20. Statement of the McDonald commission, October 13, 1978, p. 1.

21. *The Globe and Mail*, October 10, 1978.
22. *Maclean's*, October 23, 1978.
23. *The Globe and Mail*, February 9, 1978.
24. Ibid., December 24, 1977.
25. Statement of the McDonald commission, October 13, 1978, p. 26.
26. *The Globe and Mail*, October 31, 1978.
27. Ibid., November 1, 1978.
28. *Toronto Telegram*, June 3, 1965.
29. *Toronto Star*, October 2, 1965.
30. *The Globe and Mail*, June 13, 1963.
31. *Weekend Magazine*, vol. 11, no. 40, 1961.
32. *Star Weekly*, October 2, 1965.
33. *Toronto Telegram*, June 30, 1969.
34. "Observations on the McKenzie Report," *Toronto Star*, June 30, 1969.
35. Mckenzie, 1969, p. 129.
36. Ibid., p. 130.
37. *Toronto Telegram*, June 30, 1969.
38. *The Globe and Mail*, June 30, 1969.
39. Marin, 1976, p. 40.
40. Ibid., p. 41.
41. *Ottawa Gazette*, December 21, 1977.
42. *The Globe and Mail*, September 29, 1978.

Chapter 14

1. See for example Kelly and Kelly, 1976, Preface; Bent, 1974, p. x.
2. Hansard, October 31, 1977, p. 460.
3. Quoted in Halperin, 1976, p. 225.
4. Hoover Commission, *Report on Security*, 1954, cited by Stockwell, 1978, p. 252.
5. *The Globe and Mail*, June 30, 1978.
6. Ibid., November 9, 1978.
7. Ibid.
8. McKenzie, 1969, p. 21.
9. Ibid., p. 22.
10. Institute for the Study of Conflict, London, England; cited in *Maclean's*, November 6, 1978.
11. *Star Weekly*, October 25, 1965.
12. See Tannenbaum, 1938; Schur, 1971.
13. *The Globe and Mail*, June 30, 1978.

14. Kelly and Kelly, 1976, p. 525.
15. *Law and Order in Canadian Democracy*, King's Printer, 1949, p. 118.
16. Earle, 1967, p. 131.
17. *Ottawa Journal*, May 7, 1969.
18. Quoted by *Society*, (previously called *Trans-action*), vol. 12, no. 3 (April 1975), p. 56.
19. Copeland, 1974, p. 75.
20. Penrose and Courtiour, 1978.
21. Lower, 1957.
22. Cited by Wise, 1976, p. 30.
23. Chambliss, 1973.
24. Fines in recent years have exceeded $500,000 per corporation. See Snider, 1978 for a detailed discussion.
25. See Agee, 1975; Marchetti, 1974; Copeland, 1974.
26. See Quinney, 1969; Taylor, Walton, Young, 1973.
27. See Kelly and Kelly, 1976, p. 275-287 for arguments supporting use of conspiracy law.
28. Wolff, 1971.
29. Quinney, 1970; Chambliss, 1976.
30. *The Globe and Mail*, February 24, 1978.
31. See Porter, 1965; Clement, 1975; Freitag, 1975.
32. See Wise, 1976, p. 30.
33. Hagan, 1977, p. 94.
34. See Lipset, 1964; Hagan, *Sociological Inquiry*.
35. *The Globe and Mail*, January 22, 1979.

Chapter 15

1. McKenzie, 1969, p. 22.
2. McDonald Commission, October 1978, p. 3.
3. Quoted in *Society* (previously called *Trans-action*), vol. 12, no. 3 (April 1965), p. 7.
4. Stockwell, 1978, p. 252.
5. Letter to the media.
6. Etzioni, 1969.
7. Foucault, 1965; Szasz, 1970.
8. Royal Commission on the Police, Report, London: Her Majesty's Stationery Office, 1962.
9. Penrose and Courtiour, 1978.
10. Chapman, 1970, p. 92.
11. Stockwell, 1978, p. 250.

12. Bullock, 1963; a history of the British MI5, cited by Elmer MacKay, M.P. in a brief to the McDonald commission, January 1979, p. 31.
13. Colby, 1978, p. 59, p. 315.
14. Denning, 1963, p. 91.
15. Colby, 1978, p. 184.
16. Ibid., p. 417.
17. *Toronto Star*, November 11, 1977; *Globe and Mail*, December 1, 1978.
18. Dulles, 1963, p. 238.
19. Colby, 1978, p. 459.
20. Anderson, 1973.
21. Colby, 1978, p. 460.
22. See Hagan, 1977 for an insightful survey.
23. Sanders, 1974.
24. See Humphreys, 1975, Appendix, for a discussion of the ethics involved.
25. See Bent, 1974 for a discussion of civilian control, and Marin, 1976 for a discussion of civilian review.
26. *The Globe and Mail*, January 24, 1979.
27. Marin, 1976, Recommendations.
28. Lockhart, 1974, p. 5.
29. *The Canadian*, September 23, 1978.
30. Hugessen; page 22 of judgment re Keable commission, December 9, 1977; translated by the authors.

Appendix

Formal structure of Canada's security system

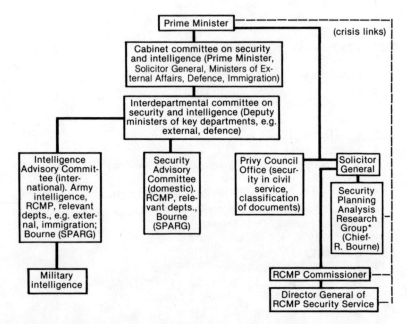

* SPARG was formerly called Police and Security Planning and Analysis

Who's in charge here?

The present study devotes little attention to the formal structure of Canada's security system, for two reasons:

1. Canadians are allowed to know very little about it. The government has consistently held that in matters of security, we must be governed without our informed consent. The above chart was contributed by a high-ranking RCMP officer.

2. The formal organization does not tell us much about the way power flows, unless we also know who are "the persons to see." Of course, we can make some guesses on the basis of those who hold positions on several key committees.

Index

Mail, illegal opening of, 64, 65, 81, 101–102
Make-work. *See* Efficiency
Marin commission, 131, 141, 154, 229–30
Masonic Order, 151
McCleery, Don, 16, 57, 145
McDonald commission, 14, 17, 23, 48, 50, 64, 84, 94–96, 142, 208, 217–25, 244
McKenzie commission, 124, 132, 162–65, 227–29, 234, 252
Mens rea (criminal intent), 77–80
MI5, MI6. *See* British intelligence
Montreal police, 29, 34, 36, 47, 60, 188
Moral career, 128
Morale, 128–29
Morand Report, 131

National security, 17, 18, 22, 24, 36, 50, 66, 80, 83, 88, 93–97, 161, 209, 213, 218, 229, 233, 238, 240, 243
Need not to know, 26, 28, 32, Chapter 6, 188, 201
Neutralization, 30, 58, 60, 63, 69, 206
New Democratic Party, 40, 45, 211
Nixon, Richard, 18, 43, 94, 209–10
North West Mounted Police (NWMP), 107–109

October crisis (1970), 22, 26, 41, 45, 62, 183, 226
Officer hierarchy, 126, 137, 141, 150, 152, 154
Official deviance, 17–18
Official Secrets Act, 23, 42, 49, 84, Chapter 10, 225, 256
Ontario Provincial Police, 130, 135, 153
Opportunity theory, 80–81
Orderly room. *See* Discipline
Orders, illegal, 55–56, 147

Parliament, 13, 45, 113, 120, 145, 148, 159, 175, 207–209, 211–12
Parti Québébois, 26–27, Chapter 3, 60–62
Person to see, 89–92, 286
Phony communiqué. *See* Disinformation
Plea bargaining, 216–17
Police force size and distribution, 170, 173–76
Power elite, 21, 79, 109, 111, 169, 214, 216–17, 235, 237–42, 252, 254
Praxis break-in, 65–66
Privy Council Office, 40, 42, 101
Professionalism, 130–32, 187, 253
Promotions, 55, 63, 127, 129, 135–37, 148
Public as enemy, 186–88, 193
Public's right not to know, 84, 103–105, 218–19, 223
PUMA. *See* Bag job

Quebec Provincial Police (SQ), 29, 33, 34, 36, 188

Recruitment, 122–27, 132, 150, 187, 189
Role strain, 143–45
Rule of law, 20, 24, 35, 55, 109, 136, 146–49, 187, 197, 232–33, 238–40, 254
Rules of RCMP, 70, 140–43, 229

Samson, Robert, 13, 25, 31, 36
Secrecy, 17, 23, 34, 43, 81, 85, 138, 144, 147, Chapter 10, 209–10, 216–19, 228–29, 244, 250, 252, 256
Secret police, 15, 24, 39, 50, 55, 60, 63, 115, 228–29, 234, 237, 246–47
Section 98 (Criminal Code), 114–17